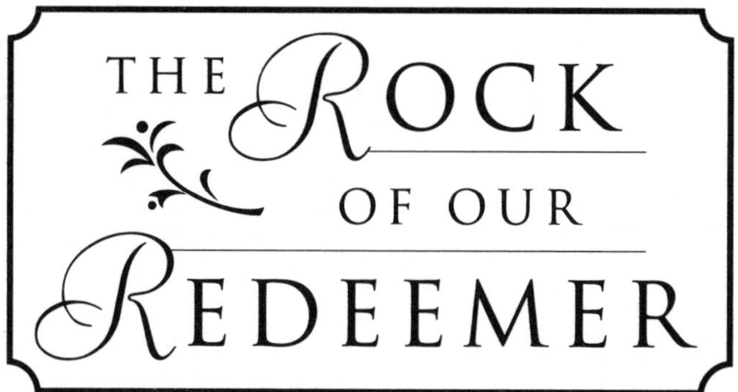
THE ROCK
OF OUR
REDEEMER

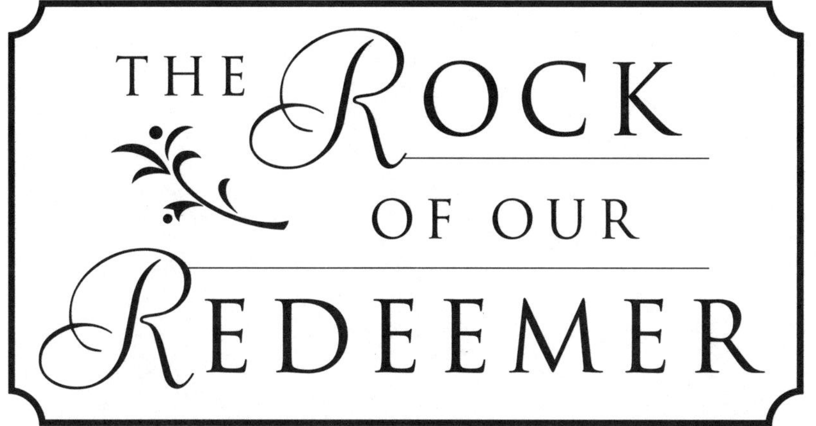

The Rock of Our Redeemer

TALKS FROM THE 2002 BYU WOMEN'S CONFERENCE

DESERET BOOK

SALT LAKE CITY, UTAH

Visit us at deseretbook.com

Library of Congress Cataloging-in-Publication Data

Women's Conference (2002 : Brigham Young University)
The rock of our Redeemer : talks from the 2002 BYU Women's Conference.
p. cm.
Includes bibliographical references and index.
ISBN 1-57008-911-6 (alk. paper)
1. Mormon women—Religious life—Congresses. 2. Church of Jesus Christ of Latter-day Saints—Congresses. I. Title.

BX8641.W73 2003
289.3'32'082—dc21 2002156208

Printed in the United States of America 72076-7048
Publishers Printing, Salt Lake City, UT

10 9 8 7 6 5 4 3 2 1

CONTENTS

WISE STEWARDS: ENGAGED WITH LIFE

HIS OWN DUE TIME

ON FIRM FOUNDATIONS

Preface

This volume, the seventeenth in the series, is a compilation of selected addresses from the 2002 BYU Women's Conference. We are grateful for the time, energy, and prayer the authors put into preparing their presentations at the conference, and we are pleased to share in this volume a sampling of their ideas and feelings on subjects that will appeal to sisters throughout our worldwide Church.

Here you will find an introduction to the Relief Society General Presidency sustained in April 2002 and inspirational insights about building upon the rock of our Redeemer, reaching out to individuals of other faiths, building unity in our families and communities, developing closer relationships with children and spouses, drawing hope and faith from scripture study and temple worship, and in other ways living as women of God.

We are grateful for the efforts of the conference planning committee, who made both the conference and this volume possible. We acknowledge the dedication and skill of our editorial team—Dawn Anderson, Suzanne Brady, Rebecca Chambers, Dlora Dalton, and Susette Green—who compiled this work.

As you read, may you receive strength and encouragement from the message in the Book of Mormon recorded by Helaman: "Remember, remember that it is upon the rock of our Redeemer, who is Christ, the Son of God, that ye must build your foundation" (Helaman 5:12). When we build upon the "rock of our Redeemer," we bear testimony of the Savior's atonement, we turn to Him for guidance, we look to Him for truth, we receive direction from His prophet, we see His hand in our lives, we feel His Spirit with us, we do His work. This is our testimony to you.

—Janet S. Scharman
Chair, 2002 BYU Women's Conference

The Precious Promise

Neal A. Maxwell

"Remember, remember that it is upon the rock of our Redeemer, who is Christ, the Son of God, that ye must build your foundation; . . . whereon if men build they cannot fall" (Helaman 5:12). A more relevant promise is hard to imagine when so many mortals are falling and being dragged down. The Great Deliverer, Jesus Christ, can deliver on this precious promise as well as on all His other reassurances. Regarding divine determination, "there is nothing that the Lord thy God shall take in his heart to do but what he will do it," and the scriptures so assure (Abraham 3:17). Imagine what it would be like if we worshiped a lesser god who, like us, had problems of his own!

Building on His firm foundation requires us, however, to emulate Christ's character. There is no joy, nor is there any security, in giving Him mere lip service. Emulating Him is the key, and our emerging character is the refined structure of our souls. After all the circumstantial scaffolding comes down, character is what is left.

Now, my beloved sisters, I have one reservation in speaking to you. You are already so conscientious, and my desire is to lift you up, not to weigh you down. Please remember, therefore, that as I speak, preceding any exhortation is admiration! You are likely to be doing much better than you realize.

First some words, however, about the precious process of character

---

Neal A. Maxwell, a member of the Quorum of the Twelve Apostles, received his bachelor's and master's degrees in political science from the University of Utah. A beloved speaker and a prolific writer, he has served as Church commissioner of education, a member of the YMMIA General Board, and a bishop. He and his wife, Colleen Hinckley Maxwell, are the parents of four children and the grandparents of twenty-four.

building. The traits of character to be focused on are all interactive, and they hasten the development of each other. Paul notes one spiritual sequence when he says, "Tribulation worketh patience; and patience, experience; and experience, hope," and hope brings more of the love of God (Romans 5:3–4). If you and I will meekly submit to "our light affliction," whatever it is, this will lead later to a far greater "weight of glory" (2 Corinthians 4:17).

So it is that while the "intelligence we attain unto in this life . . . will rise with us in the resurrection" (D&C 130:18), the gospel definition of intelligence isn't one's scholastic I.Q. Instead, intelligence signifies the totality of the soul and reflects "the divine nature" (2 Peter 1:4). If we are diligent, we can develop faith, patience, godliness, kindliness, and charity in greater abundance in our lives. These qualities, in turn, will make us fruitful "in the knowledge of our Lord Jesus Christ" (2 Peter 1:8).

Note how we differ from the world. Added knowledge of spiritual things follows better behavior! When we lack this knowledge, however, Peter warns us, we will not be able to see "afar off" (2 Peter 1:9).

When we emerge from a fiery furnace or trial, we don't run around to find another fiery furnace so we can stand in line to get an extra turn.[1] We will be amply supplied with tests and tribulations. There's no need to search for them! So, now, my saying a few things about character should be more in the nature of a caress of confirmation than an excess of exhortation.

Furthermore, when in the midst of these things, we should not be surprised if, at times, we are faithful but mute: "Be still and know that I am God" (D&C 101:16). That's sometimes the best class participation, given Who is our Tutor.

The particular developmental challenge that we face may arise from the steady drumbeat of disappointment over a poor relationship in life, or a dramatic intervening event may focus us. In a way, it doesn't matter, if we understand and value the process with all of its stepping-stones.

When we raise a blind on a window, only to be struck by a burst of bright sunlight, it makes us wince and squint and almost turn away. Sometimes doctrines are like that—they strike us with sudden illumination in ways for which we do not feel quite prepared. Such is Paul's teaching that we "glory in tribulations" (Romans 5:3). Why would anybody glory in tribulation? We find, however, that as doctrine dilates our discipleship, we can handle the added incandescence and benefit therefrom.

The women disciples in my life, especially Colleen, are often further along the developmental path of some attributes. When I finally arrive at a developmental rendezvous, Colleen is already there! Because we are further along or further behind on the path of life in some respect or another from others, we need one another's help in the journey. We realize, too, that the premortal world actually accounts for some of these striking, spiritual differences among us. Whether Jacob, Paul, or Peter—they all want us to see things more clearly. Such is the process I'm attempting to describe—seeing "things as they really are, and . . . as they really will be" (Jacob 4:13) in order for us to enjoy a supernal advantage.

Furthermore, the development of Christlike character clearly qualifies as truly being "about [our] Father's business" (Luke 2:49). The wonderful thing about this process is that amid the seeming mundaneness of daily life we can be about our Father's business, day by day, achieving imperishable things to be taken with us through the veil of death and to rise with us in the resurrection.

Jacob wrote of "looking beyond the mark" by failing to see Christ as the center of it all, and Jacob added ominously that people so blinded and diverted "must needs fall" because they are looking beyond the mark (Jacob 4:14). Ignoring the Savior includes failing to build Christlike character in order to be more rocklike ourselves.

Of course, conversion to the gospel and the Church can happen all at once in a burst of recognition and through the testifying of the Holy Spirit; however, the subsequent mentoring in order to develop further, for instance, a quality like patience, takes time. Yes, patience does not come "right now"! Do not expect the world to understand or help in the precious process I'm attempting to describe.

Mercifully, the whisperings of the Spirit nudge us along the path in an almost private process. Through it all we will need to be strong enough for ourselves but also strong enough to help others, because there will be immigrants arriving from Babylon, including some defectors from the "great and spacious building" (1 Nephi 8:26), and they need to encounter women like you.

A few examples of the character of Christ will illustrate what we are to emulate, even for the already conscientious. Because we view Christ as the Light of the World, it is by His light that we should see everything else. Disciples are the real realists, whatever irreligionists may say or think.

Unlike God and Jesus, who are omniscient, you and I are often perplexed. We can be unsettled by the unexpected or made uneasy by the unknown. We surely need all of this added perspective! Furthermore, whereas Jesus paid the full price in order to ransom us, you and I may still hesitate over paying the full costs of discipleship, including developing the key attributes of a disciple.

Likewise, though Christ successfully resisted all temptations, we still dally, and we may take some temptations under advisement. No wonder the eloquence of His example is so powerful, for the scriptures say He gave "no heed" to temptation (D&C 20:22).

We also tend to shrug off the persistent reminders of our sins of omission, as if our avoidance of the super sins of transgression and commission were enough. It is my opinion that in the realm of the sins of omission we can make more major, though quiet, progress than in any other place. That is particularly true of conscientious people.

Like His Father, Jesus exemplifies love perfectly. He so loved the Father and us that He meekly and submissively let His will be completely swallowed up in the will of the Father in order to accomplish the Atonement, including blessing billions and billions of us with the unmerited, universal resurrection. What He did is staggering even to contemplate. No wonder He can help us along. He knows the way.

So profound and comprehensive is Christ's love, that even during His infinite suffering, He still noticed and nurtured finite sufferers who endured so much less anguish than He had to bear. For instance, He noticed and restored an assailant's severed ear in the Garden of Gethsemane. On the cross, He directed John to take care of His mother, Mary. He comforted a thief on a nearby cross.

In contrast, when you and I let ourselves get stuck in the ooze of our own self-pity, we fail to notice the needs of others. Still, with a little more effort, we can become a little more noticing and a little more nurturing. Let us reflect on our circles of love. Are they increasing in size, or are they static? What is the quality of our caring for those within those circles? Do we avoid lazy stereotyping? It's so easy to deal with people as functions and stereotypes instead of as individuals. Are we lovingly patient with others who are also striving to develop? Or do we, judgmentally and impatiently, constantly pull up the daisies to see how their roots are doing?

President Brigham Young declared of love, so fundamental to everything else, "There is one virtue [or] attribute, . . . which, if cherished and practiced by the Saints, would prove salvation to thousands upon thousands. I allude," he continued, "to charity, or love, from which proceed forgiveness, long-suffering, kindness, and patience."[2] All other virtues are derivatives and reflections of love! Again, since the sisters have such an instinctive, even reflexive love, you are probably further along this trail than you now realize.

Jesus likewise exemplifies perfect patience and long-suffering. Think of the implications of the Lord's course, which, He tells us, "is one eternal round" (D&C 3:2). Routine and repetition may bother us, may bore us. But God and His Son, Jesus, are never bored with Their "one eternal round," whatever that phrase is meant to convey, because of Their perfect love. God is patient with us in process of time. He also helps by trying our patience and our faith (Mosiah 23:21).

If left untried, those qualities, which are portable and eternal, would remain underdeveloped. There's something about the isometrics that are involved when we're putting off the natural man or the natural woman while striving to become the man or the woman of Christ. These isometrics are a blessing in disguise, though I grant you sometimes it's well disguised.

As striving disciples, therefore, are we willing to be so mentored? Tutoringly, the Lord has said, "Ye cannot bear all things now; . . . I will lead you along" (D&C 78:18). He knows our bearing capacities. Though we ourselves may feel pushed to the breaking point, yet, ere long, thanks to Him, these once-daunting challenges become receding milestones.

Even outstanding and courageous Jeremiah was once discouraged. Being mocked and persecuted, he briefly considered refraining from speaking out anymore. But then he said God's word was "as a burning fire shut up in my bones . . . , and I could not stay" (Jeremiah 20:9). Jeremiah reached a breaking point, but he did not break!

Jesus also exemplifies meekness and humility. Though ever supernal in His achievements, Christ always, always, gave the glory to the Father whether in the first, second, or now in the third estate. He was and is Lord of the Universe, who under the direction of the Father created "worlds without number" (Moses 1:33). Yet, He was willingly known as Jesus of Nazareth, the carpenter's son. The Lord of the Universe. He always knew who He was! He meekly partook of history's most bitter cup without becoming bitter!

Can we, in turn, partake of our tiny, bitter cups without becoming bitter? What a wonderful way for us to witness, especially to those we love the most! Can we overcome our drives for status and preeminence or our mundane desires merely to be one up on other people?

In the ebb and flow of life, can we meekly respond as did the preparer of the Way, John the Baptist? Unselfishly, he said, "[Jesus] must increase, but I must decrease" (John 3:30).

How about meekness in our marriages? Is the pronoun *me* yielding ever more often to the pronoun *we?* The vertical pronoun *I* is best used in such situations as "I love you," "I care for you," "I hear you." Otherwise, *I* can be drenched in ego: "I demand," "I want," "I need."

Seemingly small, positive adjustments can make large differences in process of time. In our families, in the Church, and in other relationships, will we stop letting yesterday hold tomorrow hostage? Will we reclassify others, knowing that forgetting is part of forgiving?

So we see that building character is the most difficult form of construction. It requires faith and patience, using divinely given blueprints. There are also the overruns resulting from overcharged emotions. It's not easy to be meekly resilient after experiencing failures. It's not easy to retrofit by repentance, especially when our pride suggests that we are doing pretty well.

Likewise, it is ever tempting to try to use cheap, mortal substitutes instead of building Christlike character. The substitutes—such as cleverness instead of goodness, and smoothness instead of substance—do not survive when the winds and the rains pound on crumbling foundations. Furthermore, when we follow shortcuts, there is that awful subsidence, or sinking. Hence we can fall! All serious discipleship, therefore, requires our serious remodeling.

Christ is characterized as the Rock for so many reasons. We will find no fissures in His foundation. He never disappoints us. He never falters. His love never fails. He never fails to bring to pass His purposes.

We can follow Peter's counsel: Cast all your cares upon Christ, for "he careth for you" (1 Peter 5:7). We mustn't be reluctant to do that. We may need to do it again and again! Christ told His disciples to catch a particular fish with a particular coin in its mouth in order to pay taxes, or tribute. Upon finding the fish, the disciples so did! Such incredible awareness about a single fish and a single coin should console us regarding the Master's full awareness of the details in the lives of each of us.

So, "we talk of Christ, we rejoice in Christ, we preach of Christ, we prophesy of Christ." Why? So that those we love the most "may know to what source they may look for a remission of their sins" (2 Nephi 25:26).

A word now about our own families. Some of us are older; some are in mid passage; others have yet to begin. Some of us are parents, and some, grandparents. Grandparents have empty nests. Such emptyings are part of the plan, of course. Yet, since our flocks have left their nests, we find ourselves remembering and savoring precious days now irrevocably past. We listen in vain but with eager ears for children's voices we once thought too shrill, too constant—even irritating. Yet that cacophony of children, which we once called noise, was actually sweet sound, a sound we yearn to hear again if we but could.

Let us, amid the cacophony, seize the defining moments. Make more Mary-like choices and show less Martha-like anxiety. What are calories anyway, compared to special conversations? Of course, meals need to be served and consumed, but the mentoring memories will not be taken from you.

Whether old or young, married or unmarried, and with full or empty nests, the love of atoning Jesus for us is simply inestimable! Mercifully, the Lord tells us, "mine arm is lengthened out all the day long" (2 Nephi 28:32). He waits with open arms to receive us, and on a later day, says the prophet Mormon, we can be "clasped in the arms of Jesus" (Mormon 5:11).

Whatever the remaining distance between us and Him, it is ours to travel! The beckoning stepping-stones are there. We have come thus far by faith in Him, though we have "miles to go before [we] sleep,"[3] and our faith will take us even further.

Please ponder this eloquent pleading to the Father. It is by the same Jesus who volunteered in the premortal world by saying meekly and simply, "Here am I, send me" (Abraham 3:27). Here are the pleading words: "Listen to him who is the advocate with the Father, who is pleading your cause before him—Saying: Father, behold the sufferings and death of him who did no sin, in whom thou wast well pleased; behold the blood of thy Son which was shed, the blood of him whom thou gavest that thyself might be glorified; wherefore, Father, spare these my brethren that believe on my name, that they may come unto me and have everlasting life" (D&C 45:3–5).

He is always thinking of us! As one of His apostles, I so testify.

Notes

1. Neal A. Maxwell, "'From Whom All Blessings Flow,'" *Ensign*, May 1997, 11–12.
2. Brigham Young, *Journal of Discourses*, 26 vols. (London: Latter-day Saints' Book Depot, 1854–86), 7:133–34.
3. Robert Frost, "Stopping by Woods on a Snowy Evening," in *An Introduction to Poetry*, ed. X. J. Kennedy and Dana Gioia, 8th ed. (New York: HarperCollins College Publishers, 1994), 341.

The Rock: A Sure Foundation

Merrill J. Bateman and Marilyn S. Bateman

President Bateman: Helaman named his sons Nephi and Lehi in honor of their early ancestors with the expectation that they would honor their names and emulate their good works. But as good as their ancestors were, Helaman knew that the works of men, even prophets, are not sufficient for salvation. Consequently, Helaman tells Nephi and Lehi that the only way they can be saved is through faith in the atoning blood of Jesus Christ. They must look to the Savior of the world and base their lives on his teachings if they wish to attain eternal life.

In this regard, Helaman's counsel in verse 12 (and the theme of our conference) reads: "And now, my sons, remember, remember that it is upon the rock of our Redeemer, who is Christ, the Son of God, that ye must build your foundation . . . , a foundation whereon if men [and women] build they cannot fall" (Helaman 5:12).

Using imagery similar to Jesus' imagery in the meridian of time, Helaman likens the quest for eternal life to building a house (Matthew 7:24–27). The foundation of the house must be built not only upon ground that is permanent, solid, and steadfast, but upon ground that is sacred—the rock of the Redeemer. During the Savior's appearance to the Nephites following his resurrection, he explained the meaning of

---

Merrill J. Bateman, a member of the First Quorum of the Seventy, has served as president of Brigham Young University since January 1996. He previously served as Presiding Bishop of the Church and as dean of the College of Business and School of Management at BYU. Marilyn S. Bateman has served in leadership and teaching positions in ward and stake auxiliaries. Elder and Sister Bateman are the parents of seven children and the grandparents of twenty.

"the rock." After inviting the multitude to feel the wounds in his hands and feet and to thrust their hand into his side, he taught the doctrine given him by the Father. The doctrine, Jesus said, is that the Father commands men and women everywhere to believe in Christ, repent, be baptized, and receive the Holy Ghost (3 Nephi 11:31–38).

And then the Savior states: "Verily, verily, I say unto you, that this is my doctrine, and whoso buildeth upon this buildeth upon my rock, and the gates of hell shall not prevail against them" (3 Nephi 11:39).

Thus, to build one's house on the "rock of our Redeemer" is to build one's faith in the Father and the Son, to repent, to be baptized by immersion for the remission of sins, and to receive the Holy Ghost. In brief, it is to accept and live the gospel (D&C 11:24).

THE PARTNERSHIP

Moreover, the building process is a partnership. We do not build alone. Our Father in Heaven is the architect, the designer of the plan, and the Savior is the executor and mediator of the contract. He provides the tools and supervises the construction. Because each person has been given the gift of agency, each person must determine for himself whether or not he will enter into the covenant.

A clear statement by Christ indicating that he is a partner in constructing the building was given to the eleven apostles near the end of the Last Supper. He said: "In my Father's house are many mansions: if it were not so, I would have told you. I go to prepare a place for you" (John 14:2).

And then to the Missouri Saints in 1833, he said: "Let not your hearts be troubled; for in my Father's house are many mansions, and I have prepared a place for you; and where my Father and I am, there ye shall be also" (D&C 98:18).

Do you notice the difference in the two statements? To the eleven apostles prior to Gethsemane and the cross, the Savior said that he *would prepare* a place. After the Crucifixion and the Resurrection, he told the Saints in Missouri that he *had prepared* a place for them.

Through his atonement and resurrection, the Lord makes possible the construction of an eternal home for every person.

The prophets state that those who reject the master builder and his plan find his teachings "a stone of stumbling, and a rock of offence" (1 Peter 2:8; Isaiah 8:14). From the beginning of time, most people who reject the gospel are not neutral. They take offense and fight against the Lord's servants, and, therefore, against the Lord. They build their houses on sand, and the storms of life cause them to fall because their lack of faith provides little sustenance in times of adversity (Matthew 7:26–27). In the meridian of time, Jewish leaders were expecting a savior who would free them from Roman oppression—someone who would establish an earthly kingdom. Instead, the Lord offered to free them from sin and give them thrones of their own in a celestial realm. The near-sighted Jewish leaders stumbled over the rock and took offense. The Sanhedrin, fearing the loss of their position of power, voted in council to take Jesus' life (John 11:46–53). When Peter and the other apostles continued to preach after the Savior's ascension, they were threatened again and again by the same Jewish leaders. Eventually, the apostles lost their lives or were banished to a far-off isle as the Great Apostasy took hold.

The pattern of opposition to those engaged in the Lord's work continued in this dispensation. The Saints were persecuted in New York, Ohio, Missouri, and Illinois. Nevertheless, the kingdom established in this day will "never be destroyed" as the "stone . . . cut out of the mountain without hands" will roll across the earth until the work is done (Daniel 2:44–45). The stone is "the only sure foundation, upon which [people] can build" (Jacob 4:16).

Sister Bateman: President Bateman has suggested that building on the rock of the Redeemer is not a solitary effort. If we put our trust in the Lord, we learn that the Master Builder provides assistance throughout the building process. First, we receive help in pouring the foundation and in laying the cornerstone.

In speaking to the new converts in Ephesus, Paul declared: "Now therefore ye are no more strangers and foreigners, but fellowcitizens with the saints, and of the household of God; and are built upon the foundation of the apostles and prophets, Jesus Christ himself being the chief corner stone" (Ephesians 2:19–20).

Just as apostles and prophets are the foundation of the Church, so the Lord's servants assist us in building our eternal homes. They are the oracles through whom God communicates his plan. In this spirit, the apostle Paul told the Saints in Corinth that he and they were "labourers together," that he was a master builder who had laid the foundation, and they were to build upon it. He then warned them to be careful as they added to the building (1 Corinthians 3:9–10).

As the scriptures note, Jesus is the chief cornerstone of the building. In his day, "a large stone [was] placed in a corner of the building's foundation to secure it, to provide stability and strength to the structure . . . , and to serve as a guide for laying all other foundation stones."[1] Christ's atonement is the central act in history and the foundation stone in the gospel plan. His sacrifice and resurrection are also the keystone and capstone of the building. He is at the beginning of the process and at the end. When our eternal homes are completed, they will carry his name, just as the temple does. Through faith and baptism, we take his name upon us and renew our covenants weekly through the sacrament (Mosiah 18:8–10). In time, we become his begotten sons and daughters (D&C 76:24).

Christ also assists in building the house by giving the gift of the Holy Ghost to the faithful. The Holy Spirit is a guide, a comforter, a revealer of truth, a witness, a cleanser, a sanctifier, and a sealer. As a guide and revealer, the Holy Ghost explains the Father's plan "line upon line and precept upon precept." He witnesses the truthfulness of the plan. As a comforter, he provides inner peace and strength to endure the building process. In his role as cleanser, he keeps the house clean by encouraging us to be faithful, even in the little things. As a sanctifier, his purpose is to turn the house into a temple, to raise us from telestial to celestial people. Finally, as a sealer, he ensures the validity of the covenant by bonding the bricks together (2 Nephi 28:30; Ephesians 3:16; 1 Corinthians 6:19–20).

The apostle Paul told the Corinthians: "Eye hath not seen, nor ear heard, neither have entered into the heart of man, the things which God hath prepared for them that love him. But God hath revealed them unto us by his Spirit: for the Spirit searcheth all things, yea, the deep things of God" (1 Corinthians 2:9–10).

As Paul suggests, there are surprises along the way. Although we think we know the plan, there are things not seen or heard and precepts which have not entered our hearts or minds as to the full measure of what God intends for us to be. You may have noticed from the scriptures cited earlier, we think we are building a house, but the Lord's plan calls for a mansion. The command is to be perfect even as he is. To a finite mind, perfection appears unrealistic. At best, it is a long way off. It is clear that we cannot do it on our own. Our view of our future selves is clouded by our present weaknesses. C. S. Lewis recognized that sometimes we fail to appreciate the incredible being that God intends to make of us.

Lewis said: "Imagine yourself as a living house. God comes in to rebuild that house. At first, perhaps, you can understand what He is doing. He is getting the drains right and stopping the leaks in the roof and so on: you knew that those jobs needed doing and so you are not surprised. But presently he starts knocking the house about in a way that hurts abominably and does not seem to make sense. What on earth is He up to? The explanation is that He is building quite a different house from the one you thought of—throwing out a new wing here, putting on an extra floor there, running up towers, making courtyards. You thought you were going to be made into a decent little cottage: but He is building a palace. He intends to come and live in it Himself."[2] It requires faith and trust in the Father and the Son to build a palace.

Developing Faith in the Master Builder

In addition to the rock being the gospel, the scriptures refer to Christ as the rock (2 Samuel 22:2–3, 32–33; Moses 7:53; Psalms 71:3; 78:35). He is the foundation stone upon which we build. As he said to the woman at the well, so he says to us, "If you know who I am, you will ask me for living water" (John 4:10).

We are so fortunate as Latter-day Saints to know who he is. We know him as the Jehovah of the Old Testament and Jesus of the New. We believe in him not only as an historical figure, but as a resurrected person of form and substance today. We know that he is the Son of God and operates under the direction of his Father. We know the Father and the Son appeared to Joseph Smith in a grove of trees (Joseph Smith–History 1:17). We know Joseph Smith and Sidney Rigdon saw the Great Jehovah in the Kirtland Temple (D&C 110:1–4).

But to see him is not the only way to know and build faith in him. During the 1960s, President David O. McKay granted an interview to a prominent newsman. At the close of the interview, the newsman said he would like to ask a personal question for his own information. If the president did not want to answer it, he would understand. He then asked President McKay if [he] had seen the Savior.

"The President answered that he had not, but that he had heard his voice, many times, and he had felt his presence and his influence. . . .

"Then he told how some evidences [are] stronger than . . . sight, and recalled the occasion when the Savior appeared to his disciples and told Thomas who had doubted, 'Reach hither thy finger and behold my hands: and reach hither thy hand, and thrust it into my side: and be not faithless but believing.' And then President McKay said that he liked to believe Thomas did not actually look up, but knelt at the Savior's feet and said unto him, 'My Lord and my God.' And then President McKay repeated the words of the Master, 'Because thou hast seen me, thou hast believed: blessed are they that have not seen, and yet have believed.'"[3]

Joseph Smith stated that in order to develop faith in Christ one must have a "correct idea of his character, perfections, and attributes."[4] We know that he was a God before the earth was formed. We know that he is the creator of all things under the direction of the Father, that he is the source of life and light in all things (John 1:1–4, 9;

D&C 88:7–13). We understand that in the garden and on the cross, he experienced our pains and sufferings so that he could succor us in our weaknesses and trials, and even our death. We know that he is merciful as well as just. For example, when the ten lepers asked for mercy, nine were healed, but the tenth, because of his faith, was made whole (Luke 17:12–19). Christ is kind and gracious, but firm and unchangeable. He is patient and forgiving, but willing to cleanse the temple of those who would demean it. He is the epitome of humility and meekness, but he also is all powerful.

I believe that one of the most important truths to know about the Savior is his relationship with Heavenly Father: He is the "only begotten of the Father" in the flesh (John 1:14). The apostle Paul says that we as human beings are "partakers of flesh and blood," meaning that we are mortals subject to death. In contrast, Paul indicates that Jesus "took part of the same" so that he could overcome death (Hebrews 2:14). By this, Paul meant that Jesus was part mortal and part immortal. From his mother, Mary, he inherited mortality—the seeds of death. But from his immortal Father, he inherited an endless life, which gave him the power to overcome death through the Resurrection (John 5:26; Hebrews 7:16).

As he said to the Jews: "Therefore doth my Father love me, because I lay down my life, that I might take it again. No man taketh it from me, but I lay it down of myself. I have power to lay it down, and I have power to take it again. This commandment have I received of my Father" (John 10:17–18).

I testify that Christ and the gospel plan are the foundation upon which we must build. I am so grateful for my testimony of him. I am grateful for Helaman's words, which point us as well as his sons to the atoning blood of Christ. I pray that each of us may learn the lesson taught by this great prophet.

President Bateman: In the great intercessory prayer just prior to his crucifixion, Jesus said that it is life eternal to know the Father and the Son (John 17:3). I believe that the best way to know Deity is to serve them. Through the light of Christ and the Holy Ghost, we have an inner voice, or conscience, that gives us innate feelings of right and wrong. The purpose of that light is to keep us in the right way, to light our path so that we do not stumble. That light invites us to do good and to believe in Christ (Moroni 7:15–16).

Elder Russell M. Nelson, in the April 2002 general conference, cited a scripture describing the foundational way in which women may serve the Lord: "Sisters received special gifts [before the foundation of the world]. They, according to the Lord, were empowered 'to multiply and replenish the earth, according to my commandment, and to fulfil the promise which was given by my Father before the foundation of the world, . . . for their exaltation in the eternal worlds, that they may bear the souls of men; . . . herein is the work of my Father continued, that he may be glorified' (D&C 132:63). Think of it: When a mother bears and cares for a child, she not only helps the earth answer the end of its creation (D&C 49:16–17), but she glorifies God!"[5]

Women are uniquely endowed with spiritual and physical gifts from before the foundation of the world that infuse within them elements of the divine nature. Whether a woman marries or not, whether a woman has children or not, those distinctive divine elements are part of her inheritance. If she uses them with her own children or the children of others, she will contribute to the purposes of this earth and assist God in his divine plan. Moreover, she will be blessed with an increase in faith and understanding. She will build her home upon the Rock, who is Christ.

In general, women have a greater degree of spiritual awareness and a sense of caring and love for others than do men. Often, there is a meekness and humility in women not found in men. If the history of war tells us anything, it is that women innately value life more than men. In contrast, the "natural man" (Mosiah 3:19) is less patient, less submissive, and more apt to struggle with spiritual things. These special gifts enjoyed by women are not cultural but innate. The divine elements in women draw them closer to God as they nurture the spirits of God. These elements support women in building their lives on the

Rock. For example, consider the following autobiographical story by Les Goates, a former writer for the *Deseret News*.

Les was born in a small community in this valley approximately one hundred years ago. He was born prematurely and weighed only three pounds when he was seven weeks old. In addition to his small size, the infant suffered from a serious physical deformity. The mother often wept and prayed over the tiny boy. Medicine in those days was primitive.

"There were no incubators, [so the baby] was kept in a small basket with medicated cotton for its bed. Folks came from miles around to see this tiny freak of nature—especially doctors, who shook their heads and went away. Of course, everyone knew the child would not live very long.

"But the mother never ceased to fast and pray that her little one might be spared. She never relinquished for a moment the absolute assurance that she would yet rear her babe. Her faith was astounding. Then one day . . . her husband's father . . . came down from his . . . house . . . to the little shack by the railroad track to offer . . . help . . . to the distraught mother and her child.

"The rugged old pioneer took one look at the infant in the basket, then said to the mother, 'Louie, I want you to give up this baby and let it go. We all know that only your faith and prayers are keeping it alive. The time has come now for us to look . . . after you. Why, you haven't been able to walk [but] a few steps at a time since the little thing was born. Now we must look out before we lose you, too.

"'Besides, suppose that by your faith and . . . prayers, this babe is permitted to live. Chances are, it will be a lifetime burden to you and your family all the days of its life, for the doctors say it can never amount to anything. I think it best that we give it up, and let its spirit go back where it came from.'

"[The mother] said nothing as one more tear dropped upon the old, homemade rag carpet. Her father-in-law picked up his hat and strolled . . . up the street to the town meeting house where the monthly fast and testimony meeting was about to convene. In those days fast meetings were held on Thursday afternoons.

"Presently . . . the father of the infant came into the house. [He] too looked at the baby, heaved a long sigh that seemed to convey the attitude of discouragement and despair, and said to his wife, 'I don't think I can do any good here, Mother. I'll go down to the Old Field and do some more plowing. The ground is getting dry and every day at plowing helps the crops that much.'

"He hitched his team to the wagon and drove over the railroad track and down the road to his little farm. The rattle of the wheels as they bounced over the rails had scarcely died away when the mother said to her sister-in-law, 'Sarah, we are going over to the fast meeting and get the baby a name and a blessing.'

" 'But how can we go to the meeting?' Sarah protested. 'We have no horse or buggy, and you have scarcely walked since the baby came.'

" 'We'll manage somehow,' the mother remonstrated. 'I'll take this small rocking chair, drag it along for a few steps, then sit down and rest. You can carry the baby. He is very light.'

"So, in that strange way, these two women made their arduous way to the . . . meeting house on a Thursday afternoon carrying a wee babe and a rocking chair.

"When they arrived the babies were already being blessed. The wee infant was given a name and a blessing under the hands of its maternal grandfather. . . .

"After this ordinance had been attended to, the time was given to testimony bearing and among others there arose to speak a woman of rare spirituality. . . . She spoke of the many gifts and blessings she had received through the gospel. . . .

"She then began to speak in a strange language, a smooth, melodic tongue that sounded like sweet music. As she spoke, she occasionally made a gesture toward this mother with the small baby, so that the audience understood that she was speaking about them.

"When she . . . finished, . . . the stake patriarch arose to interpret the testimony. 'This sister has spoken in the language of Adam,' he said, 'and she has conveyed a message and a promise to this mother who has fasted and prayed so long for her little one.' It was on account of the exceedingly great faith of this mother, he said, that her prayers had ascended to the high heaven and her child, who had been appointed to come into the world only long enough to receive an earthly body, would now be privileged to live, to grow to manhood and rear a family in Zion. He would perform a work of which this mother would be exceedingly well pleased, the patriarch concluded.

"How much easier and shorter were the steps back home to the little old shack by the railroad track! When they arrived there, assisted by kind neighbors and friends, Sarah undid the baby's wraps to make it comfortable and as she did so she exclaimed excitedly, 'Louie, Louie, come here quick! The baby! He's perfectly all right!'

"The mother ran quickly to her baby and found that all signs of physical deformity had disappeared; the child, in very truth, was perfectly normal."[6]

Brother Goates grew to manhood and married; he and his wife had five children. He became one of the finest sportswriters in America, served as a bishop, and was a special writer for the Public Communications Department of the Church.

The point of the story is not the miracle but the relationship between the mother and child and between the mother and the Lord. Her love for the newborn infant fostered by those special nurturing gifts caused her to plead with Heavenly Father to bless the child. In the process, the trial of her faith strengthened the bond between her and the Master.

But suppose the Lord had answered her prayer in a different way. Would her house on the Rock have been any less complete? Would it have meant that her faith was insufficient? I believe that she would have loved the Lord just as much, and her house would have remained on solid ground.

All of us are aware of prayers that have not been answered in the way we would like them to be. I have had times when I pled with the Lord for a certain blessing, and my hopes were not realized. On other occasions, my dreams were fulfilled. Faith is not the only factor in determining the location of the rooms and the design of the house. We need to remember that our Father in Heaven is the architect, and he and the Son know more about us than we do. They can see the end from the beginning (Isaiah 46:10). How wonderful it is to be in a covenant relationship with them.

We testify of the Lord's goodness, of his love and concern for each of you. He knows you. He knows your individual circumstances and will listen to your petitions and answer them. Helaman understood that Christ is the Way, the Truth, and the Life. Only by building our house on sacred ground—on the rock of the Redeemer—will we find peace, happiness, and a fulness of joy. May Helaman's words be written in our minds and hearts.

Notes

1. D. Kelly Ogden and Andrew C. Skinner, *New Testament Apostles Testify of Christ* (Salt Lake City: Deseret Book, 1998), 40.
2. C. S. Lewis, *Mere Christianity* (New York: Simon & Schuster, 1996), 176.
3. *I Know That My Redeemer Lives: Latter-day Prophets Testify of the Savior* (Salt Lake City: Deseret Book, 1990), 138.
4. Joseph Smith, *Lectures on Faith*, comp. N. B. Lundwall (Salt Lake City: Deseret Book, 1985), 38.
5. Russell M. Nelson, "How Firm Our Foundation," *Ensign*, May 2002, 75–76.
6. Harold B. Lee, *Remembering the Miracles*, comp. L. Brent Goates (American Fork, Utah: Covenant Communications, 2001), 147–49.

Becoming Perfect in Christ

Camille Fronk

Several years ago, I heard a college student relate his experience as a volunteer at a Special Olympics competition. As the starting signal sounded, five young Special Olympians took off on their 200-yard dash. The stands were filled with enthusiastic spectators who cheered all five athletes. Somehow, in Special Olympics races *every* competitor is a crowd favorite. Thus, when the boy racing in the middle lane stumbled and fell, the entire crowd of spectators voiced their disappointment and then encouraged him to get up and go again. The stands fell suddenly silent, however, as the two competitors racing in the lanes on either side of the fallen boy stopped to see what the crowd was bemoaning. This was a race, and three of the five competitors were at a standstill on the track! In a moment of pure innocence, both boys spontaneously ran back to help the fallen athlete. All three—linked arm-in-arm—finished the race together. After that race, all five boys received medals. On the bronze podium, three Special Olympians stood, grinning contagiously as if to say, "We figured out a way for everyone to win!"

As mortals living in a fallen world, we all have entered a race commissioned by God. This race is not necessarily won by the swiftest (Ecclesiastes 9:11), and more is involved than finishing. The apostle Paul invited disciples of Christ to "run with patience the race that is set before us" (Hebrews 12:1). Patient running, an oxymoron in the

---

Camille Fronk is an assistant professor of ancient scripture at Brigham Young University. She has served as a counselor in her stake Relief Society presidency, as a Primary teacher, and as a member of the Young Women General Board. Before joining the faculty at BYU, she served as dean of students at LDS Business College and as a seminary and institute instructor.

eyes of the world, is the race that leads us to God. At its completion, we will have been made "perfect"—complete, ripe, whole. When we run the race of life the Lord's way, we become like him.

According to the apostle Peter, the race of life is a process of divine transformation, or "partak[ing] of the divine nature" (2 Peter 1:4). He describes the process with masterful simplicity:

> . . . giving all diligence,
> add to your faith virtue;
> and to virtue knowledge;
> and to knowledge temperance;
> and to temperance patience;
> and to patience godliness;
> and to godliness brotherly kindness;
> and to brotherly kindness charity (2 Peter 1:5–7).

If we consider each attribute in the order Peter prescribed, the power and beauty of becoming perfect in Christ unfolds and unexpected lessons leading to full consecration appear.

GIVING ALL DILIGENCE

Note that, according to Peter, *diligence* is our responsibility throughout the process. His phrase "giving all diligence" suggests that our role is more than merely saying our prayers, going to sleep, and having perfection bestowed upon us when we awake. The word *diligence* implies perseverance, dedication, and staying power—especially when the going gets tough. When Peter calls for diligence, then, he is speaking to those who are already determined to finish the task. The fickle Israelites waited for God's law to be brought down—literally and figuratively—to their level at the foot of Mt. Sinai; by contrast, in Galilee Christ invited his disciples to *follow him up* the mountain if they would receive the fullness he had to offer (JST Matthew 5:1–2). Similarly, the enslaved people of Alma did not miraculously have their heavy burdens removed from their backs when they petitioned God.

Rather, over time their backs were strengthened "that they could bear up their burdens with ease" (Mosiah 24:15). Such examples remind us that through his mercy, merits, and grace, the Messiah makes possible even our ability to endure.

Add to your faith virtue. Peter's epistle is addressed to those Christians already grounded in the "precious faith . . . of God and . . . Jesus Christ" (2 Peter 1:1). During the final years of Nero Caesar's reign, a period of burgeoning distrust and mistreatment swelled against Christians. Well acquainted with trials of their faith, recipients of Peter's epistle would have developed a steadfast trust in Christ. Peter himself knew he would shortly die (2 Peter 1:14), martyred in Rome. "Giving all diligence," he wrote from prison, next "add to your faith virtue" (2 Peter 1:5).

Virtue is the natural fruit of faith and diligence. The word *virtue* suggests moral goodness and purity in body, mind, and deed. Tabitha, a disciple of Christ, exemplified virtue, being "full of good works and almsdeeds which she did." Many in her village, particularly among "all the widows," felt her goodness. At her death, the villagers had sent for Peter and "when he was come, . . . all the widows stood by him weeping, and shewing the coats and garments which [Tabitha] made, while she was with them" (Acts 9:36–39). They mourned her death, not because she would no longer supply the village with clothing, but because she would no longer be among them radiating her inner goodness and pure motives in rendering service. Virtue purifies our motives that in turn educate our actions, unlike checklist good works where motives are questionable and expectations for recognition are high.

And to virtue knowledge. Virtue precedes knowledge, as Peter observed. When following Christ becomes a natural part of life, we begin to understand connections among gospel principles that previously seemed unrelated. Christ taught, "If any man will *do* his will, he shall *know of the doctrine,* whether it be of God, or whether I speak of myself" (John 7:17; emphasis added). In the same vein, Alma explained that "it is given unto many to know the mysteries of God; . . . according to the heed and diligence which they give unto him" (Alma 12:9).

Virtuous obedience to God's laws increases our knowledge of his gospel because our living of gospel standards invites the Spirit to teach us.

And to knowledge temperance. Peter identified the gift of temperance or self-control as the next attribute or step in transforming our nature. Temperance enables us to more wisely manage time, material resources, and appetites, and it strengthens our will to keep the first commandment. President Ezra Taft Benson taught: "When we put God first, all other things fall into their proper place or drop out of our lives. Our love of the Lord will govern the claims for our affection, the demands on our time, the interests we pursue, and the order of our priorities."[1] These are the blessings of temperance.

And to temperance patience. We need to give patience room to develop in our busy lives. As James taught, "Let patience have her perfect work, that you may be perfect and entire" (James 1:4). We forget about checking our preconceived agenda for life while losing ourselves in helping others progress along the trail. This patient response grows out of a willingness to have patience first with God.

Blessed with the Lord's gift of patience, we rejoice at the realization that God is in control and our lives will always be better when we turn them over to him and trust in his divine timetable. We don't know all he has in store for us, but we are at peace with the confidence that it will be vastly superior to our myopically designed plan. Such patience ripens into eternal perspective.

Sarah, Rebekah, Rachel, Hannah, and Elisabeth all learned the lesson of patience when decades of heartfelt prayers were offered before they received their promised children. Isaiah valued patience, declaring: "Men have not heard, nor perceived by the ear, neither hath the eye seen, . . . what he hath prepared for him that waiteth for him" (Isaiah 64:4). The phrase *waiting upon the Lord* is related in the Hebrew to *having hope in the Lord.* We are patient with God because we have hope in what we cannot see or hear. With the Lord's gift of deep and steady patience, we gratefully set aside our agendas, trust his divine timetable, and seek his will.

And to patience godliness. Godliness is a virtue that penetrates the core of our souls, enlarging and purifying virtues previously received. We know instinctively when we stand in a holy place. With the attribute of godliness, we better understand order in the Lord's Church and willingly sustain that order. When we are a godly people, we value temple worship, and we reverence the sacrament service in new ways. For the godly, the distance between earth and heaven narrows. We feel awe for God's creations, and we reverence God in our homes. Thus, godliness is not a virtue confined to sacred settings. When godliness is added to our natures, we sincerely respect all forms of life, including our fellow strugglers on this earth. Christ blessed the "pure in heart: for they shall see God" (Matthew 5:8). With the gift of godliness, in each of his children we see their potential for godliness.

And to godliness brotherly kindness. Seeing goodness and potential all around us prepares us for brotherly—or sisterly—kindness, the next step in our spiritual development. We become true under-shepherds of the Savior, eager to encourage and support those who struggle or question. Kind people are attuned to the needs of those around them and, without fanfare or formality, serve others spontaneously. With a phone call, a letter, or an invitation for a walk, they provide healing to wounds we didn't know we had.

And to brotherly kindness charity. Seeing the preparation—the perfecting influence of all the other virtues—that must precede receiving the gift of charity makes me realize how naïve I was at twenty-one, when I believed I would pick up charity sometime during my mission and stroll back into "civilian" life a year and a half later with it checked off my goal list. Elder Jeffrey R. Holland explained, "*True* charity has been known only once. It is shown perfectly and purely in Christ's unfailing, ultimate, and atoning love for us."[2] That may be why Mormon defined charity as "the pure love of Christ," that is only "bestowed upon [the] true followers of [God's] Son," and the only way that we "may become . . . like him" (Moroni 7:47–48). Bruce C. Hafen taught that the bestowal of charity "makes possible the infusion of spiritual endowments that actually change and purify our nature."[3] The principle is clear: we can never attain a divine nature by our efforts alone. We can only become perfect *in Christ*, through his gift of atonement, through his grace that bestows "strength and assistance" beyond our natural abilities.[4]

Charity, in its selflessness, invites the divine to permeate all the preceding attributes. Paul taught that without charity, any of the other attributes can become self-serving or self-laudatory "as sounding brass, or a tinkling cymbal" (1 Corinthians 13:1). With God's gift of charity, the Lord stretches, strengthens, and solidifies all the other virtues. Those whose natures are thus divinely transformed will, according to Peter, "never fall." Their "calling and election [will be] sure" (2 Peter 1:10).

Peter's perspective on this ultimate promise should dispel worries such as "Have I run far enough in this race?" or "How close am I to the finish line?" It should also eliminate self-righteous attitudes such as "I'm obviously going to win since I'm farther along the path than she is." Like the runners who found victory by helping a companion win, we lose obsession with ourselves as we become more like Christ. Our work becomes the Father's work. President Brigham Young reflected: "I can say, truly and honestly, that the thought never came into my mind, in all my labors, what my reward will be, or whether my crown would be large or small, or any crown at all, a small possession, a large possession, or no possession. . . . All that I have had in my mind has been that it was my duty to do the will of God, and to labor to establish his Kingdom on the earth."[5]

Do these scriptural admonitions to become perfect in Christ apply to us—his everyday, rank-and-file, slow-to-change disciples? Remember Elder Holland's recent observation, "The race is against sin, *not* against each other."[6] When you feel disappointed with yourself and are tempted to drop out of the race, remember Peter, whose own life reflects the process of divine transformation. Some scholars have questioned Peter's authorship of this epistle, arguing that it is "too patient" for the impetuous apostle portrayed in the four Gospels. But Peter is not the same man at the end of his mortal life as he was at Christ's crucifixion. With the gift of the Holy Ghost, a witness of the reality of the

Resurrection, and years of service rendered through diligence and obedience, Peter was fashioned into a man of charity, a "man of Christ" (Helaman 3:29).

When we become discouraged, Elder Henry B. Eyring's words instill hope: "We can take heart that our honest effort to keep our covenants allows God to increase our power to do it. We all need that assurance at times."[7] The Lord, through the power of the Atonement, transforms not only our words and deeds but our very natures to become like his. The Lord's way is a journey to discover, not a race to conquer. The Savior "marked the path and led the way, And ev'ry point define[d]."[8] Indeed, we can join with Paul by praising, "Thanks be to God, [who] giveth us the victory through our Lord Jesus Christ" (1 Corinthians 15:57). May we learn to run with patience the race that is set before us, always looking to our Redeemer, the Author and Finisher of our faith.

Notes

1. Ezra Taft Benson, "The Great Commandment—Love the Lord," *Ensign*, May 1988, 4.
2. Jeffrey R. Holland, *Christ and the New Covenant: The Messianic Message of the Book of Mormon* (Salt Lake City: Deseret Book, 1997), 336; emphasis in original.
3. Bruce C. Hafen, *The Broken Heart: Applying the Atonement to Life's Experiences* (Salt Lake City: Deseret Book, 1989), 18.
4. LDS Bible Dictionary, s.v. "Grace," 697.
5. Brigham Young, *Discourses of Brigham Young*, sel. John A. Widtsoe (Salt Lake City: Deseret Book, 1954), 452.
6. Jeffrey R. Holland, "The Other Prodigal," *Ensign*, May 2002, 64; emphasis in original.
7. Henry B. Eyring, "Witnesses for God," *Ensign*, November 1996, 30–31.
8. "How Great the Wisdom and the Love," *Hymns of The Church of Jesus Christ of Latter-day Saints* (Salt Lake City: The Church of Jesus Christ of Latter-day Saints, 1985), no. 195.

FIRM FOOTINGS: "THE LORD IS MY LIGHT"

Kathryn Afarian

The key to building a testimony, the kind that will see us tranquilly through whatever trials may come, is coming truly to know the Savior. The Savior himself said, "And this is life eternal, that they might know thee the only true God, and Jesus Christ, whom thou hast sent"(John 17:3). So how do we come to know the Savior? I used to think there was some deep, mystical secret about it. People would give talks about knowing Christ, and I would wonder, *Well, what do you do? How do you achieve this?* But I've come to realize that there is no mystical secret. It's like everything else in the gospel—there are simple ways to accomplish it. They include reading the scriptures to learn about his life and mission, seeking to emulate him, and perhaps most important, serving him. "For how knoweth a man the master whom he has not served, and who is a stranger unto him, and is far from the thoughts and intents of his heart?" (Mosiah 5:13).

What about our testimonies of the restored gospel? Probably we've all had experiences where we've felt insecure about our testimonies, especially those of us born and raised in Latter-day Saint homes, who as young adults may have compared our experiences to someone else's and found ours different or less powerful. My sister could point to a moment in time when she knew that the Church was true. I could not because I had never questioned that truth. It never occurred to me to question

---

Kathryn Afarian received her master's degree in teaching English as a second language (TESL) and has taught at Brigham Young University. She has served as a missionary and as a counselor in her ward Relief Society.

it. I grew up in western New York state and visited the important restoration sites: Joseph Smith's birthplace, the Hill Cumorah, the Sacred Grove, and the monument at Harmony, Pennsylvania, commemorating the priesthood restoration. The inscriptions on those monuments said that these things happened right at those places. It just never occurred to me to question those statements. As a result, without a specific conversion experience to relate, I grew up wondering if I really did have a testimony. Somehow it seemed that if I had never questioned, I must not really know. Some of you might have had experiences also where you have thought, *Is my testimony good enough or is it flawed in some way because my experience wasn't like someone else's?* Later in my life, I have decided that the best way to measure the validity of a testimony is to look at the choices we make every day. That's where we see whether we have a testimony or not.

We all need to bear in mind, however, that a testimony is fragile. I used to have a mental list of all the people I thought would never go astray. And I was arrogant enough to believe that my name was very near the top. In recent years, however, two charter members of my list have encountered serious spiritual difficulties. Thankfully (I think it is a credit to my list making), both of these people have returned to full fellowship in the Church. But their experiences have taught me that there is no list. We are all vulnerable. The apostle Paul was very aware of vulnerability, and perhaps especially of his own. In 1 Corinthians 10:12, he said, "Wherefore let him that thinketh he standeth take heed lest he fall." Earlier in the same epistle, he confessed, "But I keep under my body, and bring it into subjection: lest that by any means, when I have preached to others, I myself should be a castaway" (1 Corinthians 9:27).

"Your testimony is something you have today, but you may not have it always," warned President Harold B. Lee. "Testimony is as elusive as a moonbeam; it's as fragile as an orchid; you have to recapture it every morning of your life. You have to hold on by study, and by faith, and by prayer."[1] He went on to talk about some of the things that can erode our testimonies, like keeping the wrong company, falling into sin, or becoming angry. Anger struck a chord with me. I am often guilty of anger. I have at times even been angry at the Lord because what he was doing didn't seem to make sense to me. In one of my most dark and angry periods, I was riding to work with a friend and her tape player was playing a song by a Mormon soft rock group. The words as nearly as I can remember them were: "It never had occurred to me, / But suddenly I find / That our journey through eternity / Is traveled in our mind." That really brought me up short. I thought, *You know, that's true. It isn't what happens to us, but it's how we perceive what happens to us. It's the attitudes we develop about our experiences that make us who we are.* I thought long and hard about that, made some course corrections, and decided not to be so angry.

We all have trials. They are in our past, our present, and undoubtedly will be part of our future. If we read the scriptures honestly, we know we've been promised trials. These will try our faith and wear away at our testimonies if we allow them to. My trials have been unfulfilled promises and betrayal. Perhaps yours have been something else. I came to a point once where nothing made sense. The inspiration I had received and the promises I had been given just didn't add up. And I really did feel a sense of betrayal. It never occurred to me to question the truth of the gospel, but what I did question was whether it included a place for me. And I thought, *You know, if there isn't a place for me in the picture, maybe it doesn't really matter whether the gospel is true.* As I thought along those lines, a scripture kept returning to me from the book of John. After the Savior had given the Bread of Life sermon, many went away and didn't want to follow him anymore. The Savior asked his apostles if they would also go away. Peter answered, "Lord, to whom shall we go? thou hast the words of eternal life" (John 6:68). That statement of Peter's helped me through a difficult time thirteen years ago. What happened doesn't make any more sense to me today than it did then, but I know it is the Savior who has the words of eternal life, and I've been able to go on from there. Interestingly enough, even though my questions remain unanswered, after more than a decade it doesn't matter so much anymore.

In times of trial or doubt, we frequently have an experience that William Walsham How described in these words from his hymn, "For All the Saints": "And when the strife is fierce, the warfare long, / Steals on the ear the distant triumph song. / And hearts are brave again, and arms are strong."[2] It used to be for me in those moments when everything seemed bleak, and I didn't understand what was going on, that the "distant triumph song" *I* heard was, "Just keep enduring and someday you'll be a goddess." Now, that's a great song, and maybe it's the one you hear. I'm not denigrating it in any way, but it's not the song that I hear in my soul today. Maybe right now, for me at least, that particular triumph song is just a little too distant. At this point in my life, the triumph song I hear is the one about warm sunshine, cool morning breezes, lilacs, and the robin that sings outside my bedroom window. It's about sprouting seeds and the fruit of the coming harvest. It's about the quickening of understanding that has allowed for the creation of beautiful music, sculpture, and literature. It's about health, intelligence, succor, and even life itself. The song I hear is about the present, the here and now, and about the Christ through whom each present moment is made not only possible but glorious.

Notes

1. *Harold B. Lee*, [vol. 3] in *Teachings of Presidents of the Church* series (Salt Lake City: The Church of Jesus Christ of Latter-day Saints, 2000), 43.
2. William Walsham How, "For All the Saints," *Hymns of The Church of Jesus Christ of Latter-day Saints* (Salt Lake City: The Church of Jesus Christ of Latter-day Saints, 1985), no. 82.

Jesus Christ, the Rock upon Which We Must Build

Ben B. Banks

During my life, I have benefited from the example of many great sisters. In fact, the two people who have had the greatest effect on my life have been my mother and my wife. My wonderful mother, Chloa Berry Banks, became a widow in 1934 at the age of thirty-nine. I was just two years old when my father, Ben F. Banks, was critically injured in a construction accident. Within a month, he had passed away, leaving my mother to single-handedly rear seven children.

As I look back now, I realize what an incredible example of courage in action my mother was. With her father's help, she acquired some old rental units in Salt Lake City. Mom led our fatherless family to renovate those units. She handled many of the repairs herself, fixed the plumbing and electrical systems, painted, and decorated. She even hauled the coal for heating, and she rented the properties. Her actions saved our family.

My wife, Sue, and I will celebrate our fiftieth wedding anniversary in June. I remember very clearly what my mother said to my new bride on our wedding day in June 1952. Mom turned to Sue and said, "I've raised him for the first part of his life; I now turn him over to you to raise him for the rest of his life."

I have watched Sue serve our seven sons and one daughter, twenty-five grandchildren, and nine great-grandchildren. I have realized how

---

Ben B. Banks has served as a member of the Presidency of the Seventy. He has also served as president of the Scotland Edinburgh Mission, as a stake president, and as a bishop. He and his wife, Susan Kearnes Banks, are the parents of eight children and the grandparents of twenty-five and great-grandparents of nine.

much the gospel of Jesus Christ has blessed our life together and our family. You would also be interested to know that she has carried out my mother's assignment with zeal and dedication.

I constantly try to emulate the example set by these two wonderful women by their constant living of the principles of the restored gospel.

The theme of this year's BYU Women's Conference, taken from the Book of Mormon, summarizes one verse of scripture that we must learn to live by if we are to overcome by faith the challenges we all face in mortality. In Helaman we read: "Remember, remember that it is upon the rock of our Redeemer, who is Christ, the Son of God, that ye must build your foundation; that when the devil shall send forth his mighty winds, yea, his shafts in the whirlwind, yea, when all his hail and mighty storm shall beat upon you, it shall have no power over you to drag you down to the gulf of misery and endless wo, because of the rock upon which ye are built, which is a sure foundation, a foundation whereon if men build they cannot fall" (Helaman 5:12).

Helaman's timeless counsel to his sons more than two thousand years ago instructs us that, as followers of the Savior, we *must* build our foundation on Jesus Christ, our Redeemer, if we are to avoid becoming trapped in Satan's "gulf of misery and endless wo." In today's terms, that sounds very much like the symptoms of guilt, depression, and despondency.

During our lifetime, Satan's temptations will come upon us as "winds," "hail," or a "mighty storm." Why? To make us miserable like unto himself. How we deal with that assault will determine our happiness both now and hereafter.

Many have to cope with opposition and hardship in their lives. There is nothing new about this, and yet our hardships are very different from those faced by the early Church members 150 years ago.

Today I would like to share with you a snapshot of pioneer life from the writings of Sarah Ann Jackson, a pioneer member of the Church from Britain.[1] Sarah was born to John and Alice Jackson on 25 September 1863 in Accrington, Lancashire. Her father, John, full of faith, joined the Church at the age of fifteen. Some years later, he was called with his wife to serve a mission in the city of Hull when Sarah was just four years old. Following the call, Sarah, her mother, Alice, and her father, John, walked 120 miles across the Pennine Hills of England to east Yorkshire, where John served his mission and became president of the Hull Conference. About a year into the mission, John developed appendicitis and died, leaving his wife and daughter penniless and alone.

Bereft of funds and family and pregnant with twins, Alice and her daughter, Sarah Ann, gathered their few belongings and walked back across those same hills, this time to Liverpool to join the Saints leaving for America. They arrived in time to join the *USS Constitution*, sailing on 24 June 1868. Six long and terrible weeks, the rocking ship, and Alice's condition all made for a very poor journey, as you can imagine. Four-year-old Sarah was her mother's sole nurse and constant companion.

During one very bad storm, Alice and Sarah had to wrap their legs around the mast to save themselves from being washed overboard. The sea captain is reported to have said that "if the ship had not been full of Mormons, it would have sunk!"

Eventually they arrived in New York and then traveled by railroad to Benton, Wyoming. As the time was approaching to give birth to her twins, Alice set out to walk the remaining 694 miles to Salt Lake City with four-year-old Sarah Ann. Day after day, Alice would walk until her strength gave out, and then she would be lifted into a wagon to travel until she could no longer stand the jolting. She would then get out of the wagon and start to walk again. Sarah Ann later said that she remembered day after day dragging on.

The twins were born on the plains, but Sarah Ann's excitement at having siblings was short-lived, as both of them passed away within a few days of birth. With determination and faith, Alice and Sarah Ann continued on foot, arriving in Salt Lake City on 15 September 1868.

Both Alice and Sarah Ann had endured much on their journey. Both had reason to "mourn or think [their] lot [was] hard,"[2] but both continued in the faith until the time of their passing many years later.

Women of great faith always share the same hallmark—they never give up in times of adversity. They know who they are, and they know where safety is found. Jesus Christ is their foundation of faith. If someone came along today and took a snapshot of your modern life, what would it show? Today we do not face the same challenges as our pioneer forefathers faced. Our challenges are different. Our challenge may come in the form of helping a family member cope with drug or alcohol abuse, rebellion, a weak testimony, or feelings of inadequacy, depression, and self-doubt; it could even come in handling the pain of divorce or in the suffering that comes from serious ill health.

But just like the pioneers of old, our eyes have to remain firmly fixed on the Savior and his gospel. As we cross the plains of life and bear whatever we are called upon to bear, we can overcome Satan and render him powerless, if we build our lives on the foundation of Jesus Christ.

The Book of Mormon teaches us that "men [and women] are, that they might have joy" (2 Nephi 2:25).

The Lord declared to Moroni: "If men come unto me I will show unto them their weakness. I give unto men weakness that they may be humble; and my grace is sufficient for all men that humble themselves before me; for if they humble themselves before me, and have faith in me, then will I make weak things become strong unto them" (Ether 12:27).

We cannot build our foundation on Jesus Christ if we do not know him. That knowledge comes as we "press forward, feasting upon the word of Christ, and endure to the end." And he gives us this promise: "Behold, thus saith the Father: Ye shall have eternal life" (2 Nephi 31:20).

The action of pressing forward was reinforced by the risen Lord when he said to the Nephite Saints and to us: "I am the . . . light. Look unto me, and endure to the end, and ye shall live; for unto him that endureth to the end will I give eternal life" (3 Nephi 15:9).

The Savior's admonition to come unto him, press forward, look to him, feast upon his words, and endure to the end all require us to do something.

I would like to mention one more thing that will help in our quest to build our foundation on the Savior. Moroni summed this up when he said: "Yea, come unto Christ, and be perfected in him, and deny yourselves of all ungodliness" (Moroni 10:32). If we truly want a solid foundation built on the Savior, we have to deny ourselves of all manner of ungodliness. We need to be living examples of the Savior in thought and in word and in action. This requires of us to live the law of sacrifice.

Sisters can have a great influence upon those around them—especially family members. Children look to their mothers, grandmothers, and ward members for guidance. They look to you. They watch what you watch; they speak the way you speak. Their standards often derive from your standards. We can do so much good by simply keeping the commandments and quietly living the gospel.

Cast your mind back for a moment and think about how many times you have heard individuals older than yourself talk about how wicked the world is becoming. They say, "It wasn't like that when I was young," and we laugh and joke about how times have changed.

But the stark reality that we face is that times really *have* changed.

Our world today, more than ever before, needs more temples—not just the physical temples that are being built throughout the world, but the spiritual temples of which Paul wrote in his letter to the Corinthians (1 Corinthians 3:16). The prophet today is doing his part to build more sanctuaries from the storms of life. Are we, similarly, making the temples of our bodies worthy receptacles of the Holy Ghost?

We need better prepared missionaries from homes that have a mother's righteous influence, missionaries with a sure foundation who have "been taught by their mothers, that if they did not doubt, God would deliver them" (Alma 56:47). Never before in the history of this world has there been a need for more valiant mothers, more faithful

Latter-day Saint women who are an influence for good in their homes. Sisters and mothers are entitled to inspiration.

Would you allow me to share a personal story of my wife's wonderful influence on one of our sons and how inspiration came to her? Many years ago while I was serving as a bishop, I was away early Sunday morning to a bishop's meeting. My wife's responsibility was to wake the boys for priesthood meeting. One son, seventeen at the time, had been out later than he should have been Saturday evening. As Sue made the rounds, she said to him, "If you get up now you will have time to shower and have breakfast before priesthood meeting." Our son kind of groaned and moaned and turned over in his bed and said, "Mom, I'm too tired to go to priesthood meeting. I will get up later and go to sacrament meeting, but I am *not* going to priesthood meeting this morning."

My wife knew she was not strong enough to wrestle our seventeen-year-old son out of bed. She didn't know what to do. She went into the adjoining room and pondered how she might get him out of bed, knowing where he should be. The answer came to her. She walked back into his room, grabbed the covers, pulled them off him, and said, "Okay, if you are not going to church this morning, neither am I. Move over."

She crawled into the bed beside him and cuddled him as if he were still a baby.

That lasted for about ten seconds!

He threw back the covers and said, "Okay, Mom, I'll go to priesthood meeting."

She never ever from that day had a problem getting any of our sons out of bed in time for priesthood meeting. Years later that same son, while working in Washington, D.C., as an attorney in the Justice Department and also serving in a bishopric, said to his mother over the phone, "Mom, you can't believe how hard it is to get these young men in our ward to get up in time for priesthood meeting."

His mother said, "Be patient, son. Remember how you were as a teenager."

He said, "Oh, Mom, I was never like that."

How quickly we forget.

On 1 January 2000, the First Presidency and the Quorum of the Twelve, as special witnesses of Jesus Christ, issued a remarkable proclamation to the members of the Church and to the world entitled "The Living Christ." In their historic statement, they testify that he is "the light, the life, and the hope of the world."[3]

What applies universally to all mankind applies specifically and personally to each one of us. He is our *Advocate* with the Father. He is our *Redeemer*. He is our *Savior*.

The way to happiness and a sure foundation is simple. After baptism and reception of the Holy Ghost, we are admonished to—

1. Put our confidence and trust in Jesus Christ completely. We cast our burdens on him.

2. Look to him in faith. Feast on his words and trust them.

3. Repent of unworthy thoughts and any behavior that draws us away from a righteous life.

4. Renew our promises and covenants with him each week.

5. Pray daily to be worthy to have the Holy Ghost to guide us.

We cannot be an influence for good if we treat these principles of peace casually. Faith built on this sure foundation will bring peace into our lives regardless of our circumstances.

It would be good for us to remember the lesson taught by the Lord about the simpleness of his way. Remember how the Lord sent fiery serpents among the children of Israel as they journeyed in the wilderness and then prepared a way for their escape? All they had to do was to look upon the serpent on the pole, and they would be immediately healed. Here is the lesson to us: "Because of the simpleness of the way, or the easiness of it, there were many who perished" (1 Nephi 17:41). Likewise, many today experience failure and difficult challenges because they will not build on the simple foundation of Jesus Christ and his commandments.

I am reminded of an incident recorded in Matthew: "And, behold, a woman, which was diseased with an issue of blood twelve years, came behind him, and touched the hem of his garment: for she said within herself, If I may but touch his garment, I shall be whole. But Jesus turned him about, and when he saw her, he said, Daughter, be of good comfort; thy faith hath made thee whole. And the woman was made whole from that hour" (Matthew 9:20–22).

She had the simple faith that all she had to do was touch the hem of the Savior's garment. She applied that faith and put it into action. The Savior confirmed that her faith had made her whole.

Let us not forget that her faith in a loving Savior made that miracle possible.

The scriptures and modern prophets bear witness why we must place our faith in Jesus Christ:

We know that all of us are in a lost and fallen condition without him (1 Nephi 10:6; Mosiah 16:4–9; Alma 34:9; Ether 3:2).

Only he has the power to redeem us (Alma 34:8–10, 13–17).

He is our advocate with the Father (D&C 29:5; 45:3).

Because of these truths, there are many blessings we obtain when we center our faith and hope in Christ:

We know our hearts can be changed (Mosiah 5:2).

We can obtain knowledge and great joy (Mosiah 5:3–4).

Our weaknesses can become our strengths because we rely on him (Ether 12:27).

His grace will be sufficient to bring us to a state of holiness if we place our confidence and trust in him (Moroni 10:32–33; D&C 93:1).

"A classic story of meeting adversity with a winning attitude is the account of the burning of Thomas A. Edison's laboratories," says Elaine Cannon in her book *Adversity*. She writes the following:

"A spontaneous explosion occurred and others quickly spread, in dramatic repetition of the first burst, moving across the film processing plant through freight cars and on to ignite alcohol storage tanks that sent fantastic towers of flames into the air.

"Water pressure failed, and the fire was soon out of control. It was a spectacular fire! Edison sent for his wife, telling her to bring all her friends because they'd never see anything like this fire again.

"Later, when Edison surveyed the blackened ruins of a lifetime of effort, he turned to his discouraged associates and said, 'You can always make capital out of disaster. Now we are rid of a lot of our past mistakes.'

"He was sixty-seven at the time and began rebuilding the plant before the last ember was finally subdued on the old ruin.

"He could have given up. Instead he proved that youth doesn't have the only handle on growth and that preachers aren't the only people who understand hope. Besides, if adversity helps us get rid of past mistakes, *we need it!*"[4]

I want to conclude my remarks with words from the hymn "How Firm a Foundation," particularly verses 4 through 7, which we seldom ever sing:

> When through the deep waters I call thee to go,
> The rivers of sorrow shall not thee o'erflow,
> For I will be with thee, thy troubles to bless,
> And sanctify to thee thy deepest distress.
>
> When through fiery trials thy pathway shall lie,
> My grace, all sufficient, shall be thy supply.
> The flame shall not hurt thee; I only design
> Thy dross to consume and thy gold to refine.
>
> E'en down to old age, all my people shall prove
> My sov'reign, eternal, unchangeable love;
> And then, when gray hair shall their temples adorn,
> Like lambs shall they still in my bosom be borne.
>
> The soul that on Jesus hath leaned for repose
> I will not, I cannot, desert to his foes;
> That soul, though all hell should endeavor to shake,
> I'll never, no never, no never forsake![5]

Please go forward with simple faith. Ensure that your foundation and that of your family is built on the sure rock of our Savior, even Jesus Christ. Stand fast against all forms of ungodliness. Remember where to turn when you face trials. Remember that many of those trials come from the adversary, whose sole objective is to have you be as miserable as he is.

While accompanying Elder Neal A. Maxwell on a recent assignment, I heard him say there are three kinds of experiences or trials we have in this life: those common to mankind, those self-inflicted, and those individual tutorials Heavenly Father gives to each of us to test us and help us grow.

I commend you for your goodness and your influence upon your individual families and the families of this Church. I pray that we may have a renewed determination to make the Savior our sure foundation. As we do, we will find a renewing and invigorating experience awaiting us. I testify that as we build on a firm foundation, we will enjoy the surety of the Savior's influence in our lives. It will bring us the peace that so many in this world seek after and do not seem to find.

Notes

1. Darlene Chidester Hutchison, "Three Women of Faith," manuscript copy (available in Family History Library, Salt Lake City, 1991), 10–20.
2. William Clayton, "Come, Come, Ye Saints," *Hymns of The Church of Jesus Christ of Latter-day Saints* (Salt Lake City: The Church of Jesus Christ of Latter-day Saints, 1985), no. 30.
3. "The Living Christ: The Testimony of the Apostles of The Church of Jesus Christ of Latter-day Saints," *Ensign*, April 2000, 2.
4. Elaine Cannon, *Adversity* (Salt Lake City: Bookcraft, 1987), 22–23.
5. *Hymns*, no. 85.

Transforming Transitions

Bonnie D. Parkin

When I stood last year at the podium of the Marriott Center at Brigham Young University, I secretly rejoiced that my days of speaking to enormous—albeit kind—crowds had come to an end. Four weeks ago, I stood at the Conference Center podium and learned otherwise. As the saying goes, the only constant in life is change. (Especially in Church callings!) And change can be difficult—it challenges us, tests us, refines us. It gives us experience which can be for our good (D&C 122:7) if we choose to make it so.

Change is the movement from one state of being to another. Hopefully, our movement is one of progression—*eternal* progression—from grace to grace, darkness to light, weakness to strength (D&C 93:12–13, 28). I've learned that this period between two states—the transition—is a precarious place where who the Lord knows we can become intersects with who the adversary wants us to become; we choose between diminishment or growth.

I've experienced many transitions in my life. I was raised on a farm about twenty miles north of Provo—in Herriman, Utah. I herded cows; I weeded potatoes; I gathered eggs. I was such a farm girl that my high school mascot was the Beetdiggers!

My transition to Utah State University was easier because of new friends, but quiet longings for home were sometimes almost more than

---

Bonnie Dansie Parkin was sustained as Relief Society General President in April 2002. A graduate of Utah State University in elementary education, she has served on the Relief Society General Board and as a counselor in the Young Women General Presidency. She served with her husband, James L. Parkin, as he presided over the England London South Mission. They are the parents of four sons and have fifteen grandchildren.

I could bear. After graduation I started teaching third grade: thirty-three seven-year-olds in one room. That's what I call a transition! But it was then I was introduced to my husband-to-be. Blind dates do work.

Our beginnings were in a small basement apartment in Salt Lake City while Jim was completing his schooling, and our first son joined our family. We then transitioned to Seattle, far from family and friends, where Jim finished postgraduate training. Like most young couples, we struggled to make ends meet. I remember paying our tithing with the last few dollars and wondering how we'd get by. And then we received a note to our year-old son, Jeff, from my brother Rodney, saying, "Here is some money for ice cream." It was a fifty-dollar bill, and fifty dollars went a lot further in those days.

While we were in Seattle, three more sons were born to us. As a young mother, I soon found myself herding sons, gathering toys, and weeding bubble gum from hair. For me these Seattle days were a transition with needed growth and great mentoring from good women who shared how they had weathered their transitions.

When Jim accepted a position in Utah, I cried when we had to leave that ward and those Saints. But transitions can't be escaped.

An easier transition was the addition of four daughters, whom I obtained the easy way: our sons married them. And even better was becoming the grandmother of twelve grandsons and three granddaughters.

Transitions will always be with us, stretching and shaping us. Currently, I promise, I am undergoing a *big-time* transition.

It began early on the last morning in February 2002 when our phone rang. The voice on the other end asked if Jim and I would come to downtown Salt Lake City and visit with President Gordon B. Hinckley at 11:00 A.M. Wouldn't you say that's the first sign of a big-time transition? Jim and I knelt in prayer, asking Heavenly Father's help to accept and do whatever his prophet asked of us. We reread our patriarchal blessings to remind us of who we are. And then we left for 47 East South Temple Street.

President Hinckley asked about our health and especially my hearing. I explained that eleven days after arriving in the mission field, I had lost the hearing in my right ear, which has never returned. He then asked, "How is the hearing in your other ear?"

I said, "It's fine."

"Well," he responded, "just turn your head." That's his style: do what works.

Then he extended the call that began my latest transition. The kind words of encouragement and support from many, many sisters have gratefully eased my way. Still, there are many facets of this calling that are daunting, that require great faith, that challenge growth. Transitions are an essential part of growing up. I hope I will grow up soon.

What do you remember about transitions in your life? What made them difficult? What made them easy? For me there is one sure way to weather transitions well. It is to feel that you belong, that you are not alone, that you are loved. Who do you know that's going through a difficult transition right now? Could you help them feel that they belong and are loved?

If I could have one thing happen for the women of the Church, it would be to feel the love of the Lord daily in their lives. That pure, sweet love, called charity, eases all transitions. Through living, loving prophets we have been given an organization to build our faith in the Lord Jesus Christ, to feel his love, and to extend that love to all. The Relief Society is that organization.

Have you noticed how President Hinckley shows his concern for every member of the Church? I marvel at how he constantly extends a hand of inclusion to every one of us. His travels around the globe to meet the Saints where they live can't be a cakewalk for a ninety-one-year-old. And yet by going the extra thousand miles, he's saying that each of us is loved with that pure love of Christ. How well are we saying that?

For our Relief Society sisters, two crucial transitions make a big difference between retention and lost sheep, between activity and inactivity. One is for our newly converted sisters moving into our ward or branch family; the other is for our eighteen- and nineteen-year-old sisters moving from Young Women into Relief Society. The quality of these two transitions has eternal ramifications.

One of the sweetest blessings of Relief Society is getting to know other women. How I would love to know each of you individually! And yet for a new convert or young adult woman feeling outside existing friendships, this blessing of sisterhood can be seen as a transition too tough to weather. How can we ease the way? We know that three things work: Know their name. Include them. Mentor them.

The week after being sustained, I was in the Relief Society office and a bag of sky-blue cookies arrived with a note from a sister missionary on Temple Square. She had been in a precarious transition as a young woman seeking to belong in Relief Society. It wasn't easy. She wrote, "I remember being called to teach the Brigham Young manual in Relief Society when I had just barely turned eighteen years old. I was by far the youngest in the room and more than a little scared when I stood to teach my first lesson. The responsibility to teach those who had been my teachers . . . those who knew so much more than me was overwhelming, but it made me pray a lot and depend on the Spirit and seek guidance, . . . direction and inspiration. I . . . learned to ask questions that would make them think and share their insights and knowledge and experiences in relation to the topic. In short, I realized that I didn't have to know it all or do it all myself (thank goodness!)."

These wise Relief Society leaders sensed this sister's struggle. They understood her divine worth. They reached out and got to know her. They were willing to risk a less-than-perfect lesson to include her. They mentored her and loved her as she took those first scary steps toward belonging. A precarious place became a safe place.

Each sister is of divine worth—our young sisters! Our newly baptized sisters! Our less-active sisters! Our Heavenly Father knows the value of youth. After all, he chose a fourteen-year-old to bear the awesome load of beginning the restoration of the gospel.

Some time ago I was in Munich, Germany, where I attended Relief Society. The Relief Society president had returned home to care for a sick child; the child of the only other counselor also became ill, so she too went home. At the last moment, the sister missionaries were asked to teach the lesson on personal revelation. I watched in awe as these two young women in their early twenties stood to do something that in other circles of society would be close to impossible. One conducted the meeting, and the other—with help from a ward sister—led the discussion. And do you know what? We felt the Spirit of the Lord. We were about fifteen in number, yet the sisters honestly shared their experiences of how they had received personal revelation. They spoke of how the Holy Ghost had prompted them and brought them peace.

Throughout the world, teenage girls are serving as Primary presidents, Sunday School teachers, Young Women leaders and teachers. If given an inspired call, our young women can immediately begin serving as visiting teachers, class instructors, and musicians. Young women can help us build faith in our Lord Jesus Christ and powerfully teach the doctrines of the kingdom of God. We can help them understand their divine worth and the joy of serving in Relief Society.

One recently baptized British sister wrote to us, saying she didn't feel like she belonged because she didn't have a calling like everyone else had in the Church. Then, when she was called to serve as a visiting teacher, she finally felt like she belonged because she knew the importance of having a call. She felt, also, that she was trusted.

We desire all women to feel the Savior's love and to know that he values them. We help them feel his love by the way we treat them. You sisters who are in Relief Society, do you know the names of those sisters in transition? Have you introduced yourself, gotten to know them? Have you invited them to sit by you? Have you asked them to share their talents?

To Relief Society sisters serving in Young Women: Do you express your love for this divinely inspired organization? Do you share respect for Relief Society with the young women you are teaching? Your attitude toward Relief Society influences young women's attitudes toward Relief Society.

Mothers, do you foster in your daughters a love for this wonderful sisterhood? Please do so, because a mother's feelings and expressions about Relief Society will be mirrored by her daughters.

Leaders, do you extend to those capable sisters a call to serve so they can experience charity in their lives? Are they included in meaningful ways? Do you look to them for contributions to the group? Do you mentor them? Do you pray for them? Do you take time for them?

Charity is the attribute which defines us. We must all help all our sisters to feel that charity, that true love of Christ.

Young women who go away to school and transition into a university ward seem to make the transition with ease. Why? Could it be they experience just what President Hinckley said that new converts need—what all our sisters in transition need? A friend. A responsibility. Nurturing by the good word of God.

I pray that every woman can experience a positive transition from her current position into Relief Society. I have confidence that each woman in this conference can make a difference in the life of a sister in transition.

I also believe in commitment and accountability. Each woman at this conference can assist a sister transitioning into Relief Society. Would each of you forget for just a moment about yourself and your own concerns and think specifically about just one sister in transition whom you can help feel the love of the Savior by involving her in our great sisterhood? If you have a pencil, take it out and write that sister's name whom you could personally help. If you can't think of her name, create a mental image of her face in your mind. Then put your commitment into action. Find that sister—help her make her transition with love. Now, when you've had a wonderful experience in this transition of another daughter of God, please write and share with us your success; it will enrich us also.

Each individual woman in a ward or branch Relief Society can be like the yeast in the bread dough that makes it rise. The principle is taught in Galatians 5:9: "A little leaven leaveneth the whole lump." Each one of us is that leaven. And as we feel the divine love and gain compassion, as stated in Jude 1:22—"And of some have compassion, making a difference"—we can be the "some" who truly make a difference in the lives of our sisters.

Sisters, remember, remember who we are: covenant women of divine worth with faith in the Lord Jesus Christ. We must remind our sisters in transition who they are, welcome them, help them belong, let them bless us with their gifts. As we do this, we will all feel an increased measure of His love, even the love of Jesus Christ.

Serving and Supporting One Another

Kathleen H. Hughes

Since I was called to the Relief Society General Presidency, I've spent many moments reflecting on my life and what has brought me to this place. I have specifically spent time thinking back on my experiences in Relief Society and its influence in my life. Today I would like to tell you something of myself and my life's journey. Perhaps it will cause you to remember something of yourself and thus will tie us one to another.

I had a wonderful mother, who was always active in Relief Society. For many years, she taught the monthly literature lessons, and I remember the hours and hours of time she spent reading and writing in preparation for that once-a-month moment. I truly know that the sisters in our ward, as well as our family, were blessed by the knowledge that she gained by so thoroughly preparing those lessons. She also served for many years as the secretary in our ward and stake Relief Society. My memory of this time was that she was always busy with reports, rolls, and phone calls.

In addition to that, she was a faithful visiting teacher, and I remember with particular fondness an older sister in our ward whom my mother visited. She was too infirm to participate much in church

---

Kathleen H. Hughes, first counselor in the general Relief Society presidency, earned her bachelor's degree at Weber State College and her master's degree at Central Missouri State University. After teaching school for many years, she worked as an administrator in the Provo School District. She has served on the Young Women General Board and also as a ward Young Women president. She and her husband, Dean T. Hughes, are the parents of three children and the grandparents of six.

meetings. Mother loved this woman and wanted me to know and love her as well. I often went with my mom to visit, and together we spent a great deal of time in this sister's home. I came to love her as much as my mother did. Maybe we loved her because she reminded us of the mother and grandmother we had lost so many years earlier. Maybe it was simply her loving humility. I don't recall why she became so dear to us, but she is a sweet, early memory of the joy that comes from visiting teaching.

As active as my mother was in Relief Society, she was not into grapes. Do you remember the grape period in Relief Society? Some who are younger may not, but at the time it seemed like no home was complete without glass or resin grapes on the sofa table or mantel. Mom always said things like that just gathered dust, so she never made them. I kind of wish she had.

But my mother was a good seamstress and a quilter, and she spent many hours sewing for our family and others in our neighborhood. I recall as a young adult coming home from college one afternoon and, upon entering our home, hearing laughter coming from the living room. Our living room was quite large, and on that day virtually every inch of it was taken up with quilt frames perched on the backs of dining room chairs. Around that large quilt sat about ten Relief Society sisters. It was apparent from the number of times the quilt had been turned that they had been at their task all day. I remember them greeting me and Mom telling them of my involvement in Relief Society in my student ward. She said it proudly, and I was so pleased that she was excited that I was now a member of this wonderful organization. I have one other remembrance of that day: I was touched by the love and commitment shown by those women who sat all day working at that quilt. I have no idea who received the quilt, but I do know the quilters were a group of sisters serving and supporting one another.

Years passed, and all of a sudden I was a young mother living in Seattle, Washington, while my husband attended graduate school. We were members of the student ward, which met at the institute of religion on the University of Washington campus. While that was a time of relative poverty for us, it was also a time of growth in our commitment to the gospel of Jesus Christ. I remember Relief Society and the circle of sisters who met each week in the basement of the institute. I recall with fondness the bazaars, where we bought back from each other everything we had made. And I remember the lessons, when we talked and thought together about gospel subjects and expanded our own understanding of the doctrine and governance of the Church. I particularly remember our bishop's wife and the wisdom and kindness she showed to each of us young sisters as she mentored and taught us how to lead, to teach, and to care for one another. I was experiencing an amazing growth spurt in my journey of becoming.

After graduate school, Dean and I moved to Missouri. As it did for the early sisters of the Church, Missouri represented a difficult phase of my life. We were expecting our third child during our first winter there—and we had no insurance. What had sounded like a lot of money for a first teaching position turned out not to be enough. Because we had no money to buy a coat for our two-year-old daughter, I wrapped her in a blanket and carried her so she would not get cold. After the birth of our son that winter, I sank into a horrible depression. Many of the women in my family suffer from postpartum depression and, as you may know, in those days medical professionals did very little to help women with this condition. I was left to fight my way out of the darkness.

But those hard times for me were often tempered and lightened by wonderful sisters in the ward who cared for my children and who cared for me physically, emotionally, and spiritually—helping me through that emotional battle. A missionary couple was assigned to our ward during that difficult winter, and I remember this sister missionary became the mother so many of us women were missing right then in our lives. Her loving arms held me and comforted me. On occasion she would kindly scold me, "Kathy, just be glad you have a reason to get up in the morning." While her words often brought me up short, I always felt her love. I was taught once again, by this special sister and by all the women in my ward, what it means to love and support and serve one another in and through Relief Society.

So my life has gone on. The ebbs and flows of life have come with regularity, but I have learned that Relief Society is a safe place. It's a place where my mind is cared for, where my spirit can grow, and where I can continue to experience the love of the Savior, made manifest in and through others.

The two-year-old daughter I wrapped in a blanket is now a grown woman with her own little children. And what I see in her life is a repetition of the pattern of my own: a sister comes to take a toddler so a mother and new baby can rest. The toddler is returned home later in the day, but a meal comes home as well. My daughter has also suffered from postpartum depression, and the sisters in her ward have succored her through her difficult days. One day in particular, as Amy sat crying after the birth of her daughter Katie, a sister in her ward stopped by. She wrapped her arms around Amy and simply said, "We'll get through this together."

And that's what happened. So many of the sisters in her ward, knowing that she was fighting this depression, came to support her. Not a day would go by without someone calling or stopping by. Sometimes they brought meals or took her older children for a few hours, but most often they would just bring words of love and encouragement. Through that sisterhood, Amy got through that difficult time, just as I had. And now when I look at my little sweet granddaughter Katie, I cannot help but feel gratitude for the sisters who will one day help her through whatever difficult days lie ahead.

Heavenly Father sends us challenges. We all have them, and we will continue to have them. But remember that he is a vastly loving God, and it has always been his intention to support us through these challenges. He knows that we must be tested, and it is his desire that we succeed. He wants so desperately for us to return to him one day. He also knows that the best way, the easiest way, to return to him is to do it together. He knows that we need each other, and he needs each of us to love and support one another. Remember that whenever Christ's church has been organized upon this earth, a key component to that organization has been serving and supporting one another.

Do you remember the words of Alma when he began to organize Christ's church? He invited all to come into the waters of baptism, but first he said that all who did must be "willing to bear one another's burdens, that they may be light." He went on to say, "Yea, and are willing to mourn with those that mourn; yea, and comfort those that stand in need of comfort" (Mosiah 18:8–9). The same charge is given to us today by our being a part of this Church and the Relief Society organization. We have accepted that challenge to bear one another's burdens.

Now bearing one another's burdens sounds like a chore, but it's amazing how lightened we quickly feel when we do the work. Think for a moment why that is. When we bear one another's burdens, we are acting as an agent for Christ, and by so doing we're coming to Christ. I imagine you've already thought about the words of the scripture "Come unto me, all ye that labour and are heavy laden, and I will give you rest. . . . For my yoke is easy, and my burden is light" (Matthew 11:28–30).

We are so blessed to belong to an organization that allows us to share our burdens—an organization that will nurture and care for us, one that is organized and designed to help us grow and mature spiritually, one in which we learn to love and serve and support one another. How blessed and grateful we should be that our Heavenly Father knew what we would need and then provided the means—Relief Society—where these needs could be met through the hearts and hands of others who love. I pray that we will "remember, remember" what we have been given and give thanks for the opportunity that we have through Relief Society to serve and support one another. May Heavenly Father bring to our remembrance our need for one another.

I leave you with my testimony that this Church is the true Church of Christ upon this earth, that he lives, that he loves each of us. I also send my love to each of you. Thank you for what you are doing. Thank you for your loving hands and warm hearts as you love and support each other. Thank you for who you are.

Who Is She?

Anne C. Pingree

A few days after I was called to serve in the Relief Society General Presidency, a friend tried to reach me at the Relief Society Building. She called the Relief Society office and asked to speak to Anne Pingree. The Church service missionary who answered the phone said, "Who is she?"

"Who is she?" That may be a question some of you are asking as well. Today I want to share with you something of who I am. I am a wife, mother, grandmother, daughter, sister, aunt, friend, and neighbor. Like you, I find this journey of mortality exciting and challenging—with moments of terror and hilarity along the way. And like you, I am grateful to have a testimony of the Savior and the restoration of the gospel of Jesus Christ.

Of all that has shaped who I am, nothing has more defined my heart than these twin facts: I am a woman of covenant and a sister of Relief Society. I cleave unto the covenants I have made in the waters of baptism and in the holy temple. These covenants bind me to the Lord and give me strength and courage to go and do and be all the Lord requires of me.

When I was a young mother, I received my patriarchal blessing. I was reminded of my legacy of faithful ancestors as I was given the blessing that I would have "a desire to carry forward the good work

---

Anne C. Pingree, who holds a bachelor of arts degree in English from the University of Utah, was sustained as second counselor in the Relief Society General Presidency in April 2002. She has served as a member of the Relief Society General Board and in various stake and ward leadership positions. She served with her husband, George C. Pingree, as he presided over the Nigeria Port Harcourt Mission. They are the parents of five children and grandparents of four.

performed by them in both ancient and modern times." In my youth and early adulthood, I never thought much about my heritage except when we gathered as an extended family at occasional family reunions to remember and pay tribute to our valiant forebears.

After I received my patriarchal blessing, I wondered from time to time about my responsibility in carrying forward the good work of my ancestors. I didn't really understand how my life had much to do with theirs or how theirs had much to do with mine. I didn't think what they had lived through in decades past had any real bearing on me. How mistaken I was. At a time when I didn't think I could do what the Lord required of me, my own great-great-grandmother's life of faith gave me strength and courage. I was called to serve for three years with my husband as he presided over a very challenging mission ten thousand miles from home in a troubled African nation. And I was afraid.

My apprehensions increased as well-meaning friends shared accounts they had heard about the chaotic, unsettled conditions in this third-world nation in which I would live. Soon I had difficulty sleeping. I broke out in a rash that covered my body. Fear gnawed at me as I imagined what the future would hold. Then there was the difficulty in leaving my children—two married, two unmarried, and our youngest son entering the Missionary Training Center the day before my husband and I were to leave for our missionary service in West Africa.

In the midst of my inner struggles, I remembered my Norwegian great-great-grandmother. I recalled how her covenants with the Lord sustained her, giving her the courage to consecrate her life to the Lord and to her new religion. In a very real sense, her example of commitment to her covenants steadied my heart and urged me forward.

As a young widow with six children as well as being a new convert to the Church, my great-great-grandmother longed to join a group of emigrants going to Utah. She wished to bring up her children in Zion, where they could mingle with the members of the Church she had recently embraced. She sold her home in Christiania (Oslo) along with the silver and jewelry she had. But she still did not have sufficient funds to pay for the passage of all her children. She made the wrenching decision to leave her two eldest daughters—ages twelve and fourteen—behind, promising them that she would save money and send for them later. While they remained in Norway with friends and neighbors, working to support themselves, my great-great-grandmother and her four youngest children traveled by ship to America and then by rail to Council Bluffs, Iowa, where they joined a wagon train heading west.

Then conditions took a bad turn for her young family.

After the long sea and rail journey, her two-year-old, my great-grandfather, became desperately ill. She had to carry him in her arms because he couldn't stand the jolt of the wagons over the rough plains. Undaunted by the difficult journey, she walked, carrying her child, every step of the way from Council Bluffs to Utah, a distance of more than one thousand miles. Sometimes she held an umbrella over him to keep off the blazing sun. When her arms ached, she suspended him from her back in an old shawl.

She trudged along day after day and became so tired at times that she lagged far behind the company. Being such a distance away from the others put her in danger of Indian attacks and, even worse, angered the wagon master. He reproved her and even told her to give up and let her little son die because no one felt the child could possibly live anyway. He made it clear that my great-great-grandmother was holding up the wagon train by hanging onto her son. With great courage and a mother's determination, she refused to abandon her child. She assured the wagon master she would make it—even if they decided to hurry on ahead without her.

The little family did make it to Utah. She and her children moved into an abandoned building, covering the broken windowpanes with fragments of old carpet and rugs to keep out the cold. Working from early morning to late night, she took in washing and sewing. Through conditions of extreme poverty, she wove rugs and carpets on the loom she had brought with her from Norway. It was many years later when she was finally able to keep her promise to her oldest daughters, now adults, to bring them to Utah.

As I stood at what seemed like a precipice overlooking the frightening, unknown world of West Africa, I thought about the example of my own great-great-grandmother. Who is she? Though I have never seen a photograph of her, I answer without hesitation—she is a faithful woman of covenant and a sister of Relief Society. I have taken such heart from her.

During the time I spent in Nigeria, where my husband and I served, I took heart from brand-new converts to the Church who composed the majority of the women I met with so often in Relief Society. Again and again, whether it was in the teeming cities of our mission or the most remote jungle villages, I witnessed how these new members of the Church grew as they began to understand the baptismal covenants they had recently made. These beautiful, noble, ebony-skinned pioneer Relief Society members, who are so dear to me, taught me through their examples. I watched their faith and courage in the face of unbelievable hardships and terrible trials, as they struggled just to obtain enough food each day to feed their families.

To our faithful sisters in Nigeria, the journey of life brings heavy physical burdens and denies basic comforts. Yet they carry their burdens—literally and figuratively—with patience and unfailing trust in the Lord. I recalled how my great-great-grandmother carried her child in a shawl strapped to her back as I watched my African Relief Society sisters farm small plots by hand, bent over, using short-handled hoes, with their babies firmly secured to their backs with long lengths of brightly colored fabric.

In the circumstances of my mission and the challenges of my daily life, I came to understand who I am and whose I am in the most profound sense. And who I am is all centered in my covenants. Knowing that has given me the confidence that, in whatever circumstances I may find myself, "I can do all things through Christ which strengtheneth me" (Philippians 4:13). I believe in the power of covenants. Elder Jeffrey R. Holland said, "I promise you that your covenants will be a source of strength and satisfaction and safety to you."[1] And I testify that they have been.

Covenant women, as my own great-great-grandmother learned on the Great Plains of North America and as new members of Relief Society discovered in the steamy rain forests of Nigeria, can and do rely on the Lord. In our beloved Relief Society sisterhood, we also learn that we are often the instruments the Lord uses to bless others. As women of covenant and sisters of Relief Society, we help one another and strengthen one another through the hard things we face. The journey of life remains the journey, but we are surrounded by loving, charitable women who make it richer.

And this I know: The Lord is always beside us in our journey. His promise to us is sure and clear: "I will go before your face. I will be on your right hand and on your left, and my Spirit shall be in your hearts, and mine angels round about you, to bear you up" (D&C 84:88).

Who am I? I am a woman of covenant and a sister of Relief Society.

Note

1. Jeffrey R. Holland and Patricia T. Holland, "Considering Covenants: Women, Men, Perspective, Promises," in *To Rejoice as Women: Talks from the 1994 Women's Conference*, ed. Susette Fletcher Green and Dawn Hall Anderson (Salt Lake City: Deseret Book, 1995), 113.

Holiness for the Homeward Journey

Heidi S. Swinton

Imagine Nauvoo, Illinois, in May 1844. Converts are pouring in from England; Saints are trying to finish their homes and start their businesses; politicians are courting the votes of the burgeoning population; neighbors are bristling at the spectacular growth of what has become one of the largest, if not the largest, city in Illinois; visitors by the boatload are stopping to view the curious community of religious refugees; and on the bluff overlooking the river a massive stone temple is beginning to rise. In this jumble of activity, Joseph Smith, just weeks before his murder at the hands of a mob, surveyed the needs of the Saints and stated firmly, "We need the temple more than anything else."[1]

More than roofs on their homes, grain in their barns? More than schools, roads, or watchmen on the river? More than shops or secure livelihoods? Joseph Smith's call to complete the temple—which already had been nearly four years in construction—was not a push to simply finish the landmark of carved stone with grand windows inviting light. It was what would happen inside the temple that prompted his urgency. There the Lord had promised, "I may bless you, and crown you with honor, immortality, and eternal life" (D&C 124:55).

A temple provides a spiritual presence that rivets our attention to

---

Heidi S. Swinton, a graduate of the University of Utah, has written several documentaries on Church subjects, including American Prophet: The Story of Joseph Smith, *and contributed to many others. She has been a member of general Church writing committees and serves now as a member of the Relief Society General Board. She and her husband, Jeffrey, are the parents of four sons.*

things that are eternal and uplifting in a work-a-day, mortal world. The statement "Holiness to the Lord," placed on every temple, reminds us that this is a sacred structure housing uncommon purposes. It was in the Kirtland Temple that Joseph Smith and Sidney Rigdon saw the Lord "standing upon the breastwork of the pulpit." They related: "His countenance shone above the brightness of the sun" (D&C 110:2–3). Their witness teaches the extraordinary truth that Jesus Christ lives. That knowledge has resounded in this Church as the Saints have fulfilled the Lord's command, "Build a house unto me" (D&C 124:31).

The scriptures attest that "the house of God . . . is the gate of heaven" (Genesis 28:17). William Clayton, assigned to keep the records of the original Nauvoo Temple, wrote on 20 December 1845: "Saturday . . . 564 Persons have passed through, 95 this day."[2] Clayton's reference "passed through" seems a peculiar term for the culmination of a work that took an entire community five years of sacrifice and hard labor. Passing through the temple was synonymous with opening "the gate of heaven" in the journey home to God. For those early Saints, that road "home" began in Nauvoo. It crossed the plains of America, the mountain passes of the Rockies, and came into the desert valleys of the Great Basin where the Saints began to build temples—again. When the rebuilt Nauvoo Temple was dedicated on 27 June 2002, the anniversary of Joseph Smith's martyrdom, 113 temples stood in lands across the world, each on sacred ground, each mapping the way home for the Saints of God.

Young wife and mother Sarah Rich looked back at her Nauvoo experience from the wilderness of Iowa and wrote of the temple: "Many were the blessings we had received in the House of the Lord, which has caused joy and comfort in the midst of all our sorrows, and enabled us to have faith in God, knowing He would guide us and sustain us in the unknown journey that lay before us."[3]

We aren't being driven from our homes like the early Saints, but we are under siege just the same. Evil and anger, dishonesty, selfishness, pride, lust, envy, and apathy hover around us and sometimes in us. Everyone is at risk as were the early Saints. Sarah, who had worked in the temple day after day, wrote: "To start out on such a journey in the winter as it were, and in our state of poverty it would seam like walking into the jaws of death but we had faith in our heavenly father and we put our trust in him feeling that we were his chosen people and had embraced his gospel and instead of sorrow we felt to rejoice that the day of our deliverance had come."[4]

The temple prepares us for the journey—in this life. Our daily experiences—the ups and downs, the disappointments and joys—move into perspective when we know what the Lord has promised us and what we have promised him in the temple.

Consider the significance of this teaching of Elder John A. Widtsoe: "Men grow mighty under the results of temple service; women grow strong under it; the community increases in power; until the devil has less influence than he ever had before. The opposition to truth is relatively smaller if the people are engaged actively in the ordinances of the temple."[5] Recognize how far-reaching those promises are. We built a temple in East Germany. The Iron Curtain came down. I have no doubt that each temple built in the far reaches of this world blesses those communities.

When we attend the temple, it is as if we are putting ourselves in the Lord's hands and pleading, "More holiness give me." And for what purpose? For the journey. Consider the words of that poignant hymn as measures of our worthiness to receive the blessings in the temple:

> More holiness give me, more strivings within,
> More patience in suff'ring, more sorrow for sin,
> More faith in my Savior, more sense of his care,
> More joy in his service, more purpose in prayer.[6]

Each of these poetic lines speaks of the work of the temple. The temple lifts our sights—to more strivings within. It asks us to enter worthily and to sustain that worthiness "at all times, and in all places" (D&C 24:12). The temple calls for patience; scores of patient believers wait for their sacred work to be done by a people whose time has been cluttered by less precious purpose. The temple helps us turn away from sin to find joy in truth and righteous living, because with each visit we come to value the Lord's way over the jangle of the world. However, the lines "More faith in my Savior, More sense of his care" really catch my attention. It is faith in Jesus Christ, faith in his words, faith that we are his and he is our God that draw us to temple service and elevate us far beyond our day-by-day world. In the temple, I deeply feel faith in the Atonement and our place in his suffering. Listen carefully to these words from the dedication of the Kirtland Temple; listen especially to those words that describe the Lord: "O Lord God Almighty . . . answer us from heaven, thy holy habitation, where thou sittest enthroned, with glory, honor, power, majesty, might, dominion, truth, justice, judgment, mercy, and an infinity of fulness, from everlasting to everlasting" (D&C 109:77). Is there any question that we should build our foundation—our very lives—"upon the rock of our Redeemer, who is Christ, the Son of God" (Helaman 5:12).

The hymn's next phrase "More sense of his care" is what we receive in the temple. We feel him heal our hearts as we sit in solitude—amid many others seeking that same peace. I remember a particular day when my husband and I attended the temple. It was a period of great difficulty for us. I was weary with the weight of problems and saw no relief, no resolution. I had worked to "be of good cheer" (D&C 61:36) but was less than successful. I went to the temple in lockstep mode, expecting very little, not remembering that the atonement of Jesus Christ can make up for all our inadequacies and disappointments. I experienced a peace in the temple that day that I still hold dear. Today, when I glimpse the chair where I was sitting, that feeling burns again in my heart. The Lord didn't take away my trials. But he gave me something far more stirring than ease. He gave me peace, that peace promised in the scripture: "Peace I leave with you, my peace I give unto you: not as the world giveth, give I unto you. Let not your heart be troubled, neither let it be afraid" (John 14:27).

The temple is all about peace because it is God's house. And he is peace. Peace has little to do with what is amiss in the world, what we don't have, what we look for in the mall or in the refrigerator. Often what we want has nothing to do with receiving peace. "More holiness give me" means we are willing to do as Emma Smith was counseled, "Lay aside the things of this world, and seek for the things of a better" (D&C 25:10). "Better" is measured in the peace of our hearts, what we love, what we seek, what we know, what and whom we trust. So what other reasons could there be for "need[ing] the temple more than anything else"?

The reconstruction of the Nauvoo Temple has focused great interest on temples in the Church. For the past two years, I have been writing the story of the initial building coupled with the 2002 rebuilding. One Friday I stood on a scaffold that circled the tower of the temple then under construction. I was with a film crew, there to capture the moment when the statue of the angel Moroni would "fly" to the top of the temple. It was 21 September, the 178th anniversary of the angel Moroni's first visit to Joseph Smith in the family's log home in upstate New York.

Now, nearly a century and a half later, against the backdrop of an overcast sky, the statue of Moroni was being lifted into place by a huge crane as if heralding what an early Saint described as "the beginning of a new era . . . the beginning of a homeward journey."[7] An American flag fluttered from the cable just above the figure. It had been only ten days since the United States had witnessed the horrors of 9/11, and our emotions for our nation and its symbols were tender.

The night before, buckets of rain had fallen; it was threatening to rain again. As the gold-leafed statue was being set in place, the sun burst through the clouds and light enveloped Moroni. It was a breathtaking reminder of what Joseph Smith described when Moroni stood at his bedside: "His whole person was glorious beyond description, and his countenance truly like lightning" (Joseph Smith–History 1:32). The temple is all about light, the light of Jesus Christ that lights our way home.

It was by divine design that "Holiness to the Lord" was written on the stone of the original Nauvoo Temple. Those words figure prominently on every LDS temple built since that time. The statement speaks not of the walls, but of the work within. We are better people, more holy, if we attend the temple. Elder John A. Widtsoe stated: "Once only may a person receive the temple endowment for himself, but innumerable times may he receive it for those gone from the earth. Whenever he does so, he performs an unselfish act for which no earthly recompense is available. He tastes in part the sweet joy of saviorhood. He rises toward the stature of the Lord Jesus Christ who died for all."[8]

Nearly six thousand people in six weeks "passed through" the Nauvoo Temple, and then they abandoned it and went west. They yearned for their temple; they waited years for another. Our test is different. We have a temple down the street or across the valley. We have temple nights and temple tours. We orchestrate temple attendance. The early Saints shared their food to stay alive while they built a temple for God. I find the contrast sobering.

The Lord revealed in 1842: "Let the work of my temple . . . which I have appointed unto you, be continued on and not cease; and let your diligence, and your perseverance, and patience, and your works be redoubled, and you shall in nowise lose your reward" (D&C 127:4). When I read this scripture in the midst of writing about the Nauvoo Temple, the words "Let . . . your works be redoubled" jumped right off the page. I was stirred—no, I was driven, to redouble my work in the temple. What does it mean to redouble? For me it meant more than attendance. I took a bold step and started doing family history work. I had never seen myself in the genealogy camp. I have had a skewed impression that family history is the work of those who wear "sensible shoes." Well, I "changed my shoes" and went to work on my husband's family line, a fertile field that ranged from Scotland to Australia. I learned quickly that this work was not for the fainthearted. Maybe that's why genealogists wear sensible shoes—to keep going. The work wasn't easy, and I wasn't good at it, but I received help. Miracle after miracle made a believer of me. I found names, lots of them, and started submitting them. When I got cards for temple work, I was hooked. With great excitement, our family went to the temple to do baptisms for the dead—many with the last name of Swinton. Our son Jonathan, who is serving a mission in England, had the opportunity to attend a session in the London Temple this past Christmas, and he asked me to send him a card. Jonathan Swinton, born 22 January 1981 in Salt Lake City, Utah, did ordinance work for John Swinton, born 20 February 1784 in Yester, East Lothian, Scotland.

Then my husband and I started attending the temple clutching our cards. It means so much more when the name you carry is one that you know, that you've tracked down, that you are related to. Suddenly the words of Malachi, rephrased by Moroni, make more sense: "And he shall plant in the hearts of the children the promises made to the fathers, and the hearts of the children shall turn to their fathers" (D&C 2:2). With cards in hand, I felt my heart turning.

Just a few weeks ago, I was in the temple with Alison Hutchison's pink card sitting snugly in my pocket. I was pondering the experience for Alison. Suddenly into my mind came a name: Margaret Crabbe Christie. Now that's not a name I would just think up. What was the name Margaret Crabbe Christie doing in my thoughts? I pulled the card out, thinking maybe I had misread it. No. It said Alison Hutchison. But Margaret Crabbe Christie wouldn't leave me alone. Time and again her name came to my mind. I tried to recall if she was an early Saint. Had I recently read her journal? Was she an author in the stack of books I had no time to read? Try as I might, I couldn't dismiss her. I told my husband about the experience before leaving the temple. I went home to check if Margaret Crabbe Christie might possibly be a name on one of my hundreds of pink cards. I rifled through them quickly—and there she was. We had completed her baptismal work a year ago in St. George. But since she was the daughter of a son who was the brother of a great-great-great-stepgrandfather, I hadn't gotten even close to doing her work. But she was ready—and waiting. Margaret and I went to the temple. And I witnessed this promise from Isaiah: "Sing unto the Lord; for he hath done excellent things" (2 Nephi 22:5).

When King Benjamin called his people to the temple, "they pitched their tents round about, every man according to his family, consisting of his wife, and his sons, and his daughters, and their sons, and their daughters, from the eldest down to the youngest . . . every man having his tent with the door thereof towards the temple . . . that they might . . . hear the words which king Benjamin should speak unto them" (Mosiah 2:5–6). When we circle our family together, is the door of our tent facing the temple?

When the Saints abandoned Nauvoo, they left on the wall of the temple a phrase that holds great meaning to me as I have joined the ranks of those in sensible shoes: "The Lord behold our sacrifice, come after us." Margaret Crabbe Christie has been waiting for someone to come after her. Her card is the jump start for her journey. I believe she has added her voice to the chorus: "We need the temple more than anything else."

President Boyd K. Packer has said, "Temples are the very center of the spiritual strength of the Church."[9] With each visit, we increase in holiness. With devotion to our temple covenants, we are worthy of the promised blessings of the Lord "that we may be clothed upon with robes of righteousness, with palms in our hands, and crowns of glory upon our heads, and reap eternal joy" (D&C 109:76). The words sound lofty for mortals who are having trouble just matching socks. But we are more than mortals. We are daughters and sons of God on an eternal journey. Sarah Rich caught the essence of the temple experience when she said, "Had it not been for the knowledge and blessings we received in that Temple, our journey would have been like one taking a leap in the dark."[10] It was dark on their trail then; it is dark on our trail today. But the temple can light our journey all the way home to our Father in Heaven.

The Saints left behind the Nauvoo Temple with its walls of sacred stone. But the building of the temple was never about the stone-on-stone structure. It was about what would happen inside. It is what happens inside us—while in the temple—that makes the difference. In the temple, we are touched by the Spirit; we are acquainted with divinity;

we are in just the right place to plead, "More holiness give me." Joseph Smith was so right: "We need the temple more than anything else."

Notes

1. Joseph Smith, *History of The Church of Jesus Christ of Latter-day Saints*, 7 vols. (Salt Lake City: The Church of Jesus Christ of Latter-day Saints, 1932–1951), 6:230.
2. William Clayton, "Journal Three, Nauvoo Temple 1845–1846," in *An Intimate Chronicle: The Journals of William Clayton*, ed. George D. Smith (Salt Lake City: Signature Books, 1995), 220.
3. *Journal of Sarah De Armon Pea Rich*, BYU Special Collections (Provo, Brigham Young University, 1960), 42.
4. *Journal of Sarah Rich*, 42.
5. John A. Widtsoe, "Temple Worship," *Utah Genealogical and Historical Magazine*, April 1931, 51; also in *Best-Loved Talks of the LDS People*, ed. Jay A. Parry, Jack M. Lyon, and Linda Ririe Gundry (Salt Lake City: Deseret Book, 2002), 470.
6. Philip Paul Bliss, "More Holiness Give Me," *Hymns of The Church of Jesus Christ of Latter-day Saints* (Salt Lake City: The Church of Jesus Christ of Latter-day Saints, 1985), no. 131.
7. Clayton, "Journal Three," 225.
8. John A. Widtsoe, "The House of the Lord," *Improvement Era*, April 1936, 228.
9. Boyd K. Packer, *The Holy Temple* (Salt Lake City: Bookcraft, 1980), 177.
10. Sarah Pea Rich, in *Journey to Zion: Voices from the Mormon Trail*, ed. Carol Cornwall Madsen (Salt Lake City: Deseret Book, 1997), 20.

Forgiveness: "Let the Peace of God Rule in Your Hearts"

Susan L. Gong

A mother anguishes over her teenage child's decisions. Estranged cousins have forgotten the long-ago cause. A woman is cheated out of years of hard-earned income by her most trusted friend. A wife has been scarred by her husband's repeated belittling, biting remarks. In an hour of need, a woman is abandoned by her husband. A father's first-born son is murdered. All around us people struggle to forgive, and people experience the miracle of being forgiven.

The great Russian author Alexander Solzhenitsyn has written, "We differ from all animals not in our capacity to think but in our capacity to repent and to forgive."[1] Repentance and forgiveness are miracles that allow the Savior's infinite and eternal atonement to become real. Both free us from the effects of sin—others' and our own. Each opens the way for the Lord's healing love to begin to make us whole again, to give us peace even in our pain.

But forgiving is not easy. Christian writer Philip Yancey warns, "Forgiveness is achingly difficult, and long after you've forgiven, the wound . . . lives on in memory. Forgiveness is an unnatural act. . . . The only thing harder than forgiveness is the alternative."[2] Even so, the Lord repeatedly commands us to forgive: "I, the Lord, will forgive whom I will forgive, but of you it is required to forgive all men" (D&C 64:10). Why is this very difficult behavior central to the gospel? Why must we forgive?

Susan Lindsay Gong, a mother and homemaker, serves as the Sunday School secretary in her stake. She and her husband, Garrett Gong, are the parents of four sons.

We forgive because only Christ has the authority and the wisdom to judge. In John 5:22, we read, "The Father judgeth no man, but hath committed all judgment unto the Son." God the Father gave power to judge exclusively to Christ, his only begotten son, not to the Pharisees, not to our enemies, not to our neighbors, not to our children (thank goodness), not to us, not even to himself. Only to the Redeemer.

About halfway through my mission in Taiwan, I was assigned to be the companion of a local sister—who wasn't very nice to me. She was highly critical, sometimes violent, and usually sullen. She was receiving psychiatric counseling for depression—though I was too naïve to have any idea at the time what that meant. In fairness to her, I should add that she would have been within her rights to complain that I was bossy, insensitive, and hard to work with.

One wet winter night, riding a bus home from our tracting area, we argued. Exasperated, she got off the bus in the middle of nowhere, and I quickly jumped out after her. Our argument turned into a high decibel shouting match as we hurled insults back and forth across railroad tracks laid over suburban rice fields. When we finally ran out of angry words, we stomped back to the bus stop in silence and caught the last bus home, glaring at each other all the way. Still fuming when we returned to the apartment, I quickly turned out the lights and offered a very direct, sincere, on-my-knees prayer. How was I supposed to work with this woman? How could we possibly carry a message of peace and love? She was stubborn, vindictive, hateful, lazy, maybe even crazy. She was the most despicable person I had ever known. The answer to my angry prayer came suddenly and clearly in words uttered by a voice I felt in my heart, "She is my daughter and I love her. You shall not speak of her like that."

At the same time, I felt the Savior's love for me wash over and through me. It was an immensely liberating revelation. He knew me—my sins, my arrogance, my pettiness—and he loved me anyway. He loved my companion, too, enough to tell me, her insensitive companion, that she was lovable, loved by him. This revelation didn't eliminate our problems, but it helped me want to understand her instead of judge her. It opened my heart to a new kind of compassion. As we grew closer, she confided that she had been abused by her father and brother. She had suffered things I could never truly understand. How could I have judged her?

Only Christ can judge, because only he has perfect love. Through his infinite atonement, he has paid the price for our sins. Only he knows where we are along life's path. How might we have judged Peter, warming himself outside the palace of the high priest? What if Alma, the father, had given up on Alma the Younger and the sons of Mosiah? Would we have known as Paul persecuted the early Christians that he would become a passionate missionary and compassionate minister of the flock?

Only Christ may judge, and in his merciful judgment, the lost sheep, the prodigal son, the thief on the cross, and you and I are precious and welcome in the fold.

Forgiveness opens the way to repentance. In a better world, those who hurt others would be quick to repent and ask forgiveness. Certainly that would make it easier to forgive. But in the real world often the victim is left to begin the process of reconciliation if it is to happen.

True forgiveness is not offered on condition of repentance. Yet offered without condition, forgiveness has an amazing power to transform. Philip Yancey, in his book *What's So Amazing about Grace*, suggests that sometimes "forgiveness can loosen the stranglehold of guilt in the perpetrator."[3]

I met two friends during my senior year in high school. He was creative, sensitive, and bright, a good listener, and a true friend. She was insightful, kind, articulate, and wise, a writer who laughed easily. I admired her from our first conversation. Everyone was happy when they started to date, and no one was surprised when, shortly after his mission, they married. Despite the diabetes she had suffered since childhood, she bore three adorable, energetic sons. The young father was called to be a bishop in an inner city ward. The couple worked hard to build a family business, together coping with the ups and downs of an entrepreneurial existence, health concerns, and family demands. Sometimes it was almost too much, and the husband suffered from depression.

Many years into their marriage, the couple took a cruise. She was bitten by a mosquito and became ill when they returned home. She slipped into a coma, which doctors initially attributed to her diabetic condition. For weeks she lay comatose in a hospital. Her friends and family feared she would die. Finally, physicians diagnosed her illness as encephalitis and began to treat her, but critical neuro-muscular connections in her brain had been irreparably damaged. When she finally emerged from the coma, the prognosis was grim. Impaired muscle control left her with slurred speech, diminished motor skills, and the possibility that she would be confined to a wheel chair. Even with intensive physical therapy, she might never walk again.

Through a veil of depression, her husband could not cope with this prospect and in the ensuing months left her to struggle on without him. And she has done so, courageously and valiantly. In the many years since this experience, she has battled the physical limitations imposed by the disease, struggling to regain her speech and improve her coordination. She lifts weights daily and now walks for forty-five minutes at a time with a walker. Next month she is entering her first 5K wheelchair race. Most amazing, however, are spiritual and emotional advances. She continues to write and inspire with her optimism, grit, and wisdom.

Not surprisingly, she sometimes writes about the process of forgiveness. Over the years, she has shared with me the truths she has come to understand as she struggles to forgive. Prayer has been her central, most effective help in finding courage and faith. Recently, she wrote her missionary son, "Keep praying for help. In prayer, express your desire to forgive. Let the Lord know you need his help. Trust the Lord's timing and be patient. Keep praying for help forgiving. Pray for understanding for yourself and the person who has wronged you. Pray to be able to see and love the person you are forgiving in the way the Lord does."

This process can be unimaginably difficult. Sometimes, she notes, "we are told to forgive people and that everything will be better. Recently in Relief Society we were reading from Luke 23:24 about how the Savior forgave those who crucified him, and how he didn't hold malice towards them. As I read, it struck me how Jesus' forgiveness did not remove the nails out of his palms and wrists. His pain was still real and awful. His forgiveness did not make the pain disappear. But what his forgiveness healed was the anger, malice, bitterness and unfairness he could have been feeling over his betrayal when what he was doing was sacrificing himself [on our] behalf. . . . Like the Savor, I can be surrounded by the 'nails' of my problems, and yet forgiveness will still rescue me from the emotional bitterness and scarring of the anger and unfairness I feel until I forgive."[4]

My friend's prayers have helped her heal. She has been able to let go, to move forward. Recently, she was able to say to her former husband, "You know, I am not your enemy. I am your friend." Miraculously, her genuine and generous forgiveness opened the way for a conversation between them about repentance and forgiveness. I marvel that in her pain she has offered him a redemptive choice.

Repentance and forgiveness are two sides of a coin. Either action can begin the liberating process for both the sinned against and the sinner. We must forgive because forgiving opens the way to repentance, our own as well as for those who have hurt us.

Only some of us face extremely difficult situations, but all of us struggle against mundane difficulties as we try to forgive the daily, often unintended offenses that, to borrow a Chinese expression, are like grains of sand in the rice bowl of life. Every friendship, every marriage, every parent-child relationship has its share of unpleasant grit, friction, and pain. When I take my problems to the Lord, asking for help to understand and forgive, I begin to understand how my behaviors are part of the problem. I have never, in prayer, been inspired to try to change my husband. While I often go to my knees with an agenda of how I want the Lord to "fix" other people, when I am humble, I invariably come away with a list of things *I* need to change.

In true forgiveness, we see beyond "the mote . . . in [our] brother's eye" and perceive the "beam that is in [our] own eye." We can now "cast . . . the beam out of [our] own eye; and . . . see clearly" (Matthew 7:3–5).

Let us continue our struggle to forgive offenses large and small. Let us repent, that we might bless and help one another, making the Atonement real in our lives. Jesus our Redeemer lives; he knows and loves each of us, and he will help us on this righteous journey. I leave with you an admonition of Paul found in Colossians 3:12–15: "Put on therefore, as the elect of God, holy and beloved, bowels of mercies, kindness, humbleness of mind, meekness, longsuffering; forbearing one another, and forgiving one another, if any man have a quarrel against any: even as Christ forgave you, so also do ye. And above all these things put on charity, which is the bond of perfectness. And let the peace of God rule in your hearts."

Notes

1. Alexander Solzhenitsyn, quoted in *What's So Amazing about Grace?* by Philip Yancey (Grand Rapids, Mich.: Zondervan Publishing House, 1997), 98.
2. Philip Yancey, *What's So Amazing about Grace?* 84, 100.
3. Philip Yancey, *What's So Amazing about Grace?* 100.
4. Copy in possession of author.

"Knit Together in Love"

Susan T. Laing

In Maryland I serve as Relief Society president in a ward where we are attempting to "knit together in love" a colorful design of the textures and patterns of Ghana, Peru, Nigeria, Jamaica, England, Argentina, Brazil, plus Native America, African America, Utah America, and Eastern America—to name a few. This rainbow of diversity challenges us all as we seek to be knit together in love. We who have accepted the invitation to come unto Christ are also charged to become *one* with him, as he is with his Father. So important is this principle that he also warns us, "If ye are not one ye are not mine" (D&C 38:27). Scripture introduces us to the process of achieving that oneness when the Lord, through Alma, commands "that there should be no contention one with another, but that they should look forward with one eye, having one faith and one baptism, having their hearts knit together in unity and in love one towards another" (Mosiah 18:21).

I think I understand this image of being knit together in love. Many years ago my husband, who had learned from his high school choir friends, taught me to knit. I was a willing learner and soon became adept at joining series of connected loops into a useful whole. Over those first weeks, I made several pretty good single-hued and single-stitched sweaters and then added cabling and other more complex stitches that enhanced the beauty of my work. Though the idea made me a little uncomfortable, I longed to work with multicolored yarns and intricate designs. My initial steps in that direction taught me

---

Susan T. Laing is the coordinator of Honors Writing at Brigham Young University. She and her husband, John C. Laing, are the parents of three children and the grandparents of seven.

that doing so demanded more of me, yet promised more as well. Multicolored beauty has always drawn me—in knitting *and* in life.

I am the mother of three children: one came in the usual manner, but two we went searching for in foreign lands—our daughter in Korea and our Polynesian son in New Zealand. My husband and I love the beauty that their diversity adds to the pattern of our family's lives. In later years, our diversity deepened when our daughter married a fine African-American man, and we were blessed with two grandsons. One Christmas my husband accompanied our family group picture card with a one-line message, "We hope your Christmas is as colorful as ours."

Despite our joy in the multicolored tapestry we are knitting together, I came to recognize that complex patterns of culture, language, heritage, education, and economic advantage within the broader institutions of our communities and the Church do indeed add challenges to the Lord's repeated directive to be one. My own children often feared others' rejection. I recall my feisty sixth-grade daughter fist fighting with classmates who inaccurately mocked her for being Chinese, and my young son asking prior to a move: "Do they like brown kids in Orem?" Recently I have ached for my now thirty-one-year-old, less-active daughter, just returning to the Church, who has felt overlooked rather than woven into the warp and woof of her ward. She has learned not to put up her fists to fight, though sometimes I'd like to raise mine in her defense. Elder Henry B. Eyring spoke truly when he said: "Our Heavenly Father wants our hearts to be knit together. That union in love is not simply an ideal. It is a necessity."[1]

Consider the words of John Winthrop, first governor of the Massachusetts Bay Colony, to his fellow Puritans: "We must be knit together in this work as one. . . . We must delight in each other, make others' conditions our own, rejoice together, mourn together, labour and suffer together . . . as members of the same body."[2] Governor Winthrop's list contains steps which, if followed, will lead to unity and love. May I expand his list with three additional steps:

1. For me the most important beginning step has to be the *desire* to be one with those around us, particularly those not like us. Peter

illustrated this step of faith when he taught the gospel to Cornelius (Acts 10). Although it was difficult for him, he *desired* to be obedient to the Lord's command to share the gospel with a Gentile. If charity for those unlike us does not come easily, we can begin at the beginning: we can pray for a desire to be filled with charity. After all, charity itself is a gift which the Spirit can pour out upon us if we ask for it. M. Catherine Thomas, a religious education instructor at Brigham Young University, notes that "all the people in our lives are there for important reasons. . . . They are given to us to make possible a much greater love than we would have been capable of in a situation where everybody agreed with us, everybody loved us, everybody saw everything the way we do."[3]

2. We must be willing to move out of our comfort zones, to allow ourselves room to feel awkward in new situations, and do so often enough that we become comfortable—as, with practice, we will. I think of so many uncomfortable situations in my own life that have led to happiness: I have visited with those who are dying; those who struggle with handicaps; those with too much money and those with too little; those from other lands and other races. With a little effort, I have gained a wealth of variegated friendships. This process of being willing to feel awkward and uncomfortable, believing that it will not always be so, is what I like to call building the Church from the inside out—the inside of us. And that takes an act of faith. As did Cornelius and Peter, we must be willing to set aside cultural or other barriers and reach out in faith. Too often I have seen new Church members sitting alone, understandably waiting for someone to speak to them. Yet remember it was the *investigator* Cornelius who first reached out to Peter—a useful model. When people reach out from *both* directions, distance quickly disappears.

3. No one wants to be looked down on as having nothing to offer. All people have foods and customs, attitudes and attributes that can make us richer by sharing. One service missionary new to a remote Central American Indian village, before trying to teach nutrition and hygiene (as was her task), brought down walls of resistance and distrust when she explained that she had come to learn how to make *real*

tortillas! A Nigerian friend taught me by example how to *really* pray to Heavenly Father. One Japanese friend cuts my hair and translates recipes for me from the Japanese Internet; with another I have made soy squares and sesame balls and studied alternative medicine. Amazingly, one has managed to shame me into exercising daily—though I'll never run her six miles a day or earn a black belt in Kung Fu. To our delight, my husband's Venezuelan doctor shares both her skill, her family, and herself with us. These are just a few of the bright yarns that make up the colorful pattern of my life.

Just recently, our Washington D.C. Visitors' Center participated in Black History Month with a marvelous exhibit and activities. Doing so brought a flood of people of all faiths, backgrounds, and colors to enjoy it. Many of them have been amazed to discover that the *Mormon* Church cares about such things. Some of our own African-American ward members have been gratified to discover that *their* Church cares about their culture, their history, their artifacts, their music—about them as a people. Seeing their joy in that discovery, I have wondered if we as individual members are doing as well showing that we too care?

Paul instructed the Saints at Ephesus: "Ye are no more strangers and foreigners, but fellowcitizens with the saints, and of the household of God" (Ephesians 2:19). I like that. It celebrates all that is colorful and diverse and interesting and wraps it up in the single, multiple-patterned, multicolored garment that is the Church. In the world, ignorance usually begets fear and fear becomes hatred. The Lord urges a different progression. If we choose, ignorance can beget knowledge, knowledge can beget friendship and understanding, and friendship and understanding can become love.

Notes

1. Henry B. Eyring, "That We May Be One," *Ensign*, May 1998, 66.
2. John Winthrop, "A Model of Christian Charity," in *The Norton Anthology of American Literature*, 2d ed. (New York: W. W. Norton and Co., 1986), 14.
3. M. Catherine Thomas, *Selected Writings of M. Catherine Thomas* (Salt Lake City: Deseret Book, 2000), 198.

"I Am among You As He That Serveth"

Judy Ann Pugh

Middle of the night phone calls are rarely good news. Our call, now almost five years ago, was no exception. My husband, Lorin, and I were in Seoul, Korea, to meet Jason, our youngest son, as he completed his mission. We were just a day away from returning home to Utah, where other family members were to meet us at the airport. Four sons and four missions meant that being together was a blessing our family had not enjoyed for quite some time—and a blessing that was not to be.

Our eldest son, Scott, and his wife, JoAnne, were driving from Boise to Salt Lake when an accident cut short their young lives and radically changed ours. The pain we experienced when we found out was impossible to describe. Even with the promise of resurrection and forever families, this separation brought intense suffering. There would be no more conversations, hugs, and hikes—all those mortal things we loved doing together. It was, literally, the very worst of times for me and for our family.

But in the midst of this tragedy, during the worst of times, the best of times began. How can that be?

The accident that took the lives of Scott and JoAnne spared the lives of their two children: three-year-old Hannah, and Samuel, who had just celebrated his first birthday. Heavenly Father's hand and a parental commitment to car seats saved their lives; physically, they

---

Judy Ann Pugh received her master's degree in social work from the University of Utah and has been a clinical social worker. She and her husband, Lorin Pugh, are the parents of four sons and the grandparents of seven children. She serves as an achievement day leader in her ward primary.

suffered only a few broken bones. Scott and JoAnne died within minutes of the accident, but I believe their spirits must have lingered with the children. In fact, Ellen Cooper, one of the first persons at the scene of the accident, later wrote to us: "I held Hannah and wrapped her in my daughter's blanket. I am grateful that I could meet Hannah. She is a special little girl. Hannah and I were sitting in the front of our car and I was reading to her. While I was reading I felt/heard something and I stopped reading. A sweet feeling came into the car and Hannah just sat there on my lap as if she were listening to something I couldn't hear. I felt a presence, a sorrowful, yet peaceful presence concentrating on Hannah. Soon it slipped away. Hannah started sucking her thumb and cuddled close. I started to read again. The feeling didn't last long, but I will not forget its sweet power. After the feeling left, I learned that JoAnne had just passed away. It seemed that I had felt/seen a mother hugging and kissing her child, holding her hand to the babe's face as long as she could, knowing that she had to go and trusting that all would be well. I realized then that I had witnessed a very special good-bye. When the paramedics arrived they checked Hannah and when she was willing, I handed Hannah up to the paramedics. I felt the strength that had kept me calm go with her."[1]

I, too, experienced this spiritual strength and calm when holding Hannah and also Samuel. Lorin and I were blessed to become parents, by adoption, to our two dearly loved grandchildren.

In the first months following Scott and JoAnne's deaths, I spent most of my days just rolling around the floor with Hannah and Samuel, often telling them Fiddledeewog stories. A little elf-like character who loves adventures, Fiddledeewog was my dad's story creation for me. I had told his stories to my four boys when they were little, and my son Scott had already begun making them up for Hannah and Samuel. As I told these stories, the Spirit began to heal me and my family. Nurturing the children in the simple day-to-day routines of life, I felt a closeness to the Spirit I had never experienced before and haven't since to the same extent. Those months were truly the worst and best of times all wrapped together.

My journey from the accident in Idaho to this moment has been filled with emotional and spiritual highs and lows. But out of it, three simple doctrines of service have taken on special meaning to me.

LOSING OUR LIFE TO FIND IT

We are all familiar with Matthew 10:39: "He that findeth his life shall lose it: and he that loseth his life for my sake shall find it." After the accident, I understood this scripture in a new way. I had no desire other than to do my best to care for the children. Above all, I wanted to parent the children in the same wonderful way Scott and JoAnne had. Arthur Henry King, in *The Abundance of the Heart*, affirms: "'There is that of Christ in every man' [and this is the] fundamental self . . . we need to find. And that finding is something that requires self-forgetfulness. . . . Forget yourself, and you may become yourself."[2] I experienced that process. As I cared for the children, I connected with that Spirit of Christ within me. Along with the pain and difficulty of our loss, I felt great love, joy, and peace. I felt part of something bigger than myself and in partnership with the Lord to help the children. In the process, I found that nurturing heals, and caring for others is a blessing.

BRINGING POWER TO ROUTINE TASKS

There are many different kinds of caregivers. Besides caring for young children and teenagers, many care for ill husbands, aging mothers and fathers, and children with special needs. Such caregiving isn't easy. One husband caring for his dying wife observed: "This is the hardest, best thing I have ever done."

I, too, find service in the home to be both wonderful and difficult. I have loved being Mom and Grandma to Hannah and Samuel these past almost five years. I would not change places with anyone. But, to be honest, some days I feel inadequate as a parent, and other days what

I'm doing in the home doesn't seem as eternally valuable as it did those first few months after the accident. Why is it so difficult to continue to find value in the mundane routines and constant caregiving within the home? Doesn't service done at home bring the same fulfillment as other service?

Frankly, service outside the home usually gets noticed and publicly rewarded. When you help send a hundred quilts to needy children, others see your good works and sometimes plaudits follow. Service in the home is rarely commended. A two-year-old never once praises his mom for changing his diaper or cleaning up his vomit. Nor do toilets sing praises at being soft-scrubbed. Creating a home in which family members can develop their human and divine potential on this earthly journey is an awesome task, but it affords few external recognitions. In addition, many detours and discouragements complicate the process, so it is easy to fall into the trap of feeling that service done outside the home is of greater value. When we fix a dinner for the neighbor, we recognize the part taken to the neighbor to be service but usually do not regard as service the half given to our family. In homes, doing what needs to be done is service. Clutter, left to accumulate, can take over a house. (Actually, we are in the throws of such a hostile takeover in our house right now.) I don't like taking time to cook, but if I don't prepare meals, junk food reigns supreme. Preparing meals is a service. If we can recognize the work of the home as the service it really is—and if we can be motivated and fulfilled by internal rather than external rewards—we will experience greater contentment, spiritual growth, and even energy. As Anne Morrow Lindbergh notes, "Purposeful giving is not as apt to deplete one's resources."[3]

Our many routine tasks can become meaningful if we keep in mind our part as participants with the Lord in bringing to pass the eternal salvation of man. This perspective brings power to routine tasks. Brigham Young recognized the spiritual importance of daily work: "[If a farmer] raises his grain, his cattle, and brings forth his crops to sustain man and beast, and does this with an eye single to the glory of God and for the building up of his kingdom, he is just as much entitled to the Spirit of the Lord, following his plough, as I am in this pulpit preaching."[4] If Brigham Young finds eternal purpose in raising cows and crops, we certainly ought to be able to keep this perspective as we do our daily chores and rear our children.

Following the accident, I had a strong sense of purpose and partnership with the Lord. As time passes, maintaining an eternal perspective has become more difficult. The one obstacle that probably hinders me most is busyness. Your greatest obstacles might be discouragements, but mine are all the little things. I often find myself in the thick of very thin things.

In Patricia Holland's beautiful book *A Quiet Heart*, she notes, "We must not let the modern world isolate, fragment, or distance us from those we can love and serve."[5] She counsels, "Allow yourself to turn a few things down and turn a few things off."[6] Similarly, King Benjamin notes that when we are doing charitable acts, we must "see that all these things are done in wisdom and order; for it is not requisite that a man should run faster than he has strength" (Mosiah 4:27). Clearly, my life was much simpler and more focused those first few months after the accident. I stopped doing almost everything that did not involve family and loved ones. Many Americans experienced a similar shift in values after 11 September 2001. Family ties instantly surfaced as priorities. I often think of a favorite quote from Anne Morrow Lindbergh's *Gift from the Sea:* "My life cannot implement in action the demands of all the people to whom my heart responds."[7] We can't serve everyone or be engaged in every good cause. We do have to make choices about where and when to serve.

Of course, our priorities will shift with age, health, and life circumstances. Rather than taking pride in how many things I can do in a day, something I have been guilty of, I now want to make time to do things that matter most. I've noticed, as we get older, my contemporaries and I want less "stuff," lest our time go to taking care of the stuff instead of people. We also long to simplify. We no longer try to do it all, and we certainly don't try to do it perfectly. I'm not sure if this is wisdom or just a consequence of having less energy. I do know that when I am not too hurried, at the end of the day I feel closer to Heavenly Father because of the person I have been that day.

Serving Where You Matter Most

Family life creates endless opportunities to serve in deeply meaningful ways. When I was a social worker, I would sometimes feel overwhelmed at the complex problems children were experiencing and at my own ineffectiveness in helping them. Part of the problem was that we met together just one hour per week. I would sometimes think, *If only I could take this child home with me*. In family units, we have the time and recurring, everyday opportunities to make a difference. Families offer opportunities for the highest level of service.

Let me mention a few specific top-priority ways I want to serve at home and treat others. These things don't take a lot of time but do take effort. First, I would consecrate my daily tasks to the needs of others, not just my own. For example, Samuel's kindergarten class was having a costume day. He chose to be a gingerbread man. We cut out foam rubber to make a body, sprayed it brown, and then Samuel decorated it. I knew in my head what decorations would make the gingerbread costume really cute. Of course, a "darling" costume would reflect on me and show what a clever mom I was. I tried to help until Samuel said with irritation, "I can do it." I finally squashed my own ego involvement and let him have a good time. The task of making a costume remained the same, but my motive changed.

Second, I would try to pay more attention to loved ones. A few years ago as I was busy bustling myself about the house, I caught a glimpse of Hannah and Samuel sitting together in the family room looking at a book. Fortunately, I took the time to stand nearby and listen. Hannah pointed to a picture of herself in a scrapbook and said to Samuel, "Can you say 'beautiful'?" I only wish I had taken the time to savor more such moments. How many have I missed? Children need and love to be noticed, to be described, to be paid attention to. Things quickly fall apart when I don't respond to those little human cues.

Often the phone is involved. How many of you can admit to hiding outdoors in the bushes with your portable phone while chaos reigns inside? I can. Just a couple of days ago, I said to Samuel, "I've told you many times to not talk to me when I'm on the phone. I can't hear two people talk at the same time!" His rather sassy reply was, "Why not? You have two ears."

Third, I would listen better to loved ones, trying first to understand their motivation and perspective, before wanting my viewpoint to be understood. As I watch my daughters-in-law and other young mothers of today, I am impressed at how well they calmly say to their children, "What do you want, Sweetie?" or "Tell me what happened?" Then they listen carefully to the response.

Fourth, I would try to act more on daily promptings to do good. Several years ago while driving in the car listening to Primary songs about moms and dads and families, I looked in the rearview mirror and saw Hannah in her car seat looking very pensive. I had a feeling—or thought, or impression, whatever we may choose to call it—that I should pull over and hold her. Fortunately, on this occasion, I responded to my prompting, stopped the car, and jumped in the back seat. We held each other and sobbed as she described, not the sadness she was experiencing at missing her mom and dad, but the love she was feeling toward them. There is always that instant when we make a choice: do we act or not act on what we feel prompted to do?

Finally, I would understand that caring for myself is service. As I tune into others, I must also respond to my own needs. Clearly, what's going on in my own life powerfully impacts the way I see others, respond to them, and care for them. But as we give, we must be replenished. For me right now that means time for exercise, for reading and learning, for creativity, for scriptures and prayer, for fun, for friends and family, and time alone. Of course, I won't do all these things every day; personal needs change. But as I take time for myself, I need to understand that this is not selfishness. Selfishness is doing what I want at another's expense. For example, after school the children need help with homework, some individual time, and help getting places—

lessons, sports, you know the routine. If I choose to exercise or read at this time, that would be selfish. However, I find a hot bath and good book later on in the evening terrific.

So, for now, along with all the necessary routine tasks, these are a few ways I also want to serve in our home. Your list might be different, and mine probably will be, too, at another time.

Let me end with a beautiful example of how one family served together to help Hannah and Samuel immediately after the accident. Paramedics took Hannah and Samuel by ambulance to the emergency room in Burley, Idaho, where Joe Peterson was the physician on duty. His wife, Linda, happened to be in the waiting room at that time—a rare occurrence. Linda called her family at home and asked them to put the big blowup mattress on the family room floor, cover it with some bright, happy sheets, and pile on lots of stuffed animals. Then the entire family slept together that night in one room with Hannah and Samuel. Trevor, whose birthday was the next day, whispered to his mom that she could give Hannah and Samuel his birthday presents. The youngest daughter helped Hannah eat and watched Disney movies with her. An older daughter, Marci, slept on the floor at Samuel's side. When he woke up whimpering about every half hour throughout the night, Marci rubbed his back comfortingly, just to let him know that she was there. The entire Peterson family, not just the parents, continued to care for the children, until the following afternoon when some dear neighbors drove from Salt Lake to pick them up. In Matthew 25:40, we are taught, "Inasmuch as ye have done it unto one of the least of these my brethren, ye have done it unto me." There are times we read scriptures, and there are times we experience them. For the sake of Hannah and Samuel, I am grateful that the Savior's words literally lived that night in Burley, Idaho.

Notes

1. Letter in possession of the author.
2. Arthur Henry King, *The Abundance of the Heart* (Salt Lake City: Bookcraft, 1986), 255.

3. Anne Morrow Lindbergh, *Gift from the Sea* (New York: Random House, 1955), 47.
4. Brigham Young, *Journal of Discourses*, 26 vols. (London: Latter-day Saints' Book Depot, 1854–86), 11:293.
5. Patricia T. Holland, A *Quiet Heart* (Salt Lake City: Bookcraft, 2000), 2.
6. Holland, *Quiet Heart*, 14.
7. Lindbergh, *Gift*, 124.

The Wise Woman Built Her House upon the Rock

Jolene Merica

We live in a world where many "call evil good, and good evil," putting "darkness for light, and light for darkness" (2 Nephi 15:20). Is it any wonder that for us to progress through mortality and attain eternal life we need to be able to make daily righteous judgments? When we judge, we critique, evaluate, analyze, form an opinion, interpret. *Judge* comes from the Latin word *judex*, meaning one who points out the right.[1] Our ability to point out, or choose, the right depends upon our ability to judge righteously. The choices we make will either lead us toward eternal life or toward captivity and death. Put in terms of the Sermon on the Mount, we can either found our house upon the rock or build it upon the sand. In learning to judge righteous judgment, we build ourselves and our testimonies, so that neither rain nor flood nor wind can destroy us (Matthew 7:25–27).

Righteous judgment goes beyond judging people. We judge philosophies, doctrines, and institutions. We judge cultures, programs, plans, suggestions, recommendations, and commandments of men. In 1 Corinthians 2:15, we read: "He that is spiritual judgeth all things." "We should possess the Spirit of God, and be able to discern by the power and influence of the Spirit," said President Joseph F. Smith regarding this scripture. Our job is to judge all things that come in to our lives, even foolish things—anything that interferes with our progress along the path

---

Jolene Merica, formerly the program administrator for Brigham Young University Conferences and Workshops, serves as the administrative assistant to the Relief Society General Presidency. She teaches Sunday School in her ward and "parents singly" her teenage sons.

to eternal life. "We ought not to be in the condition that a great portion of the world is in," continued President Smith. "We ought not to be dependent, as they are, upon the wisdom, or judgment of man, but we should be dependent upon the wisdom of God, and upon the judgment of the Almighty."[2]

They that are spiritual judge all things, and to judge all things, we have to do it righteously: We must move beyond the ordinary understanding of men. We strive to be spiritual in the things we judge, but in our present state of being, our ability to judge righteously the influences that we allow into our lives is impeded by personal motes and beams.

One such beam in my own life is a reluctance to be responsible for judging. On one of my infrequent visits to the grocery store, I noticed a college-aged student walking toward me, scanning the wide selection of laundry detergent on the aisle. The young man passed me, turned around, and came back down the aisle, apparently engaged in speed comparison shopping. I finished putting a thirty-pound bucket of the detergent I normally buy onto my cart and made my way to the checkout stand. As I waited to pay for my groceries, I noticed this young man in the checkout lane next to me. His only purchase? The same brand of laundry detergent as I was buying, only in a much smaller quantity.

I don't know that this young man made his choice based on the brand he saw me select—my laundry detergent is probably the cheapest brand on the shelf—but I do know that his purchase reminded me of the times when my confidence to buy something, do something, or choose something has been based on decisions I've seen others make.

Of course, following the example of others or seeking their input is a very good idea. When I have a sick child, I call a friend who is the mother of many and who has experienced every illness known to man. When my car is ailing, I ask a car-savvy colleague to take it for a lunchtime drive to give a preliminary diagnosis. That is only sensible.

But I have noticed that I am more willing to defer decision making when I don't want to, or perhaps feel unable to, expend the effort and the energy to judge things for myself. It's in these moments when I'm willing to abdicate my agency, when I'm willing to take someone else's word with no thought of my own, that I've relinquished my responsibility as judge.

Related to the beam of declining to accept responsibility to judge is the beam of wanting to have prescriptions instead of principles. On too many occasions I've heard myself say, "If the Lord would just tell me what to do, I'd do it." That's like asking for a recall of my vote on the plan of salvation. In essence I'm saying, "I don't want the right to choose. I want to be told."

A wise man said that those whom you love most may be injured by your "robbing them of the opportunity to exercise judgment."[3] In asking the Lord to instruct us in all things, we are asking him to do just that. One doesn't have to be a parent long to appreciate the divine wisdom of a plan in which we learn to govern ourselves based on gospel principles rather than on directives from a parent. On many occasions, my sons travel without me. As I take them to the airport, my mind is flooded with all the things I haven't told them, all the things I might not have taught. Our preflight conversations often turn into a list of do's and don'ts according to Mom.

On one such occasion, as I said farewell to my sons before they boarded their plane, I realized that providing a list of prescriptions for every possibility was not only impossible but also debilitating. When they were faced with the difficult daily decisions of what to watch, what to wear, and what to say, defending their positions with "because Mom told me so" was not a strong option. My teenaged sons need to ground their judgments and choices in gospel principles contained in the scriptures and in the counsel of prophets.

President Joseph Fielding Smith taught: "The word of the Lord means more to me than anything else. I place it before the teachings of men. The truth is the thing which will last. All the theory, philosophy and wisdom of the wise that is not in harmony with revealed truth from God will perish. They must change and pass away, and they are changing and passing away constantly, but when the Lord speaks that is eternal truth on which we may rely."[4] My sons are of the age and maturity level at which they should never use the rationale that something is right or wrong because their mother told them so. The only sure rationale upon which they may rely is that things are right or wrong because God says it is so.

A mote that often encumbers my ability to judge righteously is failing to recognize the point of view from which I judge. One of my sons is a runner. After returning home from one of his first races, he announced that he had "PR'd." This term was new to me, so I asked if he meant he had won. No, he had not won—he had come in last in his heat—but he had PR'd. I was amazed that he was so proud about losing, and for an instant I felt embarrassed at for him. The conversation went on. I asked, "So, just what does 'PR'd' mean?" My son said, beaming, "Personal record." He had proudly set a new personal record in his running event that day—he had PR'd. I cringed at my earlier judgment. I cringed at my earlier judgment. From my point of view, success was tied to winning; from my son's perspective, success was based on improvement.

"Our understanding is limited," pointed out the Prophet Joseph Fielding Smith, "and we judge according to the things we know and with which we are familiar."[5] Personal perspectives are the familiar frameworks upon which our judgments are based. It's difficult to judge the actions and ideas of others correctly when they are outside our past or present circumstance. Therefore, we need to be open and yet discerning to the recommendations of others. We must not forget that our judgments and the judgments of others are influenced by individual inspiration and knowledge—or the lack thereof. We need to be actively engaged in discerning the correctness of input that is often so freely given.

Discernment is a gift of the Spirit that we should seek. The understanding and enlightenment we receive through this gift is commensurate with our tasks and responsibilities. Discernment is a gift of the Spirit that we should actively seek.

Another influence on our personal perspectives is ideas endorsed and even introduced by the adversary and his cohorts. It seems as though Satan tries to influence our perspectives by promoting incorrect ideas or introducing falsehoods, especially when he senses that we are making eternal progress. It seems as though Satan senses when we are making eternal progress and increases the "shafts in the whirlwind" (Helaman 5:12). One of the adversary's most successful tactics is to pacify and lull us into "carnal security" (2 Nephi 28:21–22), into accepting the relativism of our day. We're bombarded with messages that flatter us into believing that there is no evil, that rampant individuality knows no bounds and is protected under the law of agency. Not only do we need to be diligent in discerning these ravenous wolves that come to us in sheep's clothing (Matthew 7:15) but we need to pray consistently to resist temptation and to be able to see temptations for what they really are.

Besides those distractions and lies, our own resolute self-righteousness about a situation, a policy, or a practice may prohibit an accurate evaluation. In the Sermon on the Mount, the Savior instructed his disciples to teach their followers how to ask: "Say unto them, Ask of God; ask, and it shall be given you; seek, and ye shall find; knock, and it shall be opened unto you. For everyone that asketh, receiveth; and he that seeketh, findeth; and unto him that knocketh, it shall be opened."

Joseph Smith's translation of these verses gives added insight that seems to apply to righteous judgment: "And then said [the Savior's] disciples unto him, They will say unto us, We ourselves are righteous, and need not that any man should teach us" (JST Matthew 7:12–14; Matthew 7:7–8). These scriptures teach that we are unable to hear when we are unwilling to be taught. Likewise, our ability to judge righteously requires that we set aside our overconfident, prideful opinions. If we don't, we are like those that "need not that any man should teach [them]." If we acknowledge our individual bias and abandon the belief that we are beyond needing instruction, we will be better equipped to exercise righteous judgment.

Judging righteous judgment is judging as the Father and the Son judge. The scriptures teach that God will judge according to his commandments, not according to our traditions; that he will judge according to our works and the desires of our hearts, not according to the sight of the eyes and the hearing of the ears; that he will judge everything which inviteth to do good and persuade to believe in Christ, to be of God; that he will judge whatsoever thing persuadeth men not to believe in Christ, and to deny him, and to serve not God but to be of the devil (John 7:24; Mosiah 29:11–12; D&C 137:9; 2 Nephi 21: 3–4; Moroni 7:16–17).

The judging criteria seem rather clear, and a loving Heavenly Father has given each of us a guide. As members of the Church, we know that the "light by which [we] may judge" is the light of Christ (Moroni 7:18). In Doctrine and Covenants 11:12, we read: "And now, verily, verily, I say unto thee, put your trust in that Spirit which leadeth to do good—yea, to do justly, to walk humbly, to judge righteously; and this is my Spirit." To judge righteously, we have to be righteous and judge as he would judge—by the Spirit.

Our day-to-day lives involve us in judging many things, but only after we've arrived at a decision—a judgment—will we receive confirmation through the Spirit. According to President Joseph Fielding Smith, one of the functions of the Holy Ghost is "to approve of and attest to the [truthfulness] of our ordinances, [our] actions, and [our] convictions. He . . . figuratively places His stamp of approval on our lives, just as an ancient king used his personal seal to certify the validity of a document or an action."[6]

Harold Glen Clark, first president of the Provo Utah Temple, offered this insight about how to obtain confirmation from the Spirit: "The initiative to go through the thought process and draw a conclusion [or a judgment] always rests with the problem solver. The Lord will never take to himself the toil, sweat, and sometimes the tears required to think through the challenges of one's own life. This precious, soul-building task belongs to the individual. At the end one humbly hands to God his best conclusion, asking for his guidance, with willingness to accept God's amendments, rejection, or confirmation. God will not turn a deaf ear if one prays worthily in this manner: 'Father, I have tried to use every good skill and honest effort in this decision. If it is right, may I proceed with a feeling that it is Thy will. If it is wrong, cause that I may not be permitted to proceed, but in Thy wisdom be restrained from carrying it out.'"[7]

As we learn to make judgments, come to a decision, and then confirm our decisions or choices with the Lord through the Spirit, we are applying the principle of righteous judgment. As righteous judges, we will have taken the Holy Spirit for our guide, and we will be protected from those who lie in wait to deceive us (D&C 45:57). The only way not be deceived is to judge every influence we allow into our own lives and into the lives of those we are responsible for.

At the end of the Sermon on the Mount, Jesus likened those who heard and did his words to a wise [wo]man who built her house upon the rock (Matthew 7:24–27). Reading this parable reminded me of the footrest under my desk at home: an old, worn-out dictionary. If I'm ever in need of a definition or spell check, I always know where to look—right under my feet. As I have pondered and prayed about the subject of judging, I was struck by the analogy sitting on my floor. Building upon the rock is anchoring ourselves upon the words and teachings of our Savior, Jesus Christ. If, as I do with my well-worn dictionary, we will turn to him, to his words and to the words of his servants, and if we will seek understanding through prayer, our foundation will be sure.

Notes

1. *Webster's New World Dictionary*, 3d college ed. (New York: Simon & Schuster, 1994), s.v. "judge."
2. Joseph F. Smith, "Christ Our Exemplar," in *Collected Discourses 1886–1898*, sel. Brian H. Stuy, 5 vols. (Burbank, Calif. and Woodland Hills, Utah: B. H. S. Publishing, 1987–92), 5:49–50.
3. Harold Glen Clark, *The Art of Governing Zion* (Provo: Brigham Young University Extension Publications, Division of Continuing Education, 1966), 613.
4. Joseph Fielding Smith, *Doctrines of Salvation*, ed. Bruce R. McConkie, 3 vols. (Salt Lake City: Bookcraft, 1954–56), 1:108.
5. Joseph Fielding Smith, *Doctrines of Salvation*, comp. Bruce R McConkie, 3 vols. (Salt Lake City: Bookcraft, 1954–56), 1:11.
6. *Thy People Shall Be My People and Thy God My God: The 22d Annual Sidney B. Sperry Symposium* (Salt Lake City: Deseret Book, 1994), 113.
7. Clark, *Governing Zion*, 617.

"Choose Ye This Day"

Kathy D. Pullins

A short while ago, I marked my baptismal anniversary. During this season each year, I pause to reflect upon the eternal shaping of my heart and mind the truth of the gospel has brought to my life. I am humbled as I look back on that period of studying and questioning that preceded my decision to join The Church of Jesus Christ of Latter-day Saints. Motivated by an almost urgent need for a spiritual dimension in my life, I searched for four years for something solid in a world of shifting values. Then, just before my eighteenth birthday, the light and strength of the gospel of Jesus Christ stabilized my world, and I will be forever grateful.

During my first year of college, I was a student in a large Book of Mormon class at Brigham Young University. The professor, the inimitable Ivan J. Barrett, announced one day that we could earn extra credit by attending a one-act play about the story of Korihor, the Antichrist. Because extra credit is always a good idea in school—and in life, for that matter—I decided to purchase a ticket to the production. As I watched the tragedy of a life misspent unfold on the stage, I was struck by how logical Korihor's philosophical arguments would have sounded to me not that many months earlier. But now, fortified by the gift of the Holy Ghost and my developing testimony of the Savior, I could see clearly the destructive chain that was forged as Satan deceived Korihor and he, in turn, deceived all who would heed his words.

Kathy D. Pullins, associate dean of J. Reuben Clark Law School at Brigham Young University, is a trained mediator. She chaired the BYU Women's Conference from 1996 through 1998 and teaches Gospel Doctrine in her south Orem ward. She and her husband, Gary, are the parents of four sons.

We are currently confronted by twenty-first century Korihors. Those same erroneous philosophies are being re-dressed and recycled by the adversary and delivered at rapid speed and in multiple mediums. As President Ezra Taft Benson observed: "The type of apostates in the Book of Mormon is similar to the type we have today. God, with his infinite foreknowledge, so molded the Book of Mormon that we might see the error and know how to combat false educational, political, religious, and philosophical concepts of our time."

Indeed, every generation of believers—and especially this one—encounters its Korihors, those who would twist and distort the truth. In this dispensation of great freedom and technological advances, the adversary's work is accelerated. Today a virtual army of well-trained Korihors is seeking to confuse, distract, and ultimately destroy our faith in the Savior.

Let me share an experience I had with relativism, just one of the many false philosophies Korihor promoted. At one point, Korihor offered as fact, "Whatsoever a man [does is] no crime" (Alma 30:17). In modern terms, we would call such an approach situational ethics, the practice of being a moral chameleon. Such an individual adjusts his or her ethical code and accompanying conduct, depending upon the current context and the means which achieves the desired end. One who subscribes to this philosophy espouses the view that, in both the short and the long term, we are ultimately accountable only to ourselves.

In my final year of law school, I attended a conference for female students in Los Angeles. All sessions addressed current hot topics in the law, and the presenters were well prepared. The keynote speaker was especially skillful, her style practiced, and her tone persuasive. She told stories that her large audience could relate to, and she took a clever, backdoor approach to presenting her politically charged pro-choice agenda. As I listened to her opening remarks, I started to feel uneasy and began looking around the large auditorium to see others' reactions. The women were riveted upon the presenter's every word. When her voice rose to make a point, almost every head nodded in enthusiastic agreement. My discomfort escalated as I began to notice the speaker's smooth manipulation of facts and distortion of ethical standards and values.

At the end of the first day of the proceedings, I sat at dinner with some of the representatives from other law schools. Without exception these bright, articulate young women singled out the keynote speaker's address as the highlight of the conference thus far. Moreover, they wholeheartedly endorsed her platform. They didn't state their reasoning outright because to them it seemed obvious: if you are female, intelligent, and educated in the law, you will subscribe to this wise, seasoned practitioner's views. As I listened, I soon knew I couldn't let my silence lead others to think I agreed with them.

I decided the best opportunity to express my differing opinion would be at a delegates' meeting on the second and final day of the conference. As an official representative from the Brigham Young University law school, I knew I would be asked to sign off on a resolution that endorsed many of the flawed positions first introduced in the opening keynote address. This document would be forwarded to the American Bar Association with a letter of support from our national student organization. I was certain my refusal to put my name and the name of the Brigham Young University law school at the bottom of that position statement would be met with surprise, opposition, and even anger; but I was even more certain the time had come for me to take a stand.

Then, just before the roll call was to be taken, the lead delegate announced that, due to time constraints, the resolution would be tabled until the next delegates' meeting. My initial reaction was overwhelming relief that I didn't have to oppose something that appeared to be unanimously supported. That feeling faded quickly, however, and I knew that I still needed to "weigh in." That night in my hotel room, I wrote a four-page letter informing the conference leaders that, had I been asked to vote on the resolution, I would not have endorsed the measure. I explained my stance with the perspective of a member of the Church. Looking back, I honestly don't believe my few words of dissent were likely to persuade any of the organization's leaders to change their opinion. Nevertheless, I needed to voice them; the absolutes of the gospel required me to take a stand.

As followers of Christ, we must resist such intellectual enticements and stand firm as we grip the iron rod. We must be vigilant, continually anticipating erroneous, man-made ideals and preparing to counter philosophies such as relativism, hedonism, and negativism. Let me mention two practical ways that have helped me look to eternal things and filter out anything that would obscure that view.

First, focus more personally on the sacramental experience, on the blessing it is each week to renew our commitment to follow the Savior. Because we have such frequent opportunities to partake of the sacrament, at times our observance can feel routine. And, in some seasons of our lives, such as when we are teaching young children about reverence, we must concentrate more on keeping peace than seeking it! Nonetheless, whenever possible, we should anticipate our active participation in this sacred process. I've found that if I select something in advance to ponder—a verse of scripture, a hymn, an important lesson from the past week—I am more engaged and receptive to spiritual promptings. At those times, the Atonement ceases to be merely a subject for mental contemplation and becomes a heartfelt experience. I feel my Savior's sacrifice, I feel specific remorse for anything in my life that separates me from him, and I feel deep resolve to show that I remember him in all that I do and say. I sincerely want to have that more contemplative and meaningful experience become for me the rule, rather than the exception, as I participate in the sacrament.

Recently, my husband, Gary, and I attended sacrament meeting in beautiful northern California before catching a flight back home to Utah. That particular weekend had afforded me some extra time to count my blessings and concentrate upon my gratitude for the Savior's incomprehensible gift to me. From the first notes of the sacrament hymn, I was filled with the kind of joy that literally no words can express. I wrote the following lines shortly after the meeting: "Today I felt humbled and edified in much the same way I feel in the temple as I renew essential covenants. I knew I was surrounded by fellow Saints who are literally of royal birth, and I was lifted by and with them in inexpressible appreciation for our Savior." Such an experience clears my head and strengthens my heart.

Second, contemplate how to better serve those within our stewardship. Seeking inspiration to know how to best promote growth and eternal progression for members of our families, those we serve in callings, and close friends and neighbors is the noblest and most personally sustaining of pursuits. I treasure a particular picture of our sons taken at a brief moment in time before our family entered a new season. This photograph of these four adult brothers framed by the setting sun reminds me not to be complacent or to take things for granted. It urges me to step back, clear away too familiar habits, assumptions, my own needs, or anything else that would obscure my view of how best to serve these choice spirits. Such seeking to become more finely tuned instruments in the Lord's hands aligns us with the truths of his gospel and protects us and those we serve from erroneous manmade philosophies.

We will be challenged in our beliefs and in the principles that guide our lives. Some, the Korihors of our time, will try to shake the firm foundation we stand upon. May we consider how, each day—amid challenges and, yes, even mundane circumstances—we can stand solidly and strengthen our grips on the gospel's iron rod. President Gordon B. Hinckley reminds us that our direction is set by such "small, day-to-day choices" that literally become "the substance of our lives." May we choose this day, and every day, to serve the Lord.

Notes

1. Ezra Taft Benson, *A Witness and a Warning: A Modern-day Prophet Testifies of the Book of Mormon* (Salt Lake City: Deseret Book, 1988), 3.
2. Gordon B. Hinckley, *Stand a Little Taller: Counsel and Inspiration for Each Day of the Year* (Salt Lake City: Eagle Gate, 2001), 13; see also Alma 37:6.

The House of Illusions

LaNae Valentine

One day several years ago, while reading the Book of Mormon, I felt the Spirit whisper, "LaNae, you are in the great and spacious building." My immediate reaction was one of surprise and disbelief. I thought to myself, *How can that be?* I believed that those in the large and spacious building were prideful intellectuals or rich, party-animal types who wore costly apparel and mocked the members of the Church. Here I was, a poor, struggling graduate student. All of my earthly possessions could fit into my old car that I wasn't even sure would start from day to day. I didn't have any costly apparel or any worldly honors or achievements to speak of. And, at this time in my life, I did not have a lot of confidence, so how could I be proud? I was faithfully attending my church meetings, fulfilling my callings, attending the temple, and trying to keep the commandments. How could I possibly be in the large and spacious building? After a moment's consideration, I dismissed the impression.

Unfortunately, I was not very teachable at that moment. A more humble response might have been, "I'm listening, Lord, please tell me more." I wish I had been more like the child Samuel who "did let none of [the Lord's] words fall to the ground" (1 Samuel 3:19). I once read that the word *obedience* means to listen with a discerning ear and then to respond faithfully to the personal implications of what one has heard.[1] The proud do not listen well. We have a remarkable ability to filter out what we don't want to hear, or to minimize or discount what

---

LaNae Valentine, a university teacher and clinical practitioner, has specialized in women's issues and eating disorders. She has served as coordinator of Women's Services and Resources at Brigham Young University. She has taught in her ward Sunday School and currently serves as the Laurel advisor.

we don't understand. We are not willing to change our minds to accept truth, because to do so implies we might be wrong or might need to change something—and we don't like change very much.

Since that time, I think I have come to better understand how a good LDS woman can find herself in the large and spacious building and not even know she's there. We learn from the Book of Mormon that the large and spacious building is the pride of the world (1 Nephi 11:36). President Benson noted that "pride is a sin that can readily be seen in others but is rarely admitted in ourselves." Thus, we may be heavily afflicted with pride and not even know it. He continues: "Most of us consider pride to be a sin of those on the top, such as the rich and the learned, looking down at the rest of us. (See 2 Ne. 9:42.) There is, however, a far more common ailment among us—and that is pride from the bottom looking up. It is manifest in so many ways, such as fault-finding, gossiping, backbiting, murmuring, living beyond our means, envying, coveting, withholding gratitude and praise that might lift another, and being unforgiving and jealous."[2]

Pride is the sin we wake up to every morning. Good Latter-day Saint women are not going to go out and murder, plunder, pillage, and steal, but we might be guilty of gossiping and backbiting. We might be guilty of living beyond our means, of coveting, of withholding gratitude and praise that might lift another. As President Ezra Taft Benson stressed *twice* in his great conference address on pride, "Pride is the great stumbling block to Zion."[3] He, like all our other prophets, understood that we must carefully watch for the sin of pride in our lives or we will indeed stumble.

I believe that at the root of pride is a forgetting of who we are, who our Father is, who our Savior is, and the relationship among the three of us—as well as forgetting why we are here in mortality. Carlfred Broderick, a Latter-day Saint therapist, has stated: "I think we do not understand the nature of ourselves. I think we do not understand who we are. . . . When I went to the temple, I thought I was going to learn which star was Kolob, and where the Ten Tribes were, and other such information. But those aren't the mysteries of the kingdom; the mysteries of the kingdom are who we are, and who God is, and what our relationship to him is. . . . You can tell somebody in plain English, but they still don't know in their hearts who they really are."[4]

A friend of mine who recently had a mastectomy and a series of aggressive chemotherapy and radiation treatments commented to me that in spite of the difficulty of this ordeal, for the first time in her life she feels real. When I asked her what she meant by that, she said because she has never married, and because of her not-so-functional family, she has always felt disconnected from people, like she doesn't fit in. She said, "I was always standing on the outside of my heart. Now, I'm beginning to see that I am loved and that the most important thing in life is to love. I'm beginning to find my heart." She continued, "I'm beginning to understand how much Heavenly Father loves me and how aware of me he is, by all the loving people and little miracles he has brought into my life." She concluded, "I used to get compliments about my thin, healthy body, which made me feel good about myself. Now my body is scarred and sick. But that hasn't changed who I am. I am more than my body—much more."

Satan would have us believe the illusion of "not enough," that the only way we can be enough or have enough is to perform and achieve and earn our worth. Once we've bought into this one lie, our whole foundation is in shambles. Advertisers are brilliant at capitalizing on the illusion of "not enough." They promise that more goods, more stimulation, more achievement will deliver us from the uncomfortable feelings of "not enough." Their purpose is to create feelings of deprivation and a desire for things that promise to deliver us from the hard life, the drab life—from *real* life. Women especially are bombarded with images of beautiful, thin, smart, talented women who seem to be having and doing it all. As we compare ourselves to them, we are left feeling both deprived and inadequate.

The illusion of "not enough" is insatiable. No matter how much we do, no matter how well we do it, no matter how much weight we lose, no matter how many trophies or awards we accrue—it's never enough. Paraphrasing author Mary Pipher, we simply end up fat, addicted, broke, with a house full of junk, and no time.[5] Essentially, buying into the belief of "not enough" is saying God is not enough. God cannot be trusted to provide for our needs. God does not have enough love to go around. Thus, we put ourselves at odds with God and at enmity with everyone else. Since we can't trust God, we take matters into our own hands and rely upon our own strength.

Because we have forgotten that God *is* enough, we become focused on a competitive striving to attain, accrue, and achieve. It's no longer good enough to do our best, we must do better than everyone else, too. Everywhere I go I encounter women who are busy, stressed, anxious, and worried—striving to be the perfect wife, mother, and daughter. It seems that many women are running faster than they are able by over-extending, over-scheduling, and over-achieving.

A woman I know who struggles with this problem shared this insight with me. Her bishop released her from a very demanding church calling and asked her to take a relatively low-key position: birthday coordinator for the Relief Society. All she needed to do was call each sister in the ward the day of her birthday and wish her a happy birthday or send a birthday card. Using the guise of "magnifying her calling," she turned this position into a nightmare. Instead of simply calling each sister the day of her birthday, she planned a big celebration for her. She purchased decorations, party hats, color-coordinated tablecloths, paper ware, napkins, and cups. She also provided elaborate refreshments and party favors. She admitted to me that the calling was about to do her in. When asked why she had turned a fairly low-stress calling into such a production, she admitted that this is how she does everything in her life. She has to make everything big, flashy, and wonderful because this is how she derives her sense of worth. She, like many of us, has forgotten that "our individual worth is already divinely established as 'great'; it does not fluctuate like the stock market."[6]

How can we move from this house of illusions and build upon a sure foundation? One night I watched Mike Wallace interview the real John Nash (on whom the movie *A Beautiful Mind* was based). Mr. Nash explained that one thing that helped him fight the disease of schizophrenia was to stop himself from engaging in his delusions. He remarked that they really weren't getting him anywhere. And then he said, "After awhile, I just became disillusioned with my delusions." We, too, must get to a point where we realize that our illusions aren't getting us anywhere. We must become disillusioned with *our* illusions.

Pride spawns most of our illusions. If pride is about forgetting, then perhaps the antidote to pride is remembering. Sister Virginia H. Pearce said, "I believe that *remember* is a holy word. I believe it is one that prophets have used to move us more surely to our Heavenly Father."[7] The word *remember* is used twice in Helaman 5:12: "Remember, remember that it is upon the rock of our Redeemer, who is Christ, the Son of God, that ye must build your foundation . . . which is a sure foundation, a foundation whereon if men build they *cannot fall*" (emphasis added).

What does it mean to build our foundation on Christ? How do we do it? Jesus said he did "always those things" that pleased God (John 8:29). President Benson taught, "Would we not do well to have the pleasing of God as our motive" rather than the pleasing of men?[8] A prideful person finds it difficult to do the will of God. Instead of seeking his will concerning our heavenly potential and spiritual worth, we turn to the world to make us feel better—to addictions, to work, to achievement and false security. Wouldn't it be liberating to be delivered from the bondage of other's judgments? Wouldn't it be glorious if we were not driven by the slavish need to please and to conform to the fickle fads and fashions of the day—if we did not have to depend upon the world to tell us whether or not we have value? President Benson said, "If we love God, do His will, and fear His judgment more than men's, we will have self-esteem."[9]

Coming to know the will of God and offering complete submission to him requires that we be able to hear and recognize his voice. It requires that we hold still. Elder Henry B. Eyring has said, "Pride creates a noise within us which makes the quiet voice of the Spirit hard to hear."[10]

To hear his voice, we must always "listen with the intent of doing what we are told,"[11] even though God may require of us things that are not comfortable or popular. The apostle Paul said, "Be not conformed to this world: but be ye transformed by the renewing of your mind, that ye may prove what is that good, and acceptable, and perfect will of God" (Romans 12:2). Sister Patricia Holland explains, "To connect with God and to be filled with his fulness, to not be conformed to the world, . . . requires a calm mind, a 'renewed mind.' A renewed mind is one which has been illuminated by a new spiritual perception—revelation. When our mind has been illuminated to see as God sees, it becomes a joy to accept his will."[12]

Somewhere in our lives there must be time and room for personal communion with the Lord. We must let a few things go and turn a few things off so that we might prayerfully position ourselves in solitude and serenity to receive the mind of God. To become as he is, we need to spend spiritual time with him *every day*. In doing so, we will have his image in our countenance. We will not feel anxious or inadequate. I read once that the word *discipline* comes from the same root as *disciple* and means seeing yourself through the eyes of the teacher who loves you. I thought this was a lovely definition. Could it be possible that the discipline we're trying to achieve is the ability to see ourselves and all things as God sees?

One day when I was actually holding still and pondering, an image came to my mind of the Savior sitting in a rocking chair in my home. I saw myself busily running around him, not even noticing him. In spite of my mindless activity and avoidance of him, I had an overwhelming sense of his presence and the calm assurance of his amazing love and patience for me. I sensed he is always patiently waiting for me to approach him, that he will wait as long as it takes, that he will not force or compel me to come to him. I felt no judgment or reproach for my busyness and neglect of him because I sensed he knows me and understands why I do this. I felt him inviting me to come to him, to stop this silly running around, and to lay all my anxious worries at his feet; he has a better way to show me. For a fleeting moment, I saw myself through his eyes and caught a glimpse of my weaknesses and fears. I was comforted to feel that I wasn't as bad as I had made myself out to be. If he can view me with such compassion and support, can't I do the same? And can't I offer this same compassion and support to others? I resonate with his words in Doctrine and Covenants 19:40–41: "Canst thou run about longer as a blind guide? Or canst thou be humble and meek, and conduct thyself wisely before me? Yea, come unto me thy Savior."

I think too many of us hold back or avoid the Savior's love because we fear we're lacking. It's true we are not perfect. It's true we have weaknesses. Do we believe the Lord when he says that his grace is sufficient to make weak things strong (Ether 12:27)? Are we willing to submit to this process? Elder Richard G. Scott testifies: "God is not a jealous being who delights in persecuting those who misstep. He is an absolutely perfect, compassionate, understanding, patient, and forgiving Father. He is willing to entreat, counsel, strengthen, lift, and fortify."[13] When we are transformed by his love, we have no need for greed or jealousy or envy.

We, like Jesus, must acquire a sense of who we are and who God is through study, obedience, and prayer. Jesus often withdrew to silent places—the hills, gardens, fishing boats—to have time alone to pray. As a result, Jesus knew who he was and who his Father was. Jesus overcame the veil of forgetfulness, just as we can. The Lord has promised, "Draw near unto me and I will draw near unto you; seek me diligently and ye shall find me" (D&C 88:63). As we allow ourselves to be known by the Lord, to receive his freeing and redeeming knowledge of ourselves, we learn to know others and the world in the same loving way. We eventually come to a place of peace—to the assurance that what we have (whatever that is) and who we are (whoever that is) is enough!

Notes

1. Parker J. Palmer, *To Know as We Are Known: Education as a Spiritual Journey* (San Fransisco: HarperSanFransisco, 1993), 89.
2. Ezra Taft Benson, "Beware of Pride," *Ensign*, May 1989, 5.

3. Benson, "Beware of Pride," 7.
4. Carlfred Broderick, "The Uses of Adversity," in *The Best of Women's Conference: Selected Talks from 25 Years of BYU Women's Conferences* (Salt Lake City: Deseret Book, 2000), 56; also *As Women of Faith: Talks Selected from the BYU Women's Conferences* (Salt Lake City: Deseret Book, 1989), 178.
5. Notes taken by the author at a conference at the Renfrew Center, Philadelphia, Pennsylvania, November 2001.
6. Neal A. Maxwell, "Consecrate Thy Performance," *Ensign*, May 2002, 36.
7. Virginia H. Pearce, "The Power of Remembering," in *The Arms of His Love: Talks from the 1999 Women's Conference* (Salt Lake City: Deseret Book, 2000), 76.
8. Benson, "Beware of Pride," 5.
9. Benson, "Beware of Pride," 6.
10. Henry B. Eyring, "Prayer," *Ensign*, November 2001, 16.
11. Henry B. Eyring, *To Draw Closer to God: A Collection of Discourses* (Salt Lake City: Deseret Book, 1997), 34.
12. Patricia T. Holland, "Filled With all the Fullness of God," *Brigham Young Magazine*, November 1996, 21; also in *Clothed with Charity: Talks from the 1996 Women's Conference*, ed. Dawn Hall Anderson, Susette Fletcher Green, and Dlora Hall Dalton (Salt Lake City: Deseret Book, 1997), 4.
13. Richard G. Scott, "Finding Forgiveness," *Ensign*, May 1995, 75.

The Whole Armor of God

Kathy Newton

One day last year, I accompanied my husband to the Utah State Prison, where he was serving as a bishop. A choir from our home stake was also there to perform choruses from Handel's *Messiah* at the worship service in the prison chapel. An inmate sang an opening hymn accompanied beautifully on the piano by another inmate. The pianist obviously had spent many years practicing and perfecting his musical talent. Accompanying the singers that day was a young man from our home ward, a returned missionary, just months away from completing his undergraduate degree. As the choir began to sing, the accompanist began to have some difficulty, so the inmate pianist unobtrusively walked to the piano, sat on the bench, and began turning the pages of the sheet music at the appropriate time. Tears came to my eyes as I watched these two young men, one dressed in a white prison jumpsuit, the other in a coat and tie. They shared a love of music, and each obviously had someone in their life, probably a mother, who loved them enough to give them the gift of music. But one had chosen to follow the Lord and his teachings; the other had violated the law sufficiently to put himself behind bars. I doubt that I will ever forget the image of those two young men sitting side by side, so alike in their talents, yet so opposite in their life choices.

Those two gifted pianists have become constant companions in my mind as I have thought and prayed about this question: Why was one of them able to take upon himself the "whole armor . . . to withstand

---

Kathy Newton received a bachelor's degree in sociology from Washington University (St. Louis). She has served as the Young Women president in her stake. She and her husband, Jack, are the parents of four children.

the evil day" while the other succumbed? If we could probe into each of their pasts, we no doubt would find profound differences. It is probably fair to suppose that the inmate had challenges not encountered by the college student, yet we could dissect their lives and still not arrive at a conclusive answer as to why they chose such different roads.

Whatever else happened, I believe one underlying difference existed: At some point prior to the events which resulted in his incarceration, the inmate forgot that he was a child of God. Events in his life, some in his control and others not, estranged him from his Heavenly Father and left him vulnerable to the adversary.

From the psalmist of the Old Testament who declared: "All of you are children of the most High" (Psalm 82:6), to Paul who testified: "For we are also his offspring" (Acts 17:29), to modern-day revelation given to the Prophet Joseph Smith in the Doctrine and Covenants: "The inhabitants [of the worlds created by the Savior] are begotten sons and daughters unto God" (D&C 76:24), we know that we are children of God: "children," "offspring," "sons," "daughters." Could any words be more clear?

We come to this earth knowing we are children of God and only gradually lose that knowledge. Some children seem to be born with a stronger sense of their divine nature than others. No matter how hard the world tries to beat them down, they seem to be able to hold on to the knowledge of who they are. But many lose that confidence somewhere in adolescence. How many of us have had responsible, capable, rational, confident fifth and sixth graders only to see them become irrational, irritable, disinterested, irresponsible teenagers whose entire vocabulary seems to consist of two expressions: "I dunno" and "I forgot"?

If acknowledging their divine heritage becomes more difficult for our youth during their teenage years, then it is equally likely they will also question the reality of Satan. That is where, I believe, many of our young people go astray. With a blurred perception of the power and influence of Satan, they become more vulnerable to his cunning. From the scriptures, we know three very important things about Satan: first, he "sought to destroy the agency of man" (Moses 4:3); second, when he was cast out of the Father's presence, he became "the devil, the father of all lies, to deceive and blind men, and to lead them captive at his will" (Moses 4:4); and third, "he seeketh that all men might be miserable like unto himself" (2 Nephi 2:27). Do our youth understand these three fundamental characteristics? Do they know what Satan's mission is?

In the four years that my husband has been serving at the state prison, we have learned valuable lessons. One I will always remember came from an inmate who wrote: "I want to share with you a word that I have come to know. It is called S.U.D. or short for *Seemingly Unimportant Decisions*. These are the choices we make that on the surface appear to be unimportant, but as time goes on weaken our spirit or lead us straight to sin. A poor choice here and there, a drink here or there, a lie or two . . . just a little white lie. Do you see the pattern? S.U.D.s add up, and soon you are far away from the light and in temptation's hand. They seem not so bad at first but . . . soon, though, they're not little. They become life changers."[1]

Do our youth understand that those first seemingly harmless steps can be the critical ones that lead them to more serious transgressions? This man knows the danger from sad experience. He goes on to warn: "Know that you have limitations to what your spirit can protect you from. . . . [Satan] is strong and knows your weaknesses. . . . Stay close to the Lord. Live to have the Spirit each and every day. Don't become a slave to sin, a prisoner of doing wrong."[2]

Making mistakes is part of life, part of the learning process. Being a parent sometimes means that you have to sit by and watch as your child suffers the consequences of poor decisions. Sometimes you have to be the one to mete out those painful consequences. But what happens when the everyday adolescent ups and downs are being replaced with choices that have the potential to cause irreparable harm? What do you do when that inner voice tells you that something serious is the matter? Elder M. Russell Ballard has counseled: "You don't have to stand idly by as those over whom you have stewardship make poor moral choices. When one of our youth stands at a moral crossroad in life, almost always there is someone—a parent, a leader, a teacher—who could make a difference by intervening with love and kindness."[3] We have a responsibility to help in whatever way we can. Sometimes that means admitting that the problem is too big for us and that we need help from other family members, a bishop, a professional counselor, or a social service agency. We can't let feelings of hurt, embarrassment, shame, or failure keep us from seeking needed help. Our youth live in an age of unparalleled temptations and pressures. Chronic depression; eating disorders; drug, alcohol and pornography addictions; and other self-destructive behaviors can rarely be handled without professional help. We must love them enough to secure their safety by accessing all means available. We need the wisdom to know when a problem is too big for us to handle and the humility to seek the necessary help.

While shopping with my daughters recently, I overheard a preschooler say to his parents and older brother, "Someone better come with me so I don't have to get lost!" Our youth don't *have* to get lost; they don't *want* to get lost. May we do everything within our power to bring them to the knowledge that they are children of God with divine attributes and potential and that much is expected of them.

Notes

1. Copy in author's possession.
2. Copy in author's possession.
3. M. Russell Ballard, "Like a Flame Unquenchable," *Ensign*, May 1999, 87.

My Scrapbook of the Future

Sharon G. Samuelson

When I was in junior high school, my teacher assigned our class to create scrapbooks of our future. We were to fill the pages with descriptions of our desires for our future families, homes, occupations, vacations, and lifestyles. We could illustrate these scrapbooks with our own artwork or pictures cut out from magazines. I recall searching for pictures of the best-looking man, the cutest children (five of them), and the fanciest house, among pictures of other wants and desires of a young teenage girl.

As I envisioned my future family during that early stage of my life, I didn't understand "that the family is central to the Creator's plan for the eternal destiny of His children."[1] I didn't think about the responsibilities I would have as a wife, mother, daughter, or sister, or about my obligation to give and receive "sacred support" within the family. At that age, creating my scrapbook of the future, family life looked romantic, exciting, and so far away.

Now that many years have passed—and I have no idea where that scrapbook is—I better understand what Captain Moroni called "the sacred support which we owe to our wives and our children" (Alma 44:5). I believe it means to do all we can as wives, husbands, fathers, mothers, siblings, aunts, uncles, and grandparents to unify, preserve, and strengthen the family so that as a family we may return to live once more with our Father in Heaven. I am still learning and struggling to integrate that understanding into my life each day.

Sharon G. Samuelson has served as a teacher or leader in all the Church auxiliaries. She and her husband, Cecil O. Samuelson of the First Quorum of the Seventy, are the parents of five children and the grandparents of three.

I recall that in my scrapbook I had two related requirements concerning the man I would marry. First, he would not be a doctor, and second, he would work eight to five so that he would be home often to help with the children and be involved in household activities. I achieved my first desire but only because my new husband was a college undergraduate and not yet in medical school. My second requirement was, of course, never met. Sustaining and supporting a husband whose work and church obligations required many hours and days away from home has been an ongoing part of my married life.

I have often turned to Doctrine and Covenants 25 as a guide, substituting my name for Emma's. Verse 5 reads: "And the office of thy calling shall be for a comfort unto . . . thy husband, in his afflictions, with consoling words, in the spirit of meekness." Even though I can't compare Emma's calling and great challenges with my own, it doesn't mean that my life hasn't been frustrating, challenging, discouraging, and often lonely. It has also been fulfilling, satisfying, and joyful.

I have also looked to Sariah in the Book of Mormon as an example. She supported her husband, Lehi, as she left her home and life in Jerusalem. She faced hardships and worries as they traveled. At one point, her concern for her sons overwhelmed her. Nephi reported: "She . . . complained against my father . . . saying: Behold thou hast led us forth from the land of our inheritance, and my sons are no more, and we perish in the wilderness" (1 Nephi 5:2). Sariah knew in her heart, however, that the Lord had inspired their flight, and she rejoiced at their sons' safe return: "I know of a surety that the Lord hath commanded my husband to flee into the wilderness" (1 Nephi 5:8). Even though it was difficult for Sariah, even if she sometimes became angry and frustrated, she knew that God loved her and would be with her and her family in their trials. When I have murmured at times concerning the support required of me so that my husband can fulfill his obligations—both secular and ecclesiastical—I take comfort in remembering Sariah. She, too, found what she was asked to do challenging and difficult, but because of her faith in God she did it.

We can also learn from the wives of our modern-day prophets. President Ezra Taft Benson commented: "A man succeeds and reaps the honors of public applause, when in truth a [steadfast and courageous] woman has in large measure made it all possible—has by her tact and encouragement held him to his best, has had faith in him when his own faith has languished, has cheered him with the unfailing assurance, 'You can, you must, you will.'"[2] Husbands and wives support one another as equal partners in the gospel of Jesus Christ. Whenever we support a spouse in a righteous endeavor, in a quiet but powerful way, we, too, serve the Lord.

Of Marjorie Hinckley, Elder L. Tom Perry observed: "Over the years, my wife and I have had the privilege of traveling on many assignments with President and Sister Hinckley. In our travels, we have always found Sister Hinckley so positive and cheerful. Her enthusiastic and supportive attitude clearly lifts her husband. . . . She has set a standard of support for priesthood-leader husbands that literally brings out the best in them."[3]

In a marriage, mutual love, respect, and support are essential, but it takes desire, time, and effort to build these attributes. Your husband may not be a Church member, or he may be a less active one. As his wife, you still have the same obligation to support him in righteousness, and you still have the same gospel teachings to guide you. Your family is the most important unit in the Church, and your goal is still to be an eternal family. Your patience, faith, and living example of the gospel of Jesus Christ is vital. Former Utah Jazz basketball player Thurl Bailey converted to the Church after marrying a Latter-day Saint. Of his wife, he says, "She never abandoned any of her beliefs; she just lived what she knew and led by example."[4]

In my scrapbook of the future, I had pictures of five children. My husband and I do have five children, but they didn't come the way I envisioned. Three came to our family the usual way, although it took surgeries, tests, a tubal pregnancy, tears, and prayers before they all arrived. Two came by the way of adoption, a circumstance that has also blessed our lives in unexpected ways.

Putting pictures in a book was easy. Raising and supporting children through the years isn't. As we learn and grow as parents, we will make mistakes and poor judgments. Keep trying. Nephi reminds us that "we talk of Christ, we rejoice in Christ, we preach of Christ . . . that our children may know to what source they may look for a remission of their sins" (2 Nephi 25:26). President Hinckley tells us that "every child is entitled to grow up in a home where there is warm and secure companionship, . . . where appreciation one for another is taught and exemplified, and where God is acknowledged."[5] This is the "sacred support" we owe our children. Remember that the role of parenting and supporting can be shared with aunts, uncles, grandparents, and other family members.

As parents we err. Our children will err, too, sometimes making disastrous choices that cause us great concern and heartbreak. We can and must still give "sacred support" and love to these children. "Pray for your careless and disobedient children; hold on to them with your faith. Hope on, trust on, till you see the salvation of God," counseled the Prophet Joseph Smith. "The eternal sealings of faithful parents and the divine promises made to them for valiant service in the Cause of Truth, [will] save not only themselves, but likewise their posterity. Though some of the sheep may wander, the eye of the Shepherd is upon them, and sooner or later they will feel the tentacles of Divine Providence reaching out after them and drawing them back to the fold. Either in this life or the life to come, they will return."[6] What a comforting doctrine and encouragement to parents to be faithful to covenants made in the temple of our Lord.

I know now what I didn't know when I was making my scrapbook of the future. I know the importance of the family in God's plan. I know that he loves us and will bless us as we strive to serve him by living gospel principles.

Notes

1. "The Family: A Proclamation to the World," *Ensign*, November 1995, 102.

2. Sheri L. Dew, *Ezra Taft Benson: A Biography* (Salt Lake City: Deseret Book, 1987), 413–14.
3. L. Tom Perry, "Elect Lady," *Ensign*, May 1995, 73, 74.
4. Thurl Bailey, in *Why I Believe* (Salt Lake City: Bookcraft, 2002), 38.
5. Gordon B. Hinckley, *Teachings of Gordon B. Hinckley* (Salt Lake City: Deseret Book, 1997), 416.
6. As cited in Orson F. Whitney, Conference Report, April 1929, 110; also in *Are My Children Going to Make It? Real Help for Teaching the Gospel in the Home*, R. Wayne Boss and Leslee S. Boss (Salt Lake City: Deseret Book, 1991), 197–98. Elder Whitney continued: "They will have to pay their debt to justice; they will suffer for their sins; and may tread a thorny path; but if it leads them at last, like a penitent Prodigal, to a loving and forgiving father's heart and home, the painful experience will not have been in vain."

Your Average, Imperfect Parents

Marsha A. Castleton

My husband, Lowell, and I are your average, imperfect, "in-the-trenches" parents who have reared a wonderful, loving, equally imperfect family. Our experiences rearing a family may strike a chord of commonality with other Latter-day Saint parents.

Questions to our seven sons and reading my journal entries over the years have given me insight into many things, especially how I have evolved and changed as a mother. I was an idealistic, type A personality in my younger days. Being achievement oriented, I thought if I just worked hard enough or pushed hard enough things would turn out the way I wanted. I married a husband who was also type A, meticulous, and organized. Children helped mellow us and plug us into what is really important or worth fretting about.

My journals reveal these high achievement tendencies spilling over into our early parenting. Well-intentioned parents that we were, we had no doubt that our children would be perfectly behaved, excel as the Castleton Family Orchestra, always work hard at whatever they were asked to do, and roll right along in their parents' timeline of high expectations. If I only had known then what I know now! Parenting isn't *pushing* children into what we want them to be. It's establishing a rich, loving environment based on your family values and beliefs and, in that environment, guiding and encouraging them to develop and

---

Marsha A. Castleton, homemaker, mother, and grandmother, is also a registered nurse. She has served as first counselor in her ward's Young Women presidency. She and her husband, Lowell, are the parents of seven sons and the grandparents of seven children.

magnify *who they already are*. They may display the family stamp in some physical characteristics, but there resemblances end. They are unique in most other ways.

We learned that our job was to be available as much as possible to celebrate our children's amazing individuality. Children need parents to help them discover and develop their *own* talents and to appreciate, and be satisfied with, who they are. Most important, parents need to tether each child to our earthly family and to their Heavenly Father, who is counting on their return. Without this firm connection, a child's eventual return trip becomes much more tentative.

My husband and I bravely sent a lengthy questionnaire to each of our sons to collect their thoughts and memories about growing up in our family. A response from one son noted the importance of family in forming lifelong values and attitudes:

"Once I became older and more independent, I remember that the family was where all my values and standards were embedded. I knew that these principles and this behavior were expected at home and always would be, and this was a large influence in keeping me grounded when I started making my own decisions and mistakes. While growing up, my family was the cornerstone of my life, and though I look back and realize that we were not a perfect family, *there were those key ingredients there* that allowed me to feel loved, to feel accepted, and that established and taught me what was right and how to live accordingly."

Gospel-Based Activities

From the beginning, Lowell and I wanted the foundation and strength of a gospel-based home. We loved the idea of family night and family prayer and implemented them both when our children were toddlers. Family night became synonymous with Monday evenings as the boys grew. We experimented with every possible approach at different times. The overall key to success, especially when the boys were older, was to have family council, or a short planning time, on Sunday to review calendars and encourage goals. That kept Monday free for family night. We had short ones and long ones, happy ones and disrupted ones, great ones and boring ones—but we almost always had them. Many times we questioned if this time did any good at all. If you have wondered the same thing, consider these responses from three of our sons to the question, "What things in our home made you feel loved and secure?"

"Though I wouldn't have admitted it at the time, family home evening was a great comfort and stabilizer for me. It showed that my parents held their family as a first priority. It also provided a place and time outside of church to spiritually grow and feel part of something. Having someone ask me on a weekly basis what I had going on in my life meant a lot to me."

"Being a shy person with a lot of difficulties that came from this characteristic, I really don't remember enjoying going to church or having a lot of friendships that I furthered by going there. What made a difference to me was the clear and concrete fact that church—the gospel—didn't end when church was over, and what I learned from my parents at family night and other events was a very real extension of what church was about. I remember *very clearly* many of the family night lessons taught by Mom and Dad and several of them had a memorable impact on me."

"Family home evening is a tradition that, while I know I didn't appreciate at the time, I am so grateful for now. And honestly, I don't remember learning a lot of specific gospel principles at family night. But I can name dozens of life's lessons that we learned. The fact that Mom and Dad took time to prepare meaningful and relevant lessons made a big impact on my mind and soul. More importantly, I remember them bearing testimony to us as kids in those family home evenings, and that went a long way in helping me to gain my testimony."

THE LORD'S LESSONS

I marvel at the Lord's wisdom in giving us particular parenting problems and challenges. Our problems often become the impetus for life's richest blessings. For example, two of our sons were born with congenital deformities: one with a severe bilateral cleft lip and palate, and the other with marked paralysis in his left arm, hand, and leg. Both have grown into amazing young men who have accomplished much and are sensitive to the needs of those around them. During their growing up years, however, especially through grade school, they often fell victim to cruel teasing and being left out. Our home had to fortify them against these assaults on their self-image and confidence. We worked hard to learn tolerance and sensitivity, not only to help build up these two sons, but also to teach their brothers to forgive those who were mean to them. Being Christlike was a theme we emphasized often, and our boys learned to watch out for others in similar circumstances.

I'll never forget when one of these sons came home from school crying because a group of boys had repeatedly teased and pushed him around that day. Furious, his older brothers initially planned a counterattack. With a little coaching from Mom and Dad, the big brothers sent their little brother back to school the next day with a challenge to the bullies to take him on with his brothers—not in a fight, but in a football game. It sounds crazy, but it worked. Four young boys showed up in our yard after school, probably more from curiosity than anything else. The game began; the big brothers helped the little brother look pretty darn good for the win and gain some credibility with those bullying classmates, who never bothered him again.

An Atmosphere of Love

Not too many years ago, a favorite child psychologist said he knew the most important key in dealing with hard-to-handle teens. I could hardly wait for him to expand on that! "Just love them," he admonished and then repeated three times, "Just love them." Loving them is sometimes hard when you don't agree with what they're doing, but that unconditional love often softens teenage hearts, allows for communication, and encourages improved behavior.

Homes don't have to be big or expensive or have quality furniture or designer bedrooms. They can even be a mess sometimes. But our homes should be *beautiful* with love and respect among family members, and, most important, with loving arms to encircle our children *under any circumstance*. How important is this? Let me share another son's thought: "The most important family memory to me was being able to go to my parents when I was struggling. I've had a lot of hard times so far in my short life and I would never have made it without them." I never imagined that this special son would ever have tough problems as a teen. I remember so clearly a morning in grade school when he bounded up the stairs into the kitchen for breakfast, whistling. "Well, how are you?" I said. He smiled and answered emphatically, "I'm just great!" "How do you know?" I asked. "The mirror told me so!" he replied. He was truly one of our happiest kids. Circumstances changed, however, as he grew older. He ran into obstacles and challenges that upset his confidence and happy nature. Since then he's been on a temporary spiritual detour, but he still loves to come home. We hold back the strong desire to lecture and correct, because we know from experience that it's much more effective to just love him.

A hard lesson for us as parents, from our first child to our last, has been looking beyond those annoyances that drive parents wild—long hair, untidy clothes, "interesting" friends—and responding to them with smiles, warm hugs, and a tone of voice that speaks love. These attitudes are much more likely to keep the kids coming home instead of making them feel unaccepted and disapproved of, feelings they are struggling with anyway.

DADS WHO CARE

As a young mother, I was haunted by a remark by President David O. McKay about his wife. He proudly pointed out that he had never heard her raise her voice to their children. I can tell you right now that if I had never raised my voice at those seven boys, I never would have been heard. At peak hours, the noise level at the Castleton house could be pretty scary. Home wasn't home without slamming doors, hoards of friends going in and out, kitchen raiding, loud music, and boisterous voices. When people ask me how I ever reared all those boys, I just smile and say, "I didn't do it alone." My marathon running partner not only kept me enduring with him until the last apron string was cut but was also a great coach and example to me when it came to helping his sons finish their own race of life.

Even though Lowell spent much time talking with or giving father's interviews to our boys throughout the years, one of his most effective communication tools was notes. There's something special about a written message that can be reviewed, reread, and thought over. I cannot tell you how often a folded note adorned the pillow of a turned-down bed awaiting a son. Whether it was recognition for a triumph or success, or a father's counsel after trouble, our boys knew their dad cared and was plugged in to the details of their lives. They listened to notes.

Then there were Dad's "yellow lists"—job assignments written on yellow legal paper and taped above the kitchen stove. Each son knew from the time he was young: *No work, no play*. The sooner their chores were finished and crossed off, the sooner they were free. If they chose not to work, the consequence was simply "house arrest." In spite of all the complaints these lists created, they had a strong impact in teaching our boys a good work ethic.

Even though Lowell was gone frequently with church or professional assignments, he always seemed to be there during the most critical times. In high school, one son who was a cross-country runner was at an out-of-town meet where he wasn't expecting either of his parents. Lowell unexpectedly managed to break away from work and arrived at the event just in time to see the latter part of the state qualifying event. This son was struggling up the last hill before the home stretch, trying to win a chance to go to state. Instead of watching from the sideline with the other parents, Lowell, in his suit and trench coat, ran up the hill to meet him and literally ran by his side the last hundred yards, coat tails flying, all the way to the finish line where they embraced and jumped with triumph together.

At-home Mom Time

I worked part time as a registered nurse to help Lowell through law school. After he graduated, I gratefully became a full-time mom. I loved being at home. But my experiences in both worlds made two things apparent to me: one, when you're working, you wish you could be home more; and, two, when you're home all the time, you miss the challenge and fulfillment of working outside the home.

When my children were all in school, Lowell was stricken with a very serious illness that almost took his life. That scare prompted us to invest time and money to reactivate my nursing license. I then worked part time to keep my license. Though this step seemed wise, I felt guilty about being unavailable for some of my children's activities. Demands on a working mother are tremendous, whether she is married or shouldering the parenting alone. In either situation, I feel strongly we will all be rewarded richly for our every effort. One son wrote:

"In my senior year, I had been doing a lot of work on the senior slide show. After the assembly where we did the show, I remember walking home after school, being very tired and a little disappointed in how it had all turned out. Just as I crossed the road I saw Mom walking on the sidewalk towards me. She had had to work that day and wasn't able to see the slide show. I could see in her eyes that she was sorry that she had to miss it but wanted to show her love and support by meeting me on the way home. That she would want to do that for me to show her love was a very special thing for me."

Looking back, I now understand how important a mom is to a child. Moms are quick to think we're always "the heavy" who has to lay down the law, repeatedly say no, give orders, and consistently discipline; we're the ones who must absorb the brunt of any given child's tantrums and displeasure. We're often so worn out and discouraged that we fail to realize our innate power to nurture, heal, and love our children. From my journal, I found this reassurance:

"No one in this world could convince me that there were joys in being a mother today! All I have done from morning until evening was say 'no' and break up fighting, mean boys . . . I couldn't tolerate one more minute of it. Before we had dinner, I went into the bathroom to try to compose myself at least a little bit. Much to my dismay, one young son followed me in. As I was combing my hair, he asked if he could have the empty Clorox bottle sitting on the cupboard in the kitchen. I told him (barked at him, actually) that he absolutely couldn't because it was to put water in for our food storage. Sounding irritated, he said, 'Why can't you just get a new one?' I was too tired to argue. Feeling like a failure, I said, 'I'll bet you could do with a new mother today, couldn't you!' He looked puzzled and said, 'No!'

"Then I asked, 'What if a man came to our door and offered you $1,000 for your mommy? Would you take it?' He then blurted out, 'No way! I wouldn't sell you for that much.'

"'How about a million?' I asked.

"'No way,' again he said. 'Why? Would you sell one of your boys for that much?' I was tempted to say something else, but I replied, 'No, I love my sons too much.' He smiled and went out of the room. In a moment, I could hear him posing the same question to his older brother. Would he sell me to a man at the door for a thousand dollars?

"He said, 'Heck no. But I'd let him come and live with us if he'd give me a $1,000. Then we could both have Mommy!'"

Even when we're at our worst, we are important to our children and are loved by them.

Children need and want us near as much as possible. I am deeply concerned as I see so many young couples buying or building homes they can afford only if both work. A couple's greatest concern when planning their lives and bringing children into the world should be how they can keep the mother at home as much as possible. No sacrifice should be too great to stay in our homes with our children if we can. Our desire for material things should never overshadow that all-important decision.

If I've learned nothing else from my sons' memories, I've learned that *little* is *BIG* to children. Little, less flashy elements of love, family, and home are important to them. It's sobering and yet encouraging to think that small kindnesses, mere proximity, willing and frequent hugs, love, and concern are what children remember and treasure most.

THE GREAT POWER OF EXAMPLE IN PARENTING

Lowell D. Castleton

Of all the things I could say about raising a family, the one I believe in most strongly and I have tried to practice for the thirty-four years of my marriage is this: the most important thing parents can do to influence the way their children will feel about men, women, marriage, homes, and many significant life principles is to genuinely, devotedly, and openly *love their spouse!*

I have often wondered if our sons ever got tired of hearing me say how blessed I was to have married such an exemplary, ideal woman as their mother. I really do feel that way about Marsha. Now I want so much for those sons to feel the very same way about their wives. I want them to unabashedly tell their wives of their love, not only in private but especially in front of their children.

I would categorize this behavior as "example," "patterning," or "modeling," all of which are undoubtedly the most important ways we teach our children. My children's words, my experiences in Church callings, and my work as a judge dealing daily with issues relating to children and parenting have all taught me that *how* parents relate to and deal with one another powerfully impacts the lives of their children—both for good and bad.

That message seems to have at least partially gotten through to our married sons. We sent them each a lengthy survey to find out their

---

Lowell D. Castleton is an Idaho State trial judge and the presiding judge of a pilot family violence court. A Scouter and former bishop, he has also served as a stake president. He and his wife, Marsha Adams, are the parents of seven sons and have seven grandchildren.

memories and thoughts about growing up in our home, and they gave the following responses:

"The things you taught us about loving each other, about putting your marriage first, about spending time with each other (as husband and wife, mother and father) are the patterns I am now trying to follow."

"I love that we are a 'touchy, feely' family. I love that we can hug each other and show our affection physically. I think that is so important. I'm so grateful that growing up I often heard the words 'I love you'—both from my parents to me, but also spoken by my parents to each other. I never fully appreciated that until I left home, met other people, and realized how many families and parents don't speak those words to each other."

The importance of expressing love has been brought home to me over the years as I have counseled with troubled couples—and often with their children—in various Church settings. The question I asked most frequently of family members was how often they had heard an expression of love from, or given an expression of love to, the person with whom they had a conflict. Often it had been so long that they could not even remember. What a tragedy!

If mothers and fathers, as spouses, are not expressing and showing their love one for another, then they are likely not doing the same with their children either. Elder Jeffrey R. Holland shared this example: "A young Laurel I met on a conference assignment not long ago wrote to me after our visit and said, 'I wish my dad knew how much I need him spiritually and emotionally. I crave any kind of comment, any warm personal gesture. I don't think he knows how much it would mean to me to have him take an active interest in what is going on in my life, to offer to give me a blessing, or just spend some time together. I know he worries that he won't do the right thing or won't say the words well. But just to have him *try* would mean more than he could ever know. I don't want to sound ungrateful because I know he loves me. He sent me a note once and signed it, "Love, Dad." I treasure that note. I hold it among my dearest possessions.'"[1]

I have seen that deep desire, and also the abject lack of it, in the eyes and hearts of many children in my courtroom during the last thirty years. They are the offspring of parents—yes, fathers *and* mothers—who cruelly abuse and neglect them, as well as of parents who are busy doing so many other "good things" that their children get lost in the priority shuffle. Often such children—without really realizing why—act out in rebellion just to get noticed. I submit that most rebellion comes from the way children have perceived their own importance in the lives of their parents.

When I became a judge in 1983, I thought I understood how inherently important parents were to their children and that a strong natural bond of love existed between them from birth. Early in my career, my eyes were opened, and my judicial experiences have reinforced that belief more powerfully than I could have ever imagined. I was involved in child protection matters, child abuse and neglect cases, foster home placements, and, especially and unfortunately, child molestation cases. I vividly recall a week-long seminar sponsored by the National College of Family and Juvenile Court Judges on the pros and cons of foster care placements for abused children. I went to the meetings with a strong bias toward removing children from abusive parents and finding loving foster care placements.

Given the egregious and almost unbelievably horrible circumstances of many of the abuse cases with which I was dealing, I was astounded when I heard a panel of some fifteen young people ages eighteen through twenty-five—now adults and pretty much on their own—discuss their foster care placement. Placement usually meant a termination of the rights of their natural parents, or at least drastically altered relationships with such parents—almost all fathers—who had molested them. All had spent their growing up years in foster homes and shelter care facilities, some in the very best foster care placements. Some had been adopted.

All of these now nearly grown, or adult, abuse victims detested the acts of their offenders. Yet almost all expressed a continuing deep love for that parent, a desire for the parent to get help, and a hope for reconciliation and a continuing relationship with him. Most wished to have lived with the abuser—provided they just could have been safe from further abuse.

Foster parents make amazing sacrifices as they love children who are not their own. But I left that seminar knowing that even the most horrible forms of parental abuse did not destroy these children's love for, and desire to be with, their parents. "I love him (or her) in spite of what happened, and I just wanted us to be a family" was the common and heartfelt theme. I have never forgotten those kids or their continued love for their offenders.

Contemplating that experience, I marveled at the power of a parent's presence in the life of a child. That is particularly true of mothers. Consistent with the divine Proclamation on the Family that "mothers are primarily responsible for the nurture of their children,"[2] I have been fascinated, but not at all surprised, at our own children's responses to a question about what things in our life and home made them feel loved and secure. One son answered: "I think above all it was Mom. She was always, always setting the tone of love in our home. Everything we did was always so important to Mom."

Marsha has indeed been a wonderful mother and wife, but I would not be completely honest if I told you she is perfect. She has experienced frustration, discouragement, and even occasional anger. And I have had to learn some very hard lessons about marriage by trial and error—as we all do—and I expect still more are ahead. Although we consider each other soul mates and each other's best friends, our relationship has been tried and tested many times.

We have tried, however, to work on our weaknesses, problems, and challenges together. We have intentionally left our children out of these problems if at all possible. In fact, we have worked hard to make sure our children were not even aware of them. Children have too many of their own challenges and problems to have to share in those of their parents. Unfortunately, I see too many parents who "parentify" their children—transfer to them adult responsibilities and decisions while they really deserve to just be kids. Such a parenting style can be counterproductive, and even sometimes destructive. In spite of the real-life problems parents might be facing, they need to create feelings of security and love for their children.

Marsha and I had been taught and believed from our training and experiences growing up that children are amazingly perceptive about what they witness in their parents' lives, perhaps especially those things modeled in unguarded moments. This power of example makes it critical that we live morally consistent lives in front of our children. If we hope to reach the goals set by the Proclamation on the Family, we cannot afford to be casual about the things we say we believe. We must truly do our best to live them, in spite of our own imperfection.

Let me conclude with three more observations from our children that seem to capture the task that faces all parents who try to follow the Savior's admonition to treasure little children as he does, remembering that they were children of our Father in Heaven before they were "loaned to us."

"What you did as parents wasn't perfect, but there was never a mistake which I saw you make that you didn't try to correct and learn from. . . . I hope my wife and I can do that, too."

"I recognize more each day that there is no one template or pattern to follow in raising children."

"I see now that raising a family isn't a performance."

The Lord doesn't expect a "performance" from any parent, but he does expect obedience, sacrifice, faith, and love. Remember Helaman 5:12: "It is upon the rock of our Redeemer, who is Christ, the Son of God, that ye must build your foundation . . . whereon if men build they cannot fall." If your foundation consists of your faith, your righteous desires and efforts, your sacrifice, and especially your love, though you and your children may never become perfect in this lifetime, I promise with a certain and deep conviction that you, too, cannot and will not fall.

Notes

1. Jeffrey R. Holland, "The Hands of the Fathers," *Ensign*, May 1999, 15; emphasis in original.
2. "The Family: A Proclamation to the World," *Ensign*, November 1995, 102.

The Day of Small Things

Nancy Young

Several years ago, my husband worked for a computer company. Usually, he took a lunch from home, but from time to time—when the cupboard was bare—he would frequent a fast-food franchise not far from work. He generally paid in cash, but one day he had only a personal check with him. When he reached the drive-up window, he handed the check to the worker and asked whether the man required any identification. "No, I don't," replied the attendant. "I know you." As my husband waded deep into his memory to recollect any past acquaintance, the worker explained, "We all know you. You're the only one of our customers who uses the word *please*."

Who could have foreseen, only a generation ago, that the most rudimentary politeness would one day render a person virtually unique? Yet, so it is in today's whirlwind life. Perhaps we should not be surprised, however, that the same culture that fails to recognize the outstretched hand of God granting them unprecedented prosperity also fails to respond with thanks to human kindnesses.

As I've pondered this phrase in Helaman 5:12—"When the devil shall send forth his mighty winds, yea, his shafts in the whirlwind"—I have wondered whether some of those "shafts in the whirlwind" might be the rude language, self-absorbed behavior, and coarse images common to society that deepen the pain and isolation we feel during whirlwind times of fear, trial, doubt, and discouragement.

Nancy Young and her husband, Al, are writers and artists whose work celebrates home and family. Publishers of The Storybook Home Newsletter, *their Internet gallery of fine art prints features a family reading list, viewing suggestions, and ideas for creating a storybook environment at home. Nancy serves as the teacher improvement coordinator in their ward. She and Al are the parents of three children.*

Shafts are usually arrows and darts but can also be bolts of lightning or anything capable of piercing or penetrating a narrow space. In a great storm, it is, in fact, not the whirlwind itself that is so dangerous, but the objects the winds propel. Debris hurled at great speed renders ordinarily friendly things like roof shingles or tree branches into dread weapons of destruction. It is such "shafts in the whirlwind" that at best smart and sting and at worst debilitate and destroy. Shafts propelled by societal whirlwinds can ferret out chinks in the walls of our homes; they can penetrate and exploit the breaches created when we deviate from the word of the Lord, chilling heart as well as hearth.

As "mighty storm[s]" beat upon our homes, it may seem that our response must be equally fierce, strong, and momentous. Yet just as the "soft [word] turneth away wrath" (Proverbs 15:1), the Lord has declared that he does not act according to the wisdom of the world. In Zechariah we learn: "Not by might, nor by power, but by my spirit, saith the Lord of hosts. . . . For who hath despised the day of small things?" (Zechariah 4:6–10). Also note these familiar words from Alma: "Now ye may suppose that this is foolishness in me; but behold I say unto you, that by small and simple things are great things brought to pass; and small means in many instances doth confound the wise" (Alma 37:6).

A few small and simple things seem particularly important in stemming the tide of rudeness and coarseness that rises around us. Let me focus particularly on things that can be done at home because, to quote my husband, "Home is the mold into which the human soul is poured." May I mention just two ways we can invite into our homes the "greater respect and appreciation" that our beloved prophet has encouraged us to create?[1]

Be still. I find myself inclined to self-absorption and sharpness when I'm pressed and harried. At such times, it is easy to let the whirlwind set the pace of life instead of hearkening to the voice that stilled the tempest. My tempests consist of those times when I feel I need to be five people, each with as many arms as a Hindu goddess. It is when I'm busy "run[ning] faster than [I have] strength" (Mosiah 4:27), certain that any slowing down would be disastrous, that I benefit most from being still. In the crosswinds of demands that rise up unexpectedly and scatter the well-ordered priorities on my to-do list, stopping a moment to notice the movement of a cloud, the fragrance of a lilac, or the sound of children's laughter blesses me. In doing so, I find myself not only regenerated, but reprioritized.

Elder Douglas L. Callister of the Seventy has declared: "A spiritual-minded man is observant of the beauty in the world around him. As the earth was organized, the Lord saw that 'it was good.' Then, 'It was very good.' It pleases our Father in Heaven when we, also, pause to note the beauty of our environment. . . . Elizabeth Barrett Browning wrote, 'Earth's crammed with heaven, And every common bush afire with God; And only he who sees takes off his shoes.'"[2] The Lord has made it possible for us—simply by slowing down—to draw strength from earth's constant reminders of his presence and love. Even if a moment seems more than we can spare, by slowing down we can "be still, and know that [he is] God" (Psalm 46:10; D&C 101:16).

I love this sentiment from the poet Phillip James Bailey:

> We live in deeds, not years; in thoughts, not breaths;
> In feelings, not in figures on a dial.
> We should count time by heart-throbs.[3]

In addition to appreciating the beauty in nature, we need to fill our homes with beauty that uplifts and inspires. The legacy of Babel continues in much of what is published and performed in our world. Many books, videos, and countless CDs are specifically designed to dull and confuse—to render us "past feeling," as Nephi described Laman and Lemuel (1 Nephi 17:45). Yet prayerful and diligent seeking can help us locate the virtuous, the lovely, and the praiseworthy. It is not sufficient simply to avoid evil. We must seek and embrace what is good.

A simple test can help us know what art and music, literature and speech, furnishings and media to bring into our homes. This test can also help us evaluate the things and thoughts already in our homes. We can simply ask: "Does it feel like heaven?" Pondering what heaven is like can be delightful. How does heaven smell, taste, look, feel, and sound? Sadly, the world would have us believe that only the wealthy can afford and enjoy beautiful homes and furnishings. It is not so in heaven's economy. So very much that is truly beautiful, the Lord has placed readily in our paths. Author and designer Tricia Foley expressed this insight: "Collections from nature—berried branches, shells and stones, birds' nests and leafy wreaths—can change with the seasons [and] they can be returned outdoors when they no longer look their best. With natural things you never feel your collection owns you instead of the other way around."[4]

President Hinckley counsels us: "Parents, work at the matter of creating an atmosphere in your homes. Let your children be exposed to great minds, great ideas, everlasting truth, and those things which will build and motivate for good."

He also offers this affectionate description of his childhood home: "When I was a boy we lived in a large old house. One room was called the library. It had a solid table and a good lamp, three or four comfortable chairs with good light, and books in cases that lined the walls. There were many volumes—the acquisitions of my father and mother over a period of many years. . . .

"We were never forced to read them, but they were placed where they were handy and where we could get at them whenever we wished. . . . There was quiet in that room. It was understood that it was a place to study.

"I would not have you believe that we were great scholars. But we were exposed to great literature, great ideas from great thinkers, and the language of men and women who thought deeply and wrote beautifully.

"In so many of our homes today there is not the possibility of such a library. . . . But with planning there can be a corner, there can be an area that becomes something of a hideaway from the noises about us where one can sit and read and think."[5]

This needn't be costly. Libraries are full of music, books, and videos that fulfill President J. Reuben Clark's counsel to choose "only those things that are worth remembering."[6] As we assiduously seek what is virtuous, lovely, of good report, and praiseworthy (Article of Faith 13), we tutor our families' sensibilities to heaven. Perhaps the angels will speak of our homes in the words of Isaac Watts: "I have been there and again would go, / 'Tis like a little heaven below."[7]

Be at the crossroads. Two modern-day prophets have counseled us to be at the crossroads. President Ezra Taft Benson instructed: "Take time to always be at the crossroads when your children are either coming or going—when they leave and return from school, when they leave and return from dates, when they bring friends home. Be there at the crossroads whether your children are six or sixteen."[8]

Being at the crossroads, President Harold B. Lee said, can help a mother perceive those often subtle, early "signs of difficulty, of danger and distress" while such things can be readily acted upon.[9] As a gardener, I know firsthand the regret of attempting to untwine bindweed from a rose whose blossoms are being forced into the mud by the weed clinging to and strangling it. Recognizing in the heat of summer that this task, which the thankless rose rewards only with thorn pricks, might have been the work of seconds had I been vigilant in the spring.

Assuaging hurts and grievances immediately or, as the Savior said, "while in the way" (Matthew 5:25), fosters greater peace because weeds are removed when they sprout instead of when they have had years to spread both roots and seeds throughout the family.

Of course, being at the crossroads, however desirable, may prove impossible in some instances. Even so there are ways of keeping the spirit of that counsel even when we cannot keep the letter of it. A young woman told me that when they were first married, she and her husband were students and both held jobs. Time together was scarce. Each morning, however, she would rise a little early and pack them both sack lunches. She would also quickly scribble a note on his paper napkin and add it to his brown bag. "I miss you," she would write, or "I'm thinking of you," or "I know you'll do well on your test," or some other message amounting to "I love you. I'm glad we're married." It was a small thing, the work of a moment.

She did this for several weeks with no comment from her husband. She wondered whether he liked it; she wondered whether his co-workers teased him about it; she even wondered whether he threw away the napkins without seeing her notes. One morning, in a particular hurry, she skipped writing the note. That evening when her husband returned home, she greeted him warmly and asked about his day. "It was terrible," he said, crestfallen, "one of the worst days of my life." Images racing through her mind of failed tests, job loss, or bad news from his family, she demanded, "Why? What went wrong?" With sincere hurt in his voice, he answered, "Today you didn't write *anything* on my napkin."

In a day of e-mails, phone messaging, Post-It notes, and Palm Pilots—not to mention paper napkins—there are a host of ways to leave what Dickens referred to as "tokens of [our] presence," illuminating the crossroads in our absence.[10] There are many ways of saying, "I love you. I want to hear about your day. Your concerns sit near my heart."

The Lord will bless us in our endeavors to be still and to be the comforting presence our families need at the crossroads. We can truly be his handmaidens to shield our families from the adversary's "shafts in the whirlwind," and our Lord will hold us close as we do so. Whatever may be the storms, he has promised, "For the mountains shall depart, and the hills be removed; but my kindness shall not depart from thee, neither shall the covenant of my peace be removed, saith the Lord that hath mercy on thee" (Isaiah 54:10).

Notes

1. Gordon B. Hinckley, "Of Missions, Temples, and Stewardship," *Ensign*, November 1995, 53.
2. Douglas L. Callister, "Seeking the Spirit of God," *Ensign*, November 2000, 30.
3. Phillip James Bailey, quoted in *Not My Will, But Thine*, by Neal A. Maxwell (Salt Lake City: Bookcraft, 1988), 116.
4. Tricia Foley, *The Natural Home* (New York: Clarkson Potter, 1995), 46.
5. Gordon B. Hinckley, "The Environment of Our Homes, *Ensign*, June 1985, 4.

6. J. Reuben Clark, Jr., quoted in Joseph L. Wirthlin, "The Kingdom of God Is Righteousness," *BYU Speeches of the Year, 1960* (Provo: Brigham Young University Press, 1960), 5.
7. Isaac Watts, "Divine Songs," song xxviii, *Familiar Quotations*, compiled by John Bartlett (Boston: Little Brown, 1919), #3262.
8. Ezra Taft Benson, *Come, Listen to a Prophet's Voice* (Salt Lake City: Deseret Book, 1990), 32.
9. Harold B. Lee, *The Teachings of Harold B. Lee* (Salt Lake City: Bookcraft, 1996), 288.
10. Charles Dickens, *Nicholas Nickleby* (1851; reprint, New York: Penguin Books, 2002), 384.

An Obsession with Perfection

Carol B. Thomas

When you make your bed in the morning, do you think to yourself, *I can't wait to come back to bed tonight?* Women work so hard, and rest can be so refreshing. The gospel teaches us to want to be perfect—and it wears us out. We think we have to do it *all* today. Perfection!

As I discussed this topic with my husband, he said, "So what are you going to tell them—to mellow out?" He's a pediatrician; he understands how women think.

Since receiving this assignment, I have tried to understand if women still worry too much about becoming perfect. Let me share with you what a few sisters have said: "I have a hard time relating to the Savior. He was so perfect, and I am so imperfect." "The Atonement applies to everyone else. I'm not good enough." "Only when I am perfect enough can I have the Lord's grace to help me."

Recently a talk was given at Brigham Young University entitled "'Be Ye Therefore Perfect'—Handling Obsession with Perfection," by Jeffrey Marsh.[1] Obviously, there is a need for the subject of perfection to be addressed. Let us ask ourselves, "What is my understanding of the principle 'Be ye therefore perfect, even as your Father which is in heaven is perfect'"? (Matthew 5:48).

Is our understanding healthy? Is it based on true doctrine?

You see, our perception of a principle matters. What we perceive

---

Carol Burdett Thomas has served as first counselor in the Young Women General Presidency and as a member of the Relief Society General Board. She and her husband, Dr. D. Ray Thomas, are the parents of seven children and the grandparents of thirty.

may be based not on fact but on our own ideas, and sometimes we get off course. When we get off course in understanding the doctrine, we can get off course in life. Regarding perception, Elder Cecil O. Samuelson said, "For some, they become so obsessed or consumed with their every thought, action, and response that they may become far too extreme in their own perceptions of what is expected of them."[2]

Speaking of perception, do you remember the talk President Gordon B. Hinckley gave about the six "B's"?[3] My granddaughter prayed that President Hinckley would do better in school. When her parents asked her why, she said, "Well, you know—it's because of his six 'B's.'" Our perception really matters.

Do we have a true understanding of the principle of perfection, or are we like the biblical Jews who didn't recognize the Savior because they looked beyond the mark? Are we so caught up in how the world sees us—having perfect children, perfect homes, and perfect lives—that we are looking beyond the mark?

Thinking we can and should be perfect *now* seems rather arrogant to me. Elder Bruce D. Porter has said: "I have often thought that perfectionism stems from pride and self-centeredness. It is what the Lord warned W. W. Phelps against in the Doctrine and Covenants: 'And also he hath need to repent, for I, the Lord, am not well pleased with him, for he seeketh to excel, and he is not sufficiently meek before me' (D&C 58:41)."[4]

Perhaps those who do not understand the principle of perfection do not have a correct understanding of the Atonement and the whole plan of salvation. It is as simple as this: we can never become perfect alone. No one can. It is only with the Lord's help that *we can be made* perfect. Perfection is a process.

And so, as we discuss the process of becoming perfect, I hope this talk is a one-size-fits-all. Let's discuss four ways that will help us become better outfitted as we work toward perfection: learn the doctrine, understand and apply the Atonement, be kind to ourselves, and keep the Spirit.

LEARN THE DOCTRINE OF PERFECTION

The Lord has said, "Be ye therefore perfect" (Matthew 5:48). That is God's standard. Each day we continually strive to do a little better than the day before. I love the way President Hinckley says it: "Do the best you can."[5]

Elder Bruce R. McConkie taught: "No man in mortality can become wholly perfect; that is, he cannot have his exaltation here in this state of frailty and uncertainty."[6] Only our Savior attained that goal. "No other mortal—not the greatest prophets nor the mightiest Apostles nor any of the righteous Saints of any . . . [age]—has ever been perfect [in this life]."[7]

We can do some things perfectly, such as paying our tithing or keeping the Sabbath day holy. But other commandments are not so easily accomplished.

The scriptures do speak of having a perfect knowledge, but even having a perfect knowledge will not save us. The devil's angels had a knowledge of who the Savior was, and they still chose to side with Satan.

President Joseph Fielding Smith said, "It will take us ages to accomplish this end [of perfection], for there will be greater progress beyond the grave."[8]

The Lord taught the Prophet Joseph Smith: "Ye are not able to abide the presence of God now, neither the ministering of angels; wherefore, continue in patience until [you] are perfected" (D&C 67:13). That is good advice for all of us.

UNDERSTAND AND APPLY THE ATONEMENT

The Atonement helps us to become perfect. It has a daily, weekly application. Sometimes we don't fully understand how to apply the Atonement; we can become confused, and then we get down on ourselves. We've been taught, "If I do my best, the Lord will make up the difference," but that statement may seem to imply that the Atonement works only at the end of this life. The Atonement is so much more—

each day the power of the Atonement is there for us to cleanse our sins and help us become perfected in Christ.

Another misunderstanding involves our taking the Atonement as a blank check to sin. This misunderstanding sometimes happens to teenagers when they don't understand the doctrine. Because they don't understand the importance of the Atonement, they think they can deliberately do something wrong and quickly repent. They mock the Atonement by taking it lightly.

The sacrament helps us apply the Atonement each day of our lives. Each week, as we figuratively kneel at the sacrament table, we sincerely repent and are cleansed of our sins—our Savior, through his grace, makes it possible for us to become holy, without spot. While we may not be perfect, we are worthy. Elder Samuelson declared: "Worthiness and perfection are not synonyms! All of us are 'works in progress.' We can be worthy while still needing improvement."[9]

This is why Elder Robert D. Hales has said—and he never said anything with more promise—"Tell the women of the Church that if they are worthy to hold a current temple recommend and can partake worthily of the sacrament each week, they will make it."[10]

Elder Melvin J. Ballard made this unforgettable statement: "I am a witness that there is a spirit attending the administration of the sacrament that warms the soul from head to foot; you feel the wounds of the spirit being healed, and the load being lifted."[11]

When I first heard that, I'm not sure I understood it. Week after week, as I sat alone in the congregation with seven children while my husband had responsibilities on the stand, it was not always easy to feel the Spirit. But I thought to myself, "If Elder Ballard said it, then I must be missing out on something." So, over the years I have put it to the test.

Dear sisters, it is my testimony that the Spirit of the Lord always attends our sacrament meetings. It warms us from head to foot. You can feel the burdens of your soul being lifted. That Spirit is given to cleanse us, to comfort us, to inspire, and to teach us. It is the reason why our Church leaders keep encouraging us to be reverent in our sacrament meetings—so that we can hear the voice of the Spirit. It is there in such rich abundance if we will have ears to hear.

The Savior gave us the Atonement to bless our lives. We cannot afford to take the Atonement lightly. When we understand the power of the Atonement and apply it daily, we are working toward perfection. Each day we do the best we can. Each night we kneel and ask for forgiveness for the mistakes we have made that day. The power of the Atonement changes our hearts gradually—as the Spirit teaches us self-mastery and takes away our desire for sin.

Our Father in Heaven wants us to understand the Atonement and teach it to our families. Take the time to teach this doctrine to your children. We want to tuck them in so they won't fall out.

BE KIND TO YOURSELF

Elder James E. Talmage said: "So great are the difficulties and dangers [of this earth life], so strong is the influence of evil in the world, and so weak is man in resistance thereto, that without the aid of a power above that of humanity no soul could find its way back [home] to God from whom [he] came. The need for a Redeemer lies in the inability of man to raise himself from the temporal to the spiritual plane, from the lower kingdom to the higher."[12]

Recognize that making mistakes is all part of the plan. Elder Joseph B. Wirthlin said, "Our Heavenly Father . . . understands that we will make mistakes at times, that we will stumble, that we will become discouraged and perhaps even wish to give up and say to ourselves [that] it is not worth the struggle."[13]

Several months ago, I was giving a short presentation in a General Authority meeting. Right in the middle, I forgot what I was saying and someone else had to pick up where I left off. I thought about it for days. It wasn't until I watched Michelle Kwan fall on the ice in her skating routine during the Olympics that I realized this: Everyone makes mistakes—it is part of living in mortality. Only then could I let it go.

Dwelling on our weaknesses can be self-defeating and harmful. Each one of us needs to be honest with ourselves. But it is absolutely essential that in our self-analysis we do not become so self-absorbed that it slows our progress. Elder Samuelson observed: "It is a tendency for too many of us to glory in or dwell on our weaknesses, [our] temptations, and [our] shortcomings. We must recognize them, get help when [it] is appropriate, but move on as soon as possible and not be preoccupied by them."[14]

A dear friend once indirectly gave some great advice. Offering an opening prayer in Sunday School, she said, "Heavenly Father, bless us that when we make mistakes we can forgive ourselves quickly, so we can get on with our lives." I have never forgotten that.

Love yourself. Focus more on the efforts you make to do good. Remember that sometimes it is more important to do the right things than it is to do things right or perfectly.

Brother Marsh said: "Often, 'our sacrifices' . . . are more sacred to the Lord than the results. Prayers we say, however imperfect, are sacred to God. Home evenings held, however much a disaster, count in the eyes of God. Your efforts and desires to be good, and to do good, never go unnoticed by our Eternal Father."[15]

Several Christmases ago, I attended a sacrament meeting put on by a ward choir. It was a beautiful program, but the timing between the musical numbers and the dialogue was unusually slow. I found myself becoming impatient and judgmental, and yet I didn't want to lose the Spirit. Heavenly Father must have known my thoughts because into my mind came the words, 'Their offering is acceptable unto me.' I learned a valuable lesson that day. It didn't matter that the program was not perfect. Their sacrifice *was* an acceptable offering to the Lord.

Keep the Spirit with You

One of the hardest things for all of us is to keep the Spirit with us all of the time. And yet, the Savior promises us that it is possible. How do we do it?

Prayer. "The most important thing [we] can do is to learn to talk to God."[16] There is nothing like it in all the world. I have heard President Hinckley say, "Prayer is a miracle." Prophets have said they do not worry about those who pray twice a day. Now, if they don't worry about us, then we don't need to worry about ourselves, as long as we sincerely pray twice a day.

One sister who went through divorce relates how she prayed to Heavenly Father and was blessed by the power of the Atonement: "I had no one to turn to, no place to go, except onto my knees. I prayed as I had never prayed before. I fasted faithfully, meaningfully, and often. I read and studied the scriptures from cover to cover for the first time in my life. . . . And He was there. He heard my humble pleadings. He put his arm of love around me. He forgave me of my sins and [He] showed me a better way. I was amazed at the happiness, [the] success, and opportunity that came into my life."[17] This sister's sincere prayer activated the Atonement in her life.

President Boyd K. Packer said, "The Atonement has practical, personal, everyday value; apply it in your life. It can be activated with so simple a beginning as prayer. You will not thereafter be free from trouble and mistakes, but [you] can erase the guilt through repentance and be at peace."[18]

For some time, I had a consuming problem in my life that I didn't understand. I had prayed about it forever. Finally in desperation, I said, "Heavenly Father, I don't get this. Please help me to fix it." And he did! The point is, we must be honest. We must pray from the depths of our heart. Heavenly Father then knows we are serious, and he is honor bound to bless us with help. He may not give us the answer we want, but he will always give us peace.

Heavenly Father loves us so. We are his children. He wants us to have a good relationship with him. He told Enoch, "Unto thy brethren have I said, and also given commandment, that they should love one another, and that they should choose me, their Father" (Moses 7:33).

Heavenly Father can and will answer your prayers. As we pray more often, the Spirit of the Lord strengthens our faith. With the prophet Moses, we can say, "I will not cease to call upon God, I have other things to inquire of him: for his glory has been upon me" (Moses 1:18).

How do we keep the Spirit? We need to pray.

Read the scriptures daily. President Spencer W. Kimball was not kidding when he said we must become sister scriptorians. Most of my generation were not raised on the scriptures. If you have teenagers, you know how well versed they are in the scriptures. We have some catching up to do. We must be examples to our children; otherwise, we are like the Israelites wandering in the wilderness. The younger generation may have to wait for us to die off before they can enjoy the promised land.

As we read the scriptures daily and apply them to our lives, we can find answers to our problems in the scriptures. A young woman sent this wonderful letter to our office:

"About a year ago, I had a seminary lesson about understanding the scriptures and receiving guidance and comfort from the Lord through them. . . . I decided that I really wanted to know the scriptures and benefit from them. At first, I was impatient that there was no difference in my reading, [but] I did not forget the yearning I had to experience the comfort the scriptures offer.

"During an especially trying time when I felt my whole world crashing down, it finally happened. I was reading no more intently than usual when I came across the words spoken in D&C 121—'My son, peace be unto thy soul, thine adversity and thine afflictions shall be but a small moment. . . .' This was the comfort I [was] searching for. The verse lit up my soul and was set off from the rest of the chapter. I knew my patience and unfailing determination to experience comfort from the Lord through the scriptures had finally been found. As I continued to read and pray with this constant desire, more and more scriptures have opened up to me."[19]

You, too, can be filled with the Spirit of the Lord as you ponder and study the sacred scriptures.

Prepare yourself for the sacrament each week. As women we are so good at preparing our meals for Sunday, but do we think about our own spiritual preparation? Perhaps on Saturday we could talk to Heavenly Father and ask him to help us prepare ourselves spiritually for Sunday worship. As we think about our need to repent and our desire to improve, the Spirit will teach us.

Elder Neal A. Maxwell has said, "Little wonder that when we partake of the sacramental bread we ask to have the Spirit always with us. Only then are we safe; otherwise, without the Spirit, we are left to ourselves. Who would ever want to solo, anyway?"[20]

Prayer, scripture study, and partaking of the sacrament each week will help us keep the Spirit as we work toward perfection.

The Savior is our greatest example of perfection. His total humility to the Father is what set him apart. He said, "I do always those things [which] please [the Father]" (John 8:29). We also have great need for humility. Because humility and perfection are inseparably intertwined, if we want to understand how we can become perfect, we must be humble.

President Spencer W. Kimball offered a formula for remaining humble:

"First, you evaluate yourself. What am I? I am the circle. I am the hole in the doughnut. I would be nothing without the Lord. My breath, my brains, my hearing, my sight, . . . my everything depends [on] the Lord. . . . That is the first step and then we pray, and pray often, and we will not get . . . [off] our knees until . . . [our] unhumbleness has dissipated, until [we] feel the humble spirit and realize, 'I could die this minute if it were not for the Lord's good grace. I am dependent upon him—totally dependent upon him.'"[21]

I want you to know how much I love the Savior. He is our Rock and our Redeemer. Like you, I am grateful for his willingness to help us become more perfect. President Hinckley said: "Now, you are not perfect. It isn't likely that there will be a great hole in the earth here as you are translated. You are not quite ready for that. But let us build Zion here. Let us cultivate the spirituality of the people. Let us teach faith."[22]

Perfection is a process. Enjoy life. Have fun. Don't waste too much time worrying about your mistakes. A little guilt goes a long way. In a recent fireside to the young adults of the Church, Elder M. Russell Ballard said: "Don't waste your days of probation. . . .

"Remember, you can be exalted . . . without a college degree. You can be exalted without being slender and beautiful. You can be exalted without having a successful career. You can be exalted if you are not rich and famous. So focus the best you can on those things in life that will lead you back to the presence of God—keeping all things in their proper balance."[23]

The Lord himself has told us: "Verily, verily, I say unto you, ye are little children . . . and [you] cannot bear all things now; nevertheless, be of good cheer, for I will lead you along. The kingdom is yours and the blessings thereof are yours, and the riches of eternity are yours" (D&C 78:17–18). In other words, dear sisters, as long as we are worthy to carry a current temple recommend and worthily partake of the sacrament each week, we will make it!

Notes

1. W. Jeffrey Marsh, "'Be Ye Therefore Perfect'—Handling Obsession with Perfection," Women's Services and Resources Addictions Conference, Provo, Utah, 6 February 2002; available online at www.meridianmagazine.com.
2. Cecil O. Samuelson, Missionary Training Center Devotional, Provo, Utah, 19 March 2002; copy in possession of author; used by permission.
3. Gordon B. Hinckley, "A Prophet's Counsel and Prayer for Youth," *Ensign*, January 2001, 2–11.
4. Bruce D. Porter to Carol B. Thomas; letter in possession of the author; used by permission.
5. Sheri L. Dew, *Go Forward with Faith: The Biography of Gordon B. Hinckley* (Salt Lake City: Deseret Book, 1996), 3.
6. Bruce R. McConkie, *Doctrines of the Restoration: Sermons and Writings of Bruce R. McConkie*, comp. Mark L. McConkie (Salt Lake City: Bookcraft, 1989), 352.
7. McConkie, *Doctrines of the Restoration*, 53.
8. Joseph Fielding Smith, *Doctrines of Salvation*, comp. Bruce R. McConkie, 3 vols. (Salt Lake City: Deseret Book, 1954–56), 2:18.
9. Samuelson, MTC Devotional address.
10. Robert D. Hales, conversation with author; used by permission.

11. Melvin J. Ballard, quoted in David B. Haight, "The Sacrament," *Ensign*, May 1983, 14; also Melvin J. Ballard, *Crusader for Righteousness* (Salt Lake City: Bookcraft, 1966), 133.
12. James E. Talmage, *Jesus the Christ* (Salt Lake City: Deseret Book, 1983), 25.
13. Joseph B. Wirthlin, "One Step after Another," *Ensign*, November 2001, 25.
14. Samuelson, MTC Devotional address.
15. Marsh, "'Be Ye Therefore Perfect.'"
16. *Harold B. Lee*, [vol. 3] in *Teachings of Presidents of the Church* series (Salt Lake City: The Church of Jesus Christ of Latter-day Saints, 2000), 55.
17. Mary Jane Knights, "After Divorce: Clearing the Hurdles," *Ensign*, August 1985, 50.
18. Boyd K. Packer, "The Touch of the Master's Hand," *Ensign*, May 2001, 24.
19. Letter on file in the Young Women office, Salt Lake City.
20. Neal A. Maxwell, *That Ye May Believe* (Salt Lake City: Bookcraft, 1992), 42; emphasis in original.
21. Spencer W. Kimball, *The Teachings of Spencer W. Kimball*, ed. Edward L. Kimball (Salt Lake City: Bookcraft, 1982) 233–34.
22. Gordon B. Hinckley, *Teachings of Gordon B. Hinckley* (Salt Lake City: Deseret Book, 1997), 727.
23. M. Russell Ballard, CES fireside, Brigham Young University, 3 March 2002; quoted in Sarah Jane Weaver, "His Purposes Cannot Be Frustrated," *Church News*, 9 March 2002.

"Be Ye Therefore Perfect"

Sydney S. Reynolds

We live in a media-rich world. Our foremothers just had to worry about keeping up with the Joneses, but we have the whole world at our fingertips. We are constantly seeing the stellar performers of our day. We have seen Olympic athletes receive a "perfect" six. We are bombarded with magazine photos of "perfect" bodies. We know women who can create beautiful wreaths for their homes out of flowers they grew and dried themselves or from weeds they gathered beside the road. We see Nobel Prize winners, young people with perfect ACT and SAT scores, stars, statesmen, pundits, sisters in our own wards and on general boards. We may think they are perfect. No, we know they are not really perfect, but do we sometimes wonder, "Now if I just had Susan's body, and Mary's sense of style, and Bonnie's homemaking skills, and Sheri's good brain and articulate expression, I would be perfect."

A lot of good can come from seeing and knowing about the gifts of so many. When it brings us to an appreciation of the gifts and achievements of others, when we ask how we can incorporate into our lives in appropriate ways the good things we see others doing, our horizons are expanded and our own lives can be blessed. That is good—it shows our understanding that every good gift cometh of Christ (Moroni 10:18).

But when we think, "I need to do all of that, I need to be all of that, I need to at least have something in which I am spectacular, or I

Sydney Smith Reynolds, who received her bachelor's degree from Brigham Young University and did graduate studies in history and educational psychology, has served as first counselor in the Primary General Presidency. She wrote the Sharing Time page for the 1998–99 issues of the Friend *and was a member of the Timpanogos Storytelling Festival Board. She and her husband, Noel B. Reynolds, are the parents of eleven children and the grandparents of sixteen.*

am a failure—I can never be perfect," that is not good. I have a friend, an immaculate housekeeper, who says, "Sometimes we think that if someone walks into our house and sees a dirty dish on the counter, we are not good homemakers. What does that come from—that we wouldn't want anyone to think we ate meals at our house?"

For me, Elder Jeffrey R. Holland's message at April general conference on the prodigal son spoke to this point of comparing ourselves with others. "Who is it," he said, "that whispers so subtly in our ear that a gift given to another somehow diminishes the blessings we have received? Who makes us feel that if God is smiling on another, then He surely must somehow be frowning on us? You and I both know who does this—it is the father of all lies."[1] Measuring our attempts to reach perfection by comparing ourselves with others or with our own idealized standards is doomed to failure and alienates us from the Spirit of the Lord.

I have a friend who is a professional counselor. In her work with clients, she deals with the negative consequences of perfectionism all the time. She observes that women have special problems with this issue. Her research leads her to conclude that girls are socialized to compare themselves with others and to base their self-worth and feelings of acceptance on what others think of them. Her insight is that the adversary has polluted the concept of perfection into something that is punishing and immobilizing rather than empowering and liberating. She believes that too many of us are influenced by the earthly perspective and find ourselves comparing ourselves with other humans, rather than seeking the eternal perfection that God expects of us.

"We're so irrational," she says. "Some women are worried about their physical bodies. Do they stand outside Wal-Mart and compare themselves with the average of the first one hundred bodies to walk through the store? No, they look at Cindy Crawford or Britney Spears and think, *Oh, that's the national average and certainly the goal I should aspire to*."

Here are her helpful suggestions about dealing with this situation:

First, stop and clarify what's going on: What is it I am really worried about? Is it that I don't have as much money as I want, that I don't dress my children as fashionably as others, that I don't look like Barbie, that we don't have regular family scripture study? Is that what's getting me down, or is it that for some reason, I cannot feel the Lord's love and need his acceptance?

Second, understand that the gospel teaching that each individual has divine worth is actually liberating. In the eternal perspective, we each have enormous potential and worth. We really don't all have to wear a big bow in our hair to be the cutest girl in the second grade—it's even OK not to like big bows. We don't need to compare ourselves on any level. We do need to have respect for others, and we do need to feel the Lord's love.

Third, brainstorm ways that help you see that you are in the straight and narrow path provided by Heavenly Father—or if you are not in his path, how you can get there. This applies to our children as well. Ask yourself, "What is my son or daughter's path with Heavenly Father? How can I help and not intrude as he or she finds that path?" For example, not every boy has to pitch for the Little League team or be an assistant to the mission president to be succeeding in life. Some are going to play defense for the soccer team, some are going to play chess, some are going to play the radio—and that's OK. All of them can "come unto Christ," and that's the only perfection we ultimately want for them and for ourselves as well. Some of us will serve missions, some will be family history experts, some will be writers of hymns and singers of songs, and few of us will be all those good things at the same time—and that's OK, too.

Let's look at the scriptural injunctions regarding perfection and the promise of God's grace. Does earthly perfectionism as urged by the adversary have anything to do with what the Savior was talking about when he said, "Be ye therefore perfect, even as your Father which is in heaven is perfect"? (Matthew 5:48). I don't think so.

What did *perfection* mean to the people in the Bible? In the Book of Mormon? In the Hebrew of the Old Testament, the word *tamim* means "upright, without blemish," as in this passage: "Noah was a just man and perfect (*tamim*) in his generations, and Noah walked with God" (Genesis 6:9). It can also mean "whole, entire, sound," and most of the times it is used in the Old Testament it is referring to a sacrifice that is without blemish. The *Interpreter's Dictionary of the Bible* also states that "wherever the word is used of men or their conduct, 'upright' or 'blameless' is a better rendering than 'perfect.'"[2]

The Greek word translated "perfection" in the New Testament is *teleios*, which means "full-grown, mature, having reached the . . . end of its development."[3] And listen to this definition: "*Teleios*—Perfect, said of those after baptism . . . said of those who have shown repentance, who have paid the penalty (or repented) to the deepest degree, and afterwards are admitted to participation in the ordinances."[4]

I would like to look at perfection from the perspective of the Book of Mormon—starting with Moroni. For it is Moroni who invites all to "come unto Christ, and be perfected in him" (Moroni 10:32). I'd like to consider what Moroni meant when he said, "Be perfected."

Don't you just love Moroni, this great, lonely fighting man? He was named after his father's hero, Captain Moroni, of whom his father, Mormon, wrote, "Yea, verily, verily I say unto you, if all men had been, and were, and ever would be, like unto Moroni, behold, the very powers of hell would have been shaken forever" (Alma 48:17). Talk about a "perfect" ideal to live up to! Young Moroni certainly had one.

And it is Moroni who is the source of many of our comforting and strengthening scriptures about overcoming weaknesses. You remember that it was Moroni who was given the task of completing the record of his father, and he knew that the plan was that he would hide up the record until the day it should come forth unto the Gentiles. He said to the Lord: "Lord, the Gentiles will mock at these things, because of our weakness in writing; for Lord thou hast made us mighty in word by faith, but thou hast not made us mighty in writing; . . . thou hast made us that we could write but little, because of the awkwardness of our hands . . . when we write we behold our weakness, and stumble because of the placing of our words; and I fear lest the Gentiles shall mock at our words" (Ether 12:23–25).

Do you think Moroni considered himself a great writer or a perfect writer? Or a clever artisan working with his hands, or even a perfect soldier? Obviously not. He probably spent much of his early life learning about weapons, military strategy, and leading armed forces. But his experience in battle was that he lost and lost and lost again, and then he saw all of his companions defeated and dead. For the last years of his life, he was on the run and just plain trying to survive. How good could he feel about his competence as a soldier? How many opportunities did he have for stimulating conversation or for discussing his ideas with anyone in the last decades of his life? Do you think there was a reason he might have been concerned about his writing? And yet here it was—a call to write a message to the nations of the Lamanites that could enable them to achieve their eternal salvation—hundreds of thousands of them. He was responsible to preserve the record so it could come forth to the whole world in the proper time. He was the last man on earth who could accomplish the task, and he was pretty certain he couldn't do it perfectly.

Moroni was finally and completely willing to do what he had to do because he had faith in the Lord. "I know that thou workest unto the children of men according to their faith," he said (Ether 12:29). The Lord gave him the promise that "my grace is sufficient for all men that humble themselves before me; for if they humble themselves before me, and have faith in me, then will I make weak things become strong unto them" (Ether 12:27). And the Lord surely did make "weak things become strong" for Moroni. Whether or not the Gentiles would mock, Moroni was comforted, and he acted because he knew the Lord understood his situation and accepted his efforts, despite their imperfections.

I assume that Moroni wrote the title page of the Book of Mormon last of all his writing. And here, once again, he points out, "And now, if there are faults they are the mistakes of men; wherefore, condemn not the things of God, that ye may be found spotless [could that be blameless, perfect?] at the judgment-seat of Christ."

The kind of perfection Moroni was talking about when he invites us to come unto Christ has nothing to do with flawless accomplishment. It does not even have anything to do with exceptional competence or skill in a given area, but it has everything to do with having faith in the Lord, repenting of sin, and keeping the Lord's commandments. It is only possible because of the Atonement of Jesus Christ. In the final analysis, Moroni knew that if we are willing to deny ourselves of all ungodliness and love God with all our might, mind, and strength (Moroni 10:32), then his grace is sufficient for us, and we may be made perfect in Christ. As Elder Neal A. Maxwell said, "The Church is 'for the perfecting of the Saints' (Eph. 4:12); it is not a well-provisioned rest home for the already perfected."[5]

What, then, are the requirements for denying ourselves of all ungodliness? How do we show that we love God with all our might, mind, and strength? Does that mean that we have to be perfect soldiers, perfect writers, perfect speakers, perfect parents? Obviously not for Moroni. I think that for Moroni it meant we must repent of anything we are doing which would alienate us from the Spirit of the Lord, and we must show our love for God by keeping his commandments and loving his children, that the Lord might forgive our sins and make us spotless by his grace.

Where did Moroni get his ideas? He got them from the scriptures that he guarded and pored over and added to and from the Lord himself. Let's look at what the Lord taught the Nephites in those scriptures and especially in 3 Nephi 11 and 12 before he invited them to "be perfect" (3 Nephi 12:48).

As Christ descended to the Nephites at the temple in the land Bountiful, he announced, "I am Jesus Christ, whom the prophets testified shall come into the world. . . . I have drunk out of that bitter cup which the Father hath given me, and . . . I have suffered the will of the Father in all things from the beginning" (3 Nephi 11:10–11). He invited the whole multitude to come unto him. One by one, they felt the prints of the nails in his hands and feet. One by one, they came forward that they might know for themselves who he was. They knew and they witnessed that he was the God of the whole earth, the promised

Messiah, who had been slain for the sins of the world—and now lived again.

Then came a wonderful opportunity for them to be taught personally by the Lord. He taught them about baptism, and he declared unto them his doctrine. "This is my doctrine," he begins in 3 Nephi 11:32. He declares that the Father bears record and the Holy Ghost likewise and that the commandment is "to repent and believe in me. And whoso believeth in me, and is baptized, the same shall be saved; and they are they who shall inherit the kingdom of God" (v. 33). "Verily, verily, I say unto you, that this is my doctrine, . . . and whoso believeth in me believeth in the Father also; and unto him will the Father bear record of me, for he will visit him with fire and with the Holy Ghost" (v. 35).

Then he repeats the doctrine: "And again I say unto you, ye must repent, and become as a little child, and be baptized in my name, or ye can in nowise receive these things. And again I say unto you, ye must repent, and be baptized in my name, and become as a little child, or ye can in nowise inherit the kingdom of God" (vv. 37–38). Are you struck as I am with the significance of that repetition?

"Verily, verily, I say unto you, that this is my doctrine, and whoso buildeth upon this buildeth upon my rock, and the gates of hell shall not prevail against them. And whoso shall declare more or less than this, and establish it for my doctrine, the same cometh of evil, and is not built upon my rock" (vv. 39–40). After explaining again the need for the baptism of water, Christ promises that he will "baptize you with fire and with the Holy Ghost" (3 Nephi 12:1), "by which comes the remission of sins" (2 Nephi 31:17).

What follows next is some practical teaching and examples of what people will do who have repented, been baptized, and received the Holy Ghost and a remission of their sins. This version of the Sermon on the Mount, or, as we sometimes call it, the Sermon at the Temple goes on to say that these people will be filled with the Spirit: they will be blessed, or happy; they will be the salt of the earth; they will know that they are the children of a Father who is in heaven (3 Nephi

12:45); and they will find that "old things are done away, and all things have become new. Therefore [says the Savior] I would that ye should be perfect even as I, or your Father who is in heaven is perfect" (3 Nephi 12:47–48).

Follow this train of logic with me. A: We are the children of God. Listen to your children sing it—it's not coincidence that the song "I Am a Child of God" is the first song in the *Children's Songbook*.[6] B: We have a divine nature. Listen to your daughters repeat it in the Young Women theme.[7] C: "We are beloved spirit daughters of God and our lives have meaning, purpose and direction" (Relief Society Declaration).[8] D: We have a Savior, who paid the price for any sin, mistake, or imperfection we may have for which we are willing to repent.

Therefore, as God created us and we have within us a divine spirit, all we need to do is turn ourselves, to repent, so that we are headed in the right direction. He has sent his Son to show us the direction, the *way*. Indeed, Jesus Christ is "the way, the truth, and the life" (John 14:6). There is no perfection necessary outside of his invitation and no perfection possible without his perfect atonement.

The Lord—and the Lord alone—has the power to make us perfect. He would teach us, as he taught the Nephites, that he came into the world to do the will of the Father and be lifted up on the cross that he might draw all men to him. We must have faith in him, repent of sins and ungodliness, be baptized, and receive the Holy Ghost. Doesn't that have a familiar ring? And aren't we all engaged in that endeavor? The scriptures promise us that after we have received the Holy Ghost, the Spirit will show us "all things what [we] should do" (2 Nephi 32:5). With the direction of the Holy Ghost, with the Comforter beside us, we can endure to the end. That is the doctrine of Christ, as Nephi says. That is the gospel, as Jesus says in 3 Nephi 27. That is the *good news*.

The last phrase in the gospel formula is "endure to the end." And even though we all know that in this life there are bound to be times and things that we will just plain have to endure, for many of us, that "endure to the end" phrase is a bit of a downer. When we talk to the children about it in Primary, we don't say, "Endure to the end." We say,

"Choose the right." And for myself, I like the phraseology from 2 Nephi, which means the same but sounds a little happier and stronger. "Wherefore, ye must press forward with a steadfastness in Christ, having a perfect brightness of hope, and a love of God and of all men" (2 Nephi 31:20). Pressing forward with a brightness of hope sounds like something we can do, especially with the Lord's assurance that his "yoke is easy, and [his] burden is light" (Matthew 11:30).

Second Nephi sounds a lot like Third Nephi, doesn't it? The message of the Book of Mormon about what we have to do—the gospel message—is consistent throughout. We are on the right path! It is faith in the Lord, repentance, baptism, receiving the Holy Ghost, and pressing forward in faith with love and a brightness of hope. How are we going to know that what we are doing is the right thing for us to be doing? How are we going to know we are in the straight and narrow path? I think the scriptures and the prophets tell us that the way we will know is by listening to the Spirit. It will help us know the truth of all things (Moroni 10:5). The Holy Ghost will never make us feel better about our "awful situation" (Mosiah 2:40), if that is what we are in, but it will comfort us and help us realize that we don't have to be famous, or rich, or ultra-talented, or "perfect" in the ways of the world to be acceptable to God. "It will show unto [us] all things what [we] should do" (2 Nephi 32:5).

Is there a litmus test for recognizing the Spirit? Here are some answers I've received as I've asked friends how they feel when the Spirit of the Lord is active in their lives. "It's easy to accept callings even when I know it will be a challenge." "I feel happy and blessed." "I feel grateful." "I don't feel critical of others." "I feel a quiet spirit of love and peace." In my experience, the Spirit bears witness of Jesus Christ and his love. If you're getting another message, it is not from the Holy Ghost.

In the past seven years, as I have served on the Primary General Board and in the Primary General Presidency, it has been my opportunity to visit many Primaries around the world. I have seen Primaries with 180 children, five wards in the building, and sixty more children in the nursery. I've seen Primaries with five children in the whole Primary. I've seen Primaries with resources galore, and Primaries where they used leftover political flyers for paper and broke five crayons into enough pieces so twelve children could each have something to draw with. I've seen Primaries where the Spirit was invited, testimony was borne, and the children sang from their hearts and were blessed and taught and edified. But one Primary I will never forget was one that was struggling. Two women were taking care of the Sharing Time, the music, and the classes. I could see a connection between their Sharing Time activity and the gospel principle they hoped they were teaching, but I would guess that none of the children could see it. It was far from "perfect," but I received from the Spirit an unmistakable impression of the Lord's love for those leaders and for those children and for all of us whom he allows to do his work. He loves us, he knows us, he gives us opportunities to work and to grow and to experience what we need to experience to bring us again to his presence. He wants us to succeed, and he has provided the way that we can. When we love him and follow him, he makes up the difference.

We prove to the Lord the desires of our hearts when we let him know that we are willing to do whatever he wants us to do. With the father of King Lamoni, we must be willing to "give away all [our] sins to know [him]" (Alma 22:18)—even if our sin is accepting from the adversary a destructive view of ourselves which keeps us from feeling the Lord's love. If our submission to the Lord is qualified, then how can we expect him to lead us? Would we say to him who has given everything, "I'm willing to do whatever you would have me do, but don't let it be in the nursery and please don't let it be in the geriatric wing"? There is, indeed, something sublimely perfect about "Thy will be done."

What a wonderful opportunity it is to join together to "remember that it is upon the rock of our Redeemer, who is Christ, the Son of God, that [we] must build [our] foundation . . . whereon if men [and women] build they cannot fall" (Helaman 5:12). Let us make sure that we are building on that foundation. Let us love the Lord with all our might and strength, and then let us rely on Him who is mighty to save. Moroni had it right—His grace really is sufficient for us. I bear my witness that He loves us and provides a way.

Notes

1. Jeffrey R. Holland, "The Other Prodigal," *Ensign*, May 2002, 63.
2. *The Interpreter's Dictionary of the Bible*, 4 vols. (New York: Abingdon Press, 1962), 3:730.
3. *Interpreter's Dictionary*, 3:730.
4. Henri Stephanus, *Thesaurus Linguae Graecae*, 9 vols. (reprint, Graz: Akademische Druck-und Verlagsanstalt, 1954), 8:1961. The author expresses thanks to Professor John Gee for the translation.
5. Neal A. Maxwell, "Brother Offended," *Ensign*, May 1982, 38.
6. Naomi W. Randall, "I Am a Child of God," in *Children's Songbook of The Church of Jesus Christ of Latter-day Saints* (Salt Lake City: The Church of Jesus Christ of Latter-day Saints, 1989), 2–3.
7. Young Women Theme, in Kathleen Lubeck, "Young Women of Value," *Ensign*, April 1989, 45.
8. "Relief Society Declaration," *Ensign*, November 1999, 92–93.

"Lay Aside the Things of This World"

Kristine Hansen

In scripture the term *world* is often synonymous with what is carnal, sensual, and devilish. It refers to the temporal as opposed to the eternal, to what is base and impure in contrast with what is refined and exalted. Scriptural synonyms for *world* in this sense are "Babylon" and the "great and spacious building"—places we should flee from (D&C 1:16; 1 Nephi 8:26). James asked, "Know ye not that the friendship of the world is enmity with God? whosoever therefore will be a friend of the world is the enemy of God" (James 4:4). Many other scriptures instruct us not to set our hearts upon the things of this world.

But *world* is also a name for this earth, a planet that was created for us to dwell on for a season, to prove ourselves to our Maker, who wants to see if we will do "all things whatsoever the Lord . . . shall command [us]" (Abraham 3:25). We are told that when "the foundations of the earth" were laid, we "shouted for joy" (Job 38:4, 7). The story of the earth's creation is detailed in three different places in scripture, alerting us to its importance. We read that God created "all things which come of the earth . . . for the benefit and the use of man, both to please the eye and to gladden the heart" (D&C 59:18). When he was finished with this creation, God pronounced his work "very good" (Genesis 1:31). Clearly, this world is dear to our Heavenly Father and his Son.

How is it that the same word—*world*—refers simultaneously to

---

Kristine Hansen, professor of English, is associate dean of Undergraduate Education at Brigham Young University. She has served as a counselor in her ward Relief Society presidency and enjoys being an aunt to fifty-two children.

things both bad and good? We must answer that question as we attempt to understand *why* and *how* we should "lay aside the things of this world, and seek for the things of a better" (D&C 25:10). That the Lord would invite us to live in this world, so lovingly and meticulously created for us, and at the same time direct us to keep ourselves unspotted from it, is a paradox. A paradox is a *seeming* contradiction, not a real one. By pondering this paradox, we can learn of God's wisdom and foresight in planning for us a mortal probation that will not only try us and refine us, but also allow us to glimpse the beauty, peace, and joy that await us in the better world of his kingdom.

God has allowed Satan to have a measure of influence in the created world.[1] With the help of his demons and the assistance of mortals who misunderstand the eternal nature and purpose of life, the adversary has erected here a carnal world, full of attractive goods, enticing entertainments, and opportunities which, though alluring, are far less substantial and enduring than the created world. Despite its fallen state and the desecration that Satan and his hosts have brought upon it, the world is still, as the poet Gerard Manley Hopkins said, "charged with the grandeur of God."[2] President Spencer W. Kimball told of bringing the cows home at dusk when he was a boy on a farm in Arizona. "Stopping by a tired old fence post," he said, "I would sometimes just stand silently in the mellow light and the fragrance of sunflowers and ask myself, 'If you were going to create a world, what would it be like?'" With a little thought, he said, "the answer seem[ed] so natural: 'Just like this one.'"[3]

The contrast between the beauty and significance of the everlasting earth and the tawdry and ultimately trivial world Satan offers is part of our Father's plan. This contrast was necessary; for as Lehi taught his son Jacob, "it must needs be, that there is an opposition in all things" (2 Nephi 2:11). Without this opposition—between sin and righteousness, misery and happiness—we would not be able to make choices, and then the world "must needs have been created for a thing of naught; wherefore there would have been no purpose in the end of its creation" (v. 12). So God has purposefully allowed the carnal world to be established in the created world because the very qualities he would have us develop during our mortal lives can best be developed here. By struggling to keep ourselves free of the carnal world's taint, we learn to overcome it and prepare ourselves to live in a better world. But how do we lay aside the things of this world while we yet live in it?

We might answer that question by contrasting what the trend-setters in the carnal world tempt us to become with what the prophets of God teach us to become. Among the messages we hear from the carnal world are these:

"Be beautiful!" By that, the seductive voices of the media usually mean we should be so absorbed with our appearance that we will pay for and do just about anything to have the right body shape, the right clothes and shoes, the right hair, the right makeup and jewelry—and change all of these as often as the winds of fashion blow a new direction.

"Be wealthy" is another siren call we hear all about us. Magazines, books, seminars all offer to show us the way to riches—both legitimate ways and some that are a little shady. The neighbors' new car or their vacation in Hawaii may also spur us to seek more money so that we can buy more of the symbols of wealth.

"Be powerful," shout strident, militant voices. Included in the invitation to be powerful is so often the opportunity to be prideful, selfish, and domineering.

"Be popular," beckon the tabloids, the women's magazines, the movies and TV, as they encourage us to admire actors, models, and other "personalities" and follow their lives simply because they are well-known, not necessarily because they have done something praiseworthy.

"Be comfortable and enjoy life" is the message behind the marketing of so many products that we are urged to buy, to fill our homes and time with, then trade them in for newer and better ones as often as we can.

In contrast to these messages are the voices of the prophets, who caution us to be wise in spending our means and the days God has given us. Sometimes the decision to reject the carnal world is easy; the lures are so transparent we see right through them. Other times the decision is hard, either because the pull of the carnal world is so strong, or because we believe that, really, little harm can come from the opportunity to have beauty, riches, power, popularity, or ease and comfort.

I do not want to suggest that, like medieval ascetics, we must pour ashes on our heads, wear hair shirts, and shut ourselves away in hovels to demonstrate that we reject the world. Nor do I mean that we should bury any talents we have. But I do think we must consider our motives in using gifts such as beauty, riches, and power so that we do not make the mistake that Elder Neal A. Maxwell describes in this statement: "Many individuals preoccupied by the cares of the world are not necessarily in *transgression*. But they are certainly in *diversion* and thus waste 'the days of [their] probation.' (2 Ne. 9:27). . . . People too caught up in themselves will inevitably let other people down!"[4] When we become preoccupied with attaining beauty, wealth, power, and prominence for their own sake, we confuse means with ends, and the potential good we might do is not realized. God gives these gifts to some so that they can bless others, not revel in them selfishly.

In no uncertain terms, President Spencer W. Kimball condemned as idolatry the pursuit of worldly things for their own sake: "The Lord has blessed us as a people with a prosperity unequaled in times past. The resources that have been placed in our power are good, and necessary to our work here on the earth. But I am afraid that many of us have been surfeited with flocks and herds and acres and barns and wealth and have begun to worship them as false gods, and they have power over us. Do we have more of these good things than our faith can stand? Many people spend most of their time working in the service of a self-image that includes sufficient money, stocks, bonds, investment portfolios, property, credit cards, furnishings, automobiles, and the like to *guarantee* carnal security throughout, it is hoped, a long and happy life. Forgotten is the fact that our assignment is to use these many resources in our families and quorums to build up the kingdom of God."[5]

Moroni suggests that we neglect our obligations to the poor and needy "because of the praise of the world" (Mormon 8:38). If, instead of the praise of the world, we want to hear the praise of the Lord, "Well done, thou good and faithful servant," we must lay aside worshiping the idols of the carnal world. One way to do this is to follow the counsel of President Howard W. Hunter, who taught us to make the temple the "great symbol of our membership" in the Lord's Church.[6]

If we make the temple the great symbol of our membership, our lives will manifest the covenants we make there. Being faithful to those covenants will keep us from confusing means with ends and falling into the trap of pride and selfishness. We will let the temple transform us from natural men and women into Saints, as King Benjamin described (Mosiah 3:19). We often speak of "going through" the temple as if it were like a museum that we visit but from which we might exit essentially unchanged. Perhaps instead we should think of the temple going through us, penetrating us to the core with its significance and transforming us so that we will never be the same again. The purpose of this transformation is not only so we can live unspotted in the world, but so we can change the world. Elder Neal A. Maxwell has written, "Temple work is not an escape from the world but a reinforcing of our need to better the world while preparing ourselves for another and far better world. . . . Being in the Lord's house can help us to be different *from* the world in order to make more difference *in* the world."[7]

The time will come when each of us has to lay aside the good and joyful things of this world and move on to another. Whether the next world we live in will be better than this one or not depends a great deal on whether we choose to shun the carnal world while we dwell in the created world. If you love the created world, remember that this earth will be renewed and become the celestial kingdom, becoming even more glorious and beautiful than it is now. Each of us is a precious daughter of God, with a heritage and a destiny more glorious than we realize. May we choose to live our mortal lives so that we can overcome the world and, through the grace of Christ, merit an inheritance in the celestial kingdom.

Notes

1. In this article, I refer to *world* in the negative sense as the carnal world. I refer to *world* in the positive sense as the created world.
2. Gerard Manley Hopkins, "God's Grandeur," in *Gerard Manley Hopkins: Poems and Prose*, ed. W. H. Gardner (New York: Penguin, 1970), 27.
3. Spencer W. Kimball, "The False Gods We Worship," *Ensign*, June 1976, 3.
4. Neal A. Maxwell, "The Tugs and Pulls of the World," *Ensign*, November 2000, 36–37; emphasis in original.
5. Kimball, "False Gods," 5; emphasis in original.
6. Howard W. Hunter, "The Great Symbol of Our Membership," *Ensign*, October 1994, 2.
7. Neal A. Maxwell, *"Not My Will but Thine"* (Salt Lake City: Bookcraft, 1988), 133; emphasis added.

"But Ye Are . . . A Peculiar People"

Mary Ellen Edmunds

It's interesting how people criticize and make fun of us if we are doing things that we know and feel are right—things that make us seem "peculiar." Have you ever had that experience? Sometimes the criticism even comes from those who are closest to us, family members and friends. *Peculiar* means "distinct from others; distinguished in nature, character, or attributes; unlike others; singular; uncommon; unusual; set apart." Today I want to say hurray for being peculiar!

In Exodus we read, "Now therefore, if ye will obey my voice indeed, and keep my covenant, then ye shall be a peculiar treasure unto me above all people" (Exodus 19:5). Brother John Tanner, who teaches at BYU, said, "*Peculiar* literally means we are his special treasure, purchased with his blood."[1] In 1 Peter we read, "But ye are a chosen generation, a royal priesthood, an holy nation, a peculiar people; that ye should shew forth the praises of him who hath called you out of darkness into his marvellous light" (2:9). That's a wonderful phrase: we are "called out of darkness into his marvellous light." No wonder we are such happy people. No wonder.

I'm convinced that the more we strive to become who we really are, children of God with the ability to become like him, the more we will seem unique to those who are choosing a different direction. President Gordon B. Hinckley has said, "Of course you are peculiar.

Mary Ellen Edmunds, author, speaker, and Relief Society teacher, earned a bachelor's degree in nursing from Brigham Young University. She has served on the Relief Society General Board, has filled four missions, and was a director of training at the Provo Missionary Training Center.

If the world continues its present trend, and if you walk in obedience to the doctrine and principles of this church, you may become even more peculiar in the eyes of others."[2] He also noted, "You have bypassed the things of the world. You are on your way to something higher and better. . . . You are something special. You must rise above the ordinary."[3] A prophet asks that we become something other than ordinary—extraordinary, out of this world, out of the ordinary. Well, maybe I am a peculiar person, but compared to whom or to what? Am I only peculiar when compared to Nehor, Attila the Hun, the Wicked Witch of the West, and Cruella D'Ville? Is it possible to be peculiar among the peculiar?

Is it peculiar, for example, to try to be better when you are already pretty good? If it's possible to be overly righteous, I would like to nominate my sister, Charlotte. After all, she's the one who used to say things like, "Oh, don't you love the commandments? Don't you wish we had more?"

Are you comfortable being peculiar? Some aren't. Some will struggle with their last minute, their last penny, their last breath to look like, behave like, talk like, dress like, and become like everyone else. To blend in. Not to stand up or stand out. Yet we have *covenanted* to stand as witnesses of Jesus Christ in all places. President James E. Faust has said, "In our society many sacred values have been eroded in the name of freedom of expression. The vulgar and the obscene are protected in the name of freedom of speech. The mainstream of society has become more tolerant, even accepting, of conduct that Jesus, Moses, the Prophet Joseph Smith, and other prophets have warned against since the beginning of human history.

"We should not allow our personal values to erode, even if others think we are peculiar. We have always been regarded as a peculiar people. However, being spiritually correct is much better than being politically correct." Then President Faust added, "We should only fear offending God and His Son, Jesus Christ, who is the head of this Church."[4] Doesn't it seem like the gulf between good and evil is wider than ever? Like there's an increasing separation between the great and spacious building and the strait and narrow path, complete with iron rod? There is much more distance between misery and happiness, and, oh, the contrast.

Why is our Heavenly Father asking us to be a peculiar people? One reason is for our safety and protection. Another is to help us return "home" to be with our heavenly parents, kind and dear, and our loved ones. But I want to focus on this reason: we're asked to be peculiar so we can be a light and an example to others; a standard, a refuge from the storm; to be there so others can lean on us if they become confused, weak, discouraged, lonely, tired, or lost.

Let me share a story with you. Brother Angel Abrea and his wife, Maria, moved to Salt Lake City from Argentina when he was called as a general authority. As soon as they moved here, Brother Abrea was in training and was gone a lot, especially on weekends. Sometimes Sister Abrea felt lonely. She didn't know English quite as well as he did, and she felt homesick. She said, "I'm the only child. I knew my mother missed me, and I missed her so much. She used to come to my home on Tuesday morning, and she always brought a bundle of Swiss chard from the garden. After living in Salt Lake for more than one year, one Tuesday morning I was particularly remembering my sweet mother." Sister Abrea sat sewing a dress for her daughter, thinking about her mother, and telling Heavenly Father how she was feeling. "Oh dear Father in Heaven," she said, "how I wish to see my mother coming with a bundle of Swiss chard." She said, "I knew my mother was thinking about me. It was Tuesday."

Do you know how she might have felt? Have you ever been away from home and felt homesick? There is no feeling like it. I set a record on my first mission. I used to wind up in the curtains in a little chapel in Taiwan and just boo-hoo.

Sister Abrea continued to talk to Heavenly Father, letting him know how she felt. Then the doorbell rang. A neighbor from the ward, whom she did not yet know very well, stood looking timid, even awkward, and said, "You're going to think I am really strange. I don't even know if you know what this is or if you like it. We call it Swiss chard."

One of the sweetest things about this experience is just an ordinary, wonderful neighbor could listen to the Holy Ghost and do something very unusual—peculiar even.

Speaking of pecularity, I find this much quoted prophecy from President Spencer W. Kimball especially meaningful: "Much of the major growth that is coming to the Church in the last days will come because many of the good women of the world (in whom there is often such an inner sense of spirituality) will be drawn to the Church in large numbers. This will happen to the degree that the women of the Church reflect righteousness and articulateness in their lives and to the degree that the women of the Church are seen as distinct and different—in happy ways—from the women of the world."[5] Cheerfulness is attractive. The scriptures contain many invitations to "be of good cheer." The Savior says, I will stand by you, don't fear (D&C 68:6). It's attractive to be optimistic, positive, and to have a perfect brightness of hope. "Be happy in that which you do. Cultivate a spirit of gladness in your homes," says President Hinckley. "Let the light of the gospel shine in your faces wherever you go and in whatever you do."[6] Do we do that enough? Are you tired of being Grumpy whenever you and your friends play Seven Dwarfs? Are you the reason somebody got caller ID? Can you imagine trying to share the gospel of Jesus Christ, the *good* news, without being happy? "Hello. I'm Elder Eeyore. I'm here to tell you about the great plan of happiness. Sure has brought a lot of joy to me. Want it?"

I have been convinced for a long, long time that we should be the happiest people in the world. I know that some experiences are hard. I know they can really get us down. But I'm saying that *over all* we have all the ingredients to be the happiest people anywhere. We really do. Listen to President Hinckley again (he's our visual aid for happiness): "I see a wonderful future in a very uncertain world," he said. Trust him. He's not just putting words together because he thinks they sound nice. Our leaders don't do that. "If we will simply live the gospel we will be blessed in a magnificent and wonderful way. We will be looked upon as a peculiar people who have found the key to a peculiar happiness."[7]

The key to having this peculiar happiness is found in the gospel of Jesus Christ. It is found in light and truth. It is found in striving to be better, even when we are already pretty good.

One of my favorite descriptions of peculiar people comes from the Pearl of Great Price: "And the Lord called his people Zion, because they were of one heart and one mind, and dwelt in righteousness; and there was no poor among them" (Moses 7:18). There was no one wanting and needing without someone to help. Imagine a whole village of people like that. No one hungry, or lonely, or in need. There must not have been cheating or lying, no stealing of irrigation water, or stuff like that. Wow! No hitting, spitting, withholding love. No road rage, or gossiping, or contending. Let's be more like Zion. Let's be good. Let's be true. Let's stand closer together and be kinder and more supportive of each other. May we do our best to share the good news with others. They need this message, and they need it now. They need the peace, the happiness, the contentment, the gratitude, the safety, and the joy, which are part of the gospel of Jesus Christ. May Jesus Christ be the light that we hold up: the Light of the World, the Son of the Living God, the Prince of Peace, our Advocate with the Father, our Savior, and our Redeemer.

Notes

1. John S. Tanner, "To Clothe a Temple," *Ensign*, August 1992, 47.
2. Gordon B. Hinckley, "A Chosen Generation," *Ensign*, May 1992, 71.
3. Gordon B. Hinckley, "Some Thoughts on Temples, Retention of Converts, and Missionary Service," *Ensign*, November 1997, 52.
4. James E. Faust, "Search Me, O God, and Know My Heart," *Ensign*, May 1998, 18–19.
5. Spencer W. Kimball, "The Role of Righteous Women," *Ensign*, November 1979, 103–4.
6. Gordon B. Hinckley, "Live the Gospel," *Ensign*, November 1984, 86.
7. Gordon B. Hinckley, "Look to the Future," *Ensign*, November 1997, 69.

Be Ye Wise Stewards

R. Kent Crookston

I was raised on a farm, the kind that had cows and horses and pigs and chickens. We had an enormous garden, a root cellar, and a hay barn. My mother made butter and cheese; my father made little tree houses for birds to nest in. We looked for them to come each spring and listened to their songs change with the seasons. We hunted ducks and pheasants. I trapped mink and muskrats.

I have spent my professional life researching to improve crops like corn and soybeans. As a scientist, I have worked with organic farmers, environmentalists, and politicians who are concerned about how food is produced and the way natural resources are managed. All of this has helped me appreciate the many dimensions of the word *stewardship*.

Consider these verses from the Doctrine and Covenants, and note the emphasis that the Lord puts on I, my, and mine: "For it is expedient that *I, the Lord*, should make every man accountable, as a steward over earthly blessings, *which I have made . . . I, the Lord*, stretched out the heavens, and built the earth, *my very handiwork*; and all things therein are *mine*. And it is *my* purpose to provide for *my* saints, for *all things are mine*" (D&C 104:13–15; emphasis added).

That's interesting, isn't it? Do we conclude from this emphasis on *my* and *mine* that the Lord wants to be sure he gets credit for what he has done? I think not. Rather, I believe he wants to make it clear that he is in charge, and we therefore have no need to fear. Note, in fact, how comforting this next verse is: "For the earth is full, and there is

---

R. Kent Crookston is dean of the College of Biology and Agriculture at Brigham Young University. He has had a lifetime of experience in his field from boyhood on a Canadian prairie farm to international research in Africa. He and his wife, Gayle, are the parents of seven children. He serves as a stake high councilman.

enough and to spare; yea, I prepared all things, and have given unto the children of men to be agents unto themselves" (D&C 104:17).

There are several messages in these verses. First, the Lord built the earth, it is his handiwork, he's in charge, everything associated with it is his. Second, he didn't set the planet in motion and then later on find out he hadn't planned well enough, or that he was running out of resources. No, the earth is full; there is enough and to spare.

Let me tell you, as a production agronomist who has researched the earth's resources, that the earth *is* full, there *is* enough and to spare. If all of the good land on the planet were put into production, it could easily feed fifty billion people. Sudan alone has enough good soil and water to feed all six billion people on the planet. The state of Iowa could easily produce enough food for *all* of the people in the United States, so could California or Texas. We would need to change our diets to eat less meat, and we'd have to work out a distribution system. But the Lord knew what he was talking about in 1834 when he said there was enough and to spare.

So, the earth is the Lord's *and* there's plenty to go around. Now the Lord does say that in order to make everything work, we need to share. "The poor shall be exalted, in that the rich are made low" are his words (D&C 104:16). I wish I could fully explore that qualifier, but it would take a book, not an article. The third point I'd like to note from these verses is that the Lord has delegated the management of his handiwork unto the children of men to be agents unto themselves. In other words, he doesn't micro-manage our stewardship. Notice that he gives us insight into the meaning of stewardship: taking care of something that belongs to someone else. In this case, taking care of the earth, which the Lord makes very clear is *his*.

Before we leave these verses, let's go back and consider something that I left out. "For it is expedient that I, the Lord, should make every man accountable, as a steward over earthly blessings, which I have made and prepared for my . . ." I left out the last word of this sentence. Think about what is being said and consider what word comes to mind to fill in the blank—for my *children?* for my *people?* for my *Saints?*

Okay, here is the word the Lord used: "For it is expedient that I, the Lord, should make every man accountable, as a steward over earthly blessings, which I have made and prepared for my *creatures*" (D&C 104:13). Isn't that interesting?

But wait. Didn't the Lord say "*all* things which come of the earth . . . are made for the benefit and the use of *man*"? (D&C 59:18). Listen to the words of the Father instructing the Son about the creation: "Let [man] have dominion over the fishes of the sea, and over the fowl of the air, and over the cattle, and over all the earth, and over every creeping thing that creepeth upon the earth" (Moses 2:26). So, what role do the creatures serve, really?

As a biologist, when I ponder the fact that "creatures" rather than "people" is the last word of that sentence, I find myself considering my relationship to those creatures. Geneticists tell us that 99% of our DNA is identical to the DNA of the mouse. It also appears that we humans have genes within us that could result in wings and feathers, or horns and hooves; they simply aren't expressed in people. Henry Eyring, probably the Church's best-known scientist a generation ago, spoke about the creatures of the earth: "Animals seem pretty wonderful to me. I'd be content to discover that I share a common heritage with them, so long as God is at the controls."[1]

As I consider my relationship to the creatures, and the fact that God prepared his earthly blessings for them, I feel a sense of awe and responsibility. Because, as a man, I have dominion over all other creatures. I am endowed with the means to sustain those creatures and their habitat, or I can destroy them. Why do I have this power? Why did the Creator share that authority with me? As you are thinking about that, let me tell you a story.

When I was just a little boy, I went out one cold night with my mother to tend to our baby chicks. When we entered the shed, we heard a terrible noise inside the brooding pen. Mother immediately yanked the lid off. "Ooohhh, you poor thing!" she soothed as she reached into the chaos and pulled forth a tiny, trembling chick. Two hundred other little yellow birds were swirling, leaping, chirping, and flapping their wings.

"What's going on?" I asked.

"They've been picking on this one," she said. "We got here just in time." The little bleeding bird nestled into her cupped hands.

"Why did they do it?" I asked.

"We don't know," she answered. "For some reason they just started picking on him."

"But why would they make him bleed?"

"It's awful, isn't it?"

"What will we do with him?"

"We'll take care of him."

"How?"

"We'll take him to the house. Here, you hold him while I change the water." I took the bird and held it close to my coat. "That's a lucky little bird," Mom said. "With a sore like that he'd have been gone in minutes." I felt like I might be going to have a bad dream about this. "We can learn something tonight," she said. "People are a lot like chickens."

"How?"

"People pick on each other, too," she said. "When one child is picked on, others follow."

"People don't peck each other like chickens do," I said.

"But they make fun, or tease, or even hit."

"Is that why we say 'pick on'?" I asked.

"Maybe so," she answered. "Some of the worst picking is saying unkind things . . . things that make people feel bad, or cry. So . . . ," she said, stepping over and opening my hands to see how the little bird was doing, "*we* won't ever pick on anyone, will we?"

"Unnh unnnh."

Back in the house, we made a cardboard box home for the battered little bird and put it behind the stove. By the end of the third week, the chick had grown too large for the box; and we could see it was a hen. "She's perfectly safe now," Mom said. "We'll put her back with the others." But I was afraid she would be attacked again and cried so hard that Dad came up with a plan. We had an empty rabbit pen in the backyard, and he said we could put her in there. My job was to make sure she had food and water. Several times a day, I picked her up, stroked her, and spoke to her. But before long Mother was protesting again. "She just stands in there," she said. "She wants to get out. She's plenty big enough to take care of herself." So we turned the bird loose. To our surprise, she didn't run after the other chickens. She followed me—right into the house, through the house, and all around the yard.

Mother was stake Relief Society president that year, and some of the sisters from the General Board came up from Utah for stake conference. They were to be guests at our home for dinner. I could tell they were extra special; Mom and Dad cleaned the house *and* the yard. Mother was concerned that we didn't have an indoor bathroom or running water. She realized there wasn't much hope that we could look sophisticated.

I helped get ready. Mom and I caught some roosters for dinner. She had her own way of killing them. She would take the big bird, hold its wings and feet together, and lay it on the ground. Then she would place a piece of broomstick over its neck. With one foot on each end of the stick, she pulled on the bird. After a muffled popping sound, Mother would grimace and step away from the stick, holding the creature's jerking body in the grass, neck down. The bird's head was left under the stick.

"Let 'im go, Mom, please . . ." I begged.

"No."

"Daddy does."

"Mother doesn't."

"Why?"

"It's gruesome; they get all covered in blood."

"Pleeeease."

"No."

After dunking the beheaded birds in scalding water, we stripped away their hot, soggy feathers. Then Mother cut them open and slipped her hand up into each warm carcass, past slippery intestines, on up toward the throat where she located the firm gizzard and heart. With these secure in her fingers, she gave an uncompromising pull. The innards were dislodged and came sliding out with a plop into a cardboard box. I don't have time to share the lessons she taught me about crops, gizzards, hearts, livers, and bile. I can see her carrying the butchered birds to the well to be washed, bumping into a couple of hollyhocks which curtsied after her as a swirl of shiny blue flies spiraled up from the box.

The next day was Sunday. The special ladies were inside the house, and fried chicken was on the table. I was in the backyard, pouting. "Mom, when can I show them Chickee?" I had asked when the ladies arrived. Mom only patted my head absentmindedly, then almost stepped on me as she shoved me toward the back porch. *Should have asked Daddy*, I thought. *He'da showed 'em*. All summer long, whenever anyone came to visit, my dad would take them out back to show them my little white hen. The routine was for me to step into the backyard and yell, "Here, Chickee!" The hen would come running and follow me wherever I went. If I stooped down, she would hop into my arms. I would then look over at Dad, who would give me that particular wink that meant, *We've got something special going here, haven't we, boy*. Sometimes Mom would even let me lead the bird into the house. Everyone would laugh.

I had the little white hen in my lap as I sat pouting that Sunday afternoon, listening to the sounds of important ladies from Salt Lake City having a meal. I decided to carry her past the dining room window, hoping someone would notice us. Nobody did. So, I entered the house and stood in the kitchen. I stayed there holding the bird in my arms for five minutes. Mother didn't come out of the dining room to check on anything like I thought she would. I approached the dining room door and carefully wedged it open, looking for my father. To my relief, he was the first one in the room to notice me. He raised his head and looked at me, questioning. I realized he couldn't see the chicken, so I lifted her up in front of my face. The bird shifted in my arms and stood up. Then, before I could stop her, she lifted into the air and flew—right into the middle of the dining room table.

I share this true story as an example of a mother teaching her son how to be a steward over some of God's creatures. Mother looked after the need and comfort of her chickens; she rescued them from trouble. And then, when it was the season, she caught, killed, cooked, and served them to important guests on the Sabbath day. In other words, she exercised dominion over them, and in my opinion she got it right. Hear the Lord's words on it: "Every herb in the season thereof, and every fruit in the season thereof; all these to be used with prudence and thanksgiving. Yea, flesh also of beasts and of the fowls of the air, I, the Lord, have ordained for the use of man" (D&C 89:11–12).

"And inasmuch as ye do these things with thanksgiving, with cheerful hearts and countenances . . . the fulness of the earth is yours, the beasts of the field and the fowls of the air, and that which climbeth upon the trees and walketh upon the earth; Yea, and the herb, and the good things which come of the earth, whether for food or for raiment, or for houses, or for barns, or for orchards, or for gardens, or for vineyards; Yea, all things which come of the earth, in the season thereof, are made for the benefit and the use of man, both to please the eye and to gladden the heart; Yea, for food and for raiment, for taste and for smell, to strengthen the body and to enliven the soul" (D&C 59:15–19). Have you considered how *you* exercise dominion over the creatures of the world? Haven't you decided exactly which plants to encourage in your yard and which to eliminate? Do you put bulbs in the soil and violets in the window to please the eye? At your house are there gerbils in cages, or fishes in bowls, and did you build a wren house and hang it in the shade of your tree so that the wren's song would gladden your heart?

Of course, some people, like me, make a living by exercising dominion over creatures. Have you heard about today's bio-engineering of plants and animals? Did you know that most of the cotton grown in the U.S. is bio-engineered with a built-in insecticide that kills the boll weevil so the farmer doesn't have to spray? Did you know that scientists have produced a banana with the polio vaccine engineered into it so that children in the tropics will be automatically vaccinated when they eat the banana? Have you heard that they are engineering tobacco to produce perfectly pure human insulin instead of nicotine? About all you have to do is imagine something anymore. The world's major chemical companies have announced that life science will be their principal focus for the twenty-first century. Business experts are predicting that the application of genetic engineering will have a bigger impact on our lives, and on our businesses, than did the application of the micro-chip in bringing us computers.

Some people are wondering, my goodness, does Heavenly Father approve? Aren't scientists carrying things a little too far? After all, this is *your* domain. Or, is this the very sort of thing the psalmist had in mind when he wrote: "What is man, that thou art mindful of him? . . . For thou hast made him a little lower than the angels, and hast crowned him with glory and honour. Thou madest him to have dominion over the works of thy hands; thou hast put all things under his feet" (Psalm 8:4–6).

Surely, like me, you begin to experience a sense of amazement and responsibility. I find myself praying that we will get it right—and that I, personally, will be a good steward over the earthly blessings that the Lord has made and prepared for his creatures, which include me. Recall these words: "We have learned by sad experience that it is the nature and disposition of *almost all* men, as soon as they get a little authority, as they suppose, they will immediately begin to exercise *unrighteous* dominion" (D&C 121:39; emphasis added). And, we are told that when men undertake to exercise control or dominion in any degree of unrighteousness, the heavens withdraw themselves, and the Spirit of the Lord is grieved (D&C 121:37).

So, what do we teach our children? I suggest two things. First, teach them to be thankful for the blessings of the earth. Show them how to follow the Lord's admonition to have a thankful heart. "And he who receiveth all things with thankfulness shall be made glorious;

and the things of this earth shall be added unto him, even an hundred fold, yea, more" (D&C 78:19).

Let me share one small thing my family does to engender a spirit of thankfulness in our home. When we sit down to a meal, we don't ask the Lord to bless our food. Let me explain. In Deuteronomy at one point, the Lord tells the people what to do when they finally get to the promised land. Listen to the remarkable description of that land and then pay attention to the use of the word *bless* in relation to eating: "For the Lord thy God bringeth thee into a good land, a land of brooks of water, of fountains and depths that spring out of valleys and hills; a land of wheat, and barley, and vines, and fig trees, and pomegranates; a land of oil olive, and honey; a land wherein thou shalt eat bread without scarceness, thou shalt not lack any thing. . . . When thou hast eaten and art full, then thou shalt bless the Lord thy God for the good land which he hath given thee" (Deuteronomy 8:7–10).

In this case, "bless" obviously means to thank. So, in our house at meals, we offer a prayer of thanks for our food. We mention specifically what we are thankful for. Our blessing might go something like this: "We thank thee for this lasagna, and this fresh bread, and this lovely salad, and this cold milk, and for that cherry pie waiting over there on the counter. And we thank thee for a lovely day, and for the peace and beauty of the valley in which we live." But in our prayer, we don't ask the Lord to bless what's on the table, in the other sense of the word *bless*, meaning to "take sickness away from the midst of" us (Exodus 23:25), because we have a sense that his hand has overseen and therefore "blessed" his own bounty which, after we have thanked him, he simply wants us to enjoy.

That was point one to teach our children: be thankful. The second point is related but goes deeper. As Latter-day Saints, we have an astonishing insight that makes this idea of stewardship extraordinarily meaningful. We understand that if we live up to our potential, we can ourselves be creators, we can become gods. Much of the world recoils at this "blasphemous" notion, but we do not. A careful observance of nature suggests that none of us should be surprised at our potential.

Consider the caterpillar—transformed into the butterfly. Should we question that our mortal bodies could be transformed into celestial bodies, with celestial powers?

The knowledge that we have dominion over all creatures, that we can build bird houses, and plant flowers, and manipulate the natural world in a way that no other creatures can, is as awesome as the fact that we can, with our marriage partners, create human life. It is my conviction that if we are wise in this stewardship, we will rise in the next world empowered to create our own butterflies, and dinosaurs, and whatever else we can imagine to please the eye and gladden the heart. I am equally confident that if we abuse that power or that stewardship in this life, we will not be allowed to exercise it in the next.

Show your children how to respect their power over plants and creatures throughout their lives. Help them to imagine being permitted to apply celestial-level power, a power beyond description, as creators in the worlds to come.

"And whoso is found a faithful, a just, and a wise steward shall enter into the joy of his Lord, and shall inherit eternal life" (D&C 51:19).

Note

1. Henry Eyring, *Reflections of a Scientist* (Salt Lake City: Deseret Book, 1983), 60.

The Evils and Designs of Conspiring Men

JoAnn Hibbert Hamilton

In the year 2000, I represented Utah at a national conference in the Cincinnati area put on by all the major organizations in the United States that fight pornography. I had no idea until then that the sellers of pornography, media, and slick magazines were so well organized. Their monthly trade magazine included an article that discussed how to increase profits by enticing the pornography addict to buy weekly instead of monthly.[1] In January 2000, the magazine noted a total of 17,500,000 Internet hits from homes to porn sites. The editors were ecstatic at this 40 percent increase from four months before.[2] I believe a wave of addiction across the United States caused the 40 percent increase.

For those who are addicted, the desire for pornography escalates. A young man said he bought a porn video for sixty dollars, watched it twice, and then it wasn't good enough. This pattern is typical. The desire is always to find something more explicit, and with the click of a mouse on the Internet in the middle of a night a person can easily accelerate the addicting process. One young LDS mother told me, "My husband is a porn addict and so are two of his brothers. I talked to

---

JoAnn Hibbert Hamilton, a popular speaker and columnist, received her bachelor's degree in English at Brigham Young University. She served with her first husband, Sherman H. Hibbert, while he presided in the Brazil Central Mission. Together they became the parents of eight children. After his death, she married Fred "A" Hamilton, a widower with thirteen children. JoAnn leads community-based family and parenting groups, has represented Utah at a national anti-pornography conference, and works extensively to educate people on this issue.

people down the street, and they have the problem, too." Then she added, "My husband is a good man. It's just that he was curious, and it happened so quickly." We must teach our children that addiction does happen quickly—sometimes with a single exposure, sometimes in only two weeks.[3] They cannot afford to be curious.

According to John Harmer, in his book *The War We Must Win*, purveyors of pornography spent thousands of dollars in 1978 to hire experts to evaluate their business and help increase sales. The experts came up with several recommendations. First, they needed to get women involved in pornography to extend their audience. Second, they needed to get porn into homes. Children exposed at young ages are more apt to become addicted later on. Third, they wanted to camouflage pornography in the form of humor, violence, or drama in films and video games, which would move more people toward addiction.[4]

Has their plan succeeded? In 1999, 40 percent of the porn videos rented were rented by women. One of the prevalent lies about pornography is that it will improve a couple's intimacy. Satan must love this lie. The truth is that pornography teaches false sexuality and desensitizes its viewer. It will destroy a marriage because the expectations of one or the other partner become impossible to fulfill. It also teaches acceptance of deviant behavior.

Magazines that used to be considered respectable magazines have, since 1978 and all in accordance with "the plan," introduced sexually explicit content and covers. They buy spots in the checkout lanes of stores where children have nothing else to look at. The next time you go grocery shopping notice the magazine covers, so many found at the eye level of children, not the eye level of adults. Besides inappropriate pictures, note also the explicit headlines.

Pornography publishers also purposely cause "accidental exposure" on the Internet. They know exactly what it does. Children can misspell a Disney word and pull up a porn site. Pornographers link the advertisements so that a person sees six to eight advertisements, roughly ten minutes of hard core or illegal pornography, before they are able to exit. Two little boys in the third grade at a Utah school accidentally pulled up a porn site when they put the name of their assignment on the computer. They knew it was a bad picture and tried to exit but could not. As a result, they saw ten minutes of hard core pornography. Did they tell anyone? No. They felt the guilt that seeing the pictures creates and kept quiet. Sixty percent of such children never tell their parents when they have an experience like this, leaving no chance for intervention.

There is a purposeful onslaught. How successful has it been?

Ninety-five percent of our children ten and under have already been exposed to pornography, mostly in grocery store checkout lanes.[5]

Four out of five teens, ages twelve to fourteen, have already seen hardcore pornography several times.[6]

In 1999, one out of four teens had an unwanted exposure to soft core porn (nudity) on the Internet.[7] Dr. Rick Hawks said that any exposure to Internet pornography during teen years pushes that teen toward porn addiction—unless there is intervention.[8] It is important to find out where our children and teens really are on this issue.

A study reported to the 1986 Attorney General's Commission on Pornography by Dr. Jennings Bryant showed that among high school students, 31 percent of the males and 18 percent of the females admitted actually doing some of the things sexually they had seen in the pornography within a few days after exposure. Sixty-seven percent of the males and 40 percent of the females reported wanting to try out some of the sexual behaviors they had witnessed.[9]

If 31 percent of high school males actually did some of the sexual things that they had seen in pornographic scenes within a few days of exposure, who would they try these things out on? One seventeen-year-old young man said to me, "Sister Hamilton, I never would have done to my girlfriend what I did if I had not seen pornography." Yes, the objects of these behaviors would be girlfriends, or younger brothers and sisters, or children being babysat. And those children, in the name of play, often play in sexual ways with other children.

Just as marijuana is a gateway to drug addiction, so pornography in any form is the gateway to sexual addiction. How much exposure have Latter-day Saint families had? A woman I know works for the police and administers the D.A.R.E. program (Drug Abuse Resistance Education) in schools in Utah. Last spring she said to a group of third grade children, "Sometimes I see a picture and the person isn't dressed properly or doesn't have clothes on, and that makes me feel really uncomfortable. Has that ever happened to you?" Sixty percent of the third graders said it had. Of the fifth graders, more than 90 percent said they had had this experience and many knew how to find pornography on the Internet. They talked openly about it.

President Hinckley has warned us over and over about pornography. Unfortunately, many Church members are reluctant to believe "we" have a problem. Because of our sexualized society, however, we all have a problem. Most of our children have already been exposed and without intervention many may end up being sexually addicted to pornography. Any cashier at your local store will tell you that teens swarm in to look at the *Sports Illustrated* swimsuit edition when it comes out. Of the many former addicts I have talked to, most were "started" by swimsuit photos.

So what can you do to protect your home from pornography? Many parents really don't know if there has ever been pornography on their computer. Many, in fact, don't know how to use the Internet. If you don't, you need to learn; you can't afford to be ignorant. One of my sons came home from college almost every weekend at 11:30 P.M. for a period of time and said, "Here I am, Mom, to teach you." The lessons went on until after 1 A.M. Exhausted, I didn't think I was ever going to learn. After months of instruction, one night, in twenty minutes, I finally understood how it worked. Once you know how to use the Internet, check the history every night to see what sites have been viewed on your computer. Has a babysitter pulled up a pornographic site and perhaps shown it to your children? What about your children's friends? To find out, turn on your computer and go to www.strengthenthefamily.net, scroll down, then click on contentwatch.com. On that homepage, you will see Content Audit. It is free. Download it and, according to those who put out this information, you will know right then everything that has ever been on your computer. Tonight you will know if you have a problem to deal with.

If you find pornography of some sort, talk calmly to your child or teen. If you say to your child, "I have told you a hundred times that that stuff is filth," you will never know where your child is on this issue because he will never tell you. Stay calm and maintain a good relationship with your child or teen so this becomes something you both can talk about. Ask your children what they have seen. Most children will frankly tell you. Often parents don't know because they don't ask. A child who won't talk often signals a problem. Those who do talk let you know right where they are.

Put your computer in a place where you can supervise it. Use a filter over and above that provided by your server level, but know the computer still needs supervision. Check that your school teaches your children how to "crash and tell." That is, if they ever accidentally pull up pornography on the computer, they should immediately turn off the computer. Then they will see just an instant of pornography instead of much more. They will feel guilt from this exposure, but it is important for them to tell so you can help them with it. Make sure they understand that you want to help them and give them support.

Role play with your six-year-old about how he is going to act when he is approached with an inappropriate story, joke, or picture. You might say, "Johnny, I have a bad picture," and practice until he knows how to react. Dr. Lynn Scoresby tells us in his book *Bringing Up Moral Children in an Immoral World* that sexually explicit pictures are in the hands of seven- and eight-year-olds in every elementary school.[10] I could hardly believe this until I questioned two second-grade teachers. Both acknowledged it was true.

"Is it all the children?" I asked.

"No, just a small percentage." I was so glad.

"How can you tell?" I asked.

"By the stories they write and the pictures they draw, we can tell who has pornography in their homes."

What do children do with a picture? They share. We need to send children to school prepared for these approaches by other children. We must make sure they know to tell us when this happens. When they tell, we need to praise and reward them. It's important to warn your eleven-year-olds that as hormones set in, curiosity levels rise. They will have a harder time resisting. Teach them what will happen if they give in to the curiosity. Explain what addiction is.

Share information with your neighbors and the parents of your children's friends. Parents and youngsters need to know that sleepovers can provide an environment where pictures are passed around and inappropriate touching is experienced.[11] Check computer disks brought into your home. A fifteen-year-old might give a twelve-year-old a disk and say, "There are really neat things on this disk." What he considers neat may be pornography. Beware of free AOL or other CDs that offer free hours of Internet service. Installed on your computer, they eliminate your filter.

Be sure that you understand the warning signs that will help you identify a problem. Does your child stay up late on the computer? Does he lock the door? Lying is almost always part of the problem. Teens who have never lied will lie about this. When you check Internet history sites, if all of them are erased, you likely have a problem. Involved teens will isolate somewhat, often be temperamental, and won't talk about what is bothering them. They won't feel good about themselves.

Once we protect our homes, we need to do what we can to make our community safe. Phil Burress, chairman of the Impact America Conference, said, "You will have a tendency to go home and want to work against hard core pornography. Know that it is the things in the grocery store checkout lanes that start kids."[12] Hard core pornography has to be dealt with legally, but soft core can be battled by establishing community standards. Amy Fielding led the way for me. She talked to the manager of her neighborhood grocery store because she felt she couldn't take her children along to shop anymore. After she "taught" first the manager and then his boss, the entire Macey's grocery chain began to cover everything "inappropriate" for children. How many people did it take? One.

An owner of a local grocery store told me, "If six to eight people make the same request in a two-week period of time, I make a change in my store."[13] *That's the key!* I know it works because I have done it. In the process, I learned a few helpful hints. Use the words "inappropriate for children" instead of "pornography." Massive debates surround the definition of pornography, but everyone seems to know what is inappropriate for children. Leave your message with the service desk, not the cashier, whether the store manager is there or not. Just say, "Would you please cover magazines that are inappropriate for children?" Then walk away. If this is difficult for you, just write that sentence on the back of your receipt and hand it to the service desk requesting that they give it to the manager. Encourage your friends to do the same. If inappropriate magazines are already covered, thank the employees at the service desk. Covering the magazines is inconvenient for stores, so your noticing will help keep the covers on.

You can also ask a store owner not to sell a certain offensive magazine. By asking him to have magazines covered, you are helping to develop a community standard. These magazines may not be against the law, but community standards regulate a community. Remember, the articles in such magazines are read by teens who tell your teen what is in them. Pornographers feed on the curiosity of youth. Internet pornography becomes the next step. Inappropriate magazines and movies are on the shelves because we have let them in. We must speak up. If a grocery store loses the trade of a family of four, it loses more money than it makes on all the magazines all month.

What help is available for those who are already caught? A prevalent lie is that once a person admits a pornography addiction, there is really no way out. Dr. Allan Roe states, "Lots of people pull out of this addiction."[14] Without doubt, addiction to pornography is difficult to conquer. An alcoholic can stay away from the store where he makes his purchases, a cocaine addict can avoid his sources, but the sexual addict has the pictures in his mind. Phil Burress said at the Impact America Conference, "I was an addict for twenty-five years. I have been off for fifteen. That means that every day, pictures surface in my mind, but I will have no part of them or that lifestyle."[15] Another man, who lingered after a meeting where I had spoken, said, "Let me tell you what it is like to be addicted. Let me tell you what it is like to love your wife and your family, love your God and honor your church responsibility and then go out and do something so vile that it defiles them all." He went on to describe the struggle as he pulled out of the clutches of his addiction and the peace in his life now.

"Does your wife trust you?" I asked.

"It took a long time, but she does," he replied.

Circumstances differ in every case, but certain basic elements are imperative for a Latter-day Saint recovery. The addict must first have a bishop who both understands the problem and can help the addict activate the atonement of Jesus Christ. Second, the addict needs a counselor who has experience with sexual addiction. You will need to hunt for such a person. Many people do not have the necessary training. Third, an addict must have a support group or person. As Dr. Victor Cline states, "Self-control, self-discipline, will power, and just wanting to quit—rarely work by themselves."[16] Once addicted, people can't just stop. Youthful addicts have told me that understanding the problem, understanding the triggers, and having someone to call really helps.

Parents who have a good relationship with their teens and the help of a concerned and loving bishop can sometimes work through this problem. The bishop will help the youth understand repentance and the Atonement in a special way. If this much support does not enable the youth to stop on his own, professional help is imperative. One young man told me, "I don't want to quit," but after some counseling he was on his way. Missionaries who had problems before their missions need to understand that often when they return, they may need the help of all four elements—their bishop, the Atonement, a counselor, and a support group or person—to maintain control. Having such a problem is not the end of the world, but it is crucial not to let embarrassment keep you from getting help. If one counselor doesn't seem to help, try another one. This tends to be a long-term problem, but many people have turned it around.

In marriages, a couple will often live in despair, on the verge of divorce. If she knows, the wife feels betrayed and without hope or trust. The husband insists there is no problem, but the wife feels distance in the relationship. Even if she doesn't know for sure, she senses something is wrong. Or she may pretend things are okay. Understanding addiction can help. Often a problem from a person's youth has triggered the addictive behavior. Once the addictive behavior sets in, as much as he tries, usually the person cannot pull out on his own. But divorce isn't the answer. Both husband and wife need to read and study. Books can help the addict realize that he is an addict. Once he admits his problem, he will be more likely to want help. However, because pornography changes the way a person thinks, often the person involved thinks everyone else is overreacting. Support groups are available for spouses as well as for the addict. Once a wife understands that the addiction came quickly and the spouse is, indeed, caught in something that by himself he cannot escape, there is hope.[17]

I would add a word of warning. If treatment is stopped too soon, the offender will often regress dramatically and then truly believe that there is no way out. One authority on this subject, Dr. Matthew Hedelius, notes that an addict over thirty who has been involved for a long period of time may take three to five years activating all four of the essential steps: the bishop, the Atonement, the counselor who has experience with sexual addiction, and the support person.[18]

We elected to come to a telestial world. Things would be unfair. We would live among murderers, whoremongers, and thieves. In the process, we would gain self-control, compassion, and understanding. People addicted to pornography need us to be informed about addiction as well as long-suffering and understanding. Author Steven Cramer said, "I discovered God's love for his children through my family's forgiveness. From the moment of my confession, my selfless wife was able to look beyond her own pain to the need of saving the family. I never felt a moment's revenge. Through the years of struggle, my family's attitude was that we were all in this together. Though I never deserved their love or forgiveness, their actions always affirmed: 'We still love you. We don't understand what you are going through, but it must be awful for you, and we want to help. We still need you, and we want you back as part of us. No matter how long it takes, you can count on us to see it through with you.'"[19] Surely this family followed the plan the Savior would recommend.

Armed with information, we can clean up our communities and protect our families. We need to teach our children that God puts ideas into our minds (D&C 100:5) but that Satan does also (D&C 10:10). We all choose whom to follow. If we teach our children to listen to their feelings, those bad ones that warn us, those peaceful ones that confirm truth to our minds and hearts, and to the joyful ones that are also God-given, we will teach them to be guided by the Spirit.

President Gordon B. Hinckley said: "Oh, how we need in this day and time men and women who will stand up for decency and truth and honesty and virtue and law and order and all of the other good qualities on which our society is founded. . . . Now, I want to say to you, and I say it with a plea in my heart, *get involved*. Get involved on the side of righteousness and truth and decency. . . . God bless you to speak up for truth and decency."[20]

We must listen to a prophet of God when he teaches us about pornography and entertainment. We must follow his counsel to safeguard our homes, our neighborhoods, and our communities.

Notes

1. This same magazine in March 2000 encouraged the sale of a five-video set that didn't sell well when it was introduced in 1989. A supposedly "hot item" in 2000, the five videos featured incest.
2. *American Family Association Journal* (June 2001): 14.
3. Personal communication with psychologist Dr. Rick Hawks.
4. John Harmer, *A War We Must Win: A Frontline Account of the Battle against the Pornography Conspiracy* (Salt Lake City: Bookcraft, 1999), 28–29.
5. Phil Burress, Impact America Conference, 14 April 2000, Fort Mitchell, Kentucky; author's personal notes.

6. John Harmer, training session, September 2000, South Kaysville Stake, Kaysville, Utah; author's personal notes.
7. *Enough is Enough Newsletter*, Fall 2002; reporting the findings of the Crimes Against Children Research Center in interviews with 1,501 youth ages ten to seventeen who used the Internet regularly.
8. Personal communication with author.
9. Victor B. Cline, *Pornography's Effects on Adults & Children* (New York: Morality in Media, 1999), 11.
10. A. Lynn Scoresby, *Bringing Up Moral Children in an Immoral World* (Salt Lake City: Shadow Mountain, 1998), 110.
11. Scoresby, *Bringing up Moral Children*, 109.
12. Phil Burress, Impact America Conference, author's personal notes.
13. Telephone conversation with author, June 2000.
14. Personal communication with author.
15. Burress, Impact America Conference, 2000; author's personal notes.
16. Personal communication with author.
17. The February 2001 *Ensign* contains a story of a couple who worked their way through this problem. The article is entitled "Breaking the Chains of Addiction." Helpful information is also available on the websites ldsmentalhealth.org and strengthenthefamily.net.
18. Personal communication, November 2002, Logan, Utah; Dr. Hedelius added that this was a general statement because no two people's needs are the same. For example, some need a support group or a person throughout their lives. Others perhaps can be successful with a shorter period of counseling.
19. Steven A. Cramer, *The Worth of a Soul: A Personal Account of Excommunication and Conversion* (Springville, Utah: Cedar Fort, 1995), back cover.
20. Gordon B. Hinckley, *Teachings of Gordon B. Hinckley* (Salt Lake City: Deseret Book, 1997), 128.

The Temples of Popular Culture

Mitch Davis

Sixteen years ago, my wife, Michelle, and I moved our young family to the suburbs of Los Angeles to chase the dream of making a difference in Hollywood, starting out with a master's degree in film production at the University of Southern California. I had to commute up to two hours to and from class each day. The academic program was very demanding, and money was scarce. It was a time of great growth and sacrifice for the Davis family.

One day on the way to school, stuck in yet another traffic jam, I began looking around at the city of Los Angeles as if through the eyes of a person from another time. Specifically, I wondered to myself just how much of the modern world would make sense to a Roman centurion from the time of Christ. I was surprised to find that most of what I surveyed through the ancient's eyes would not be that difficult to decipher. I imagined him gazing at the nearby football stadium. "Oh, yes," he nodded, "the coliseum, where your gladiators come to entertain and do great battle." I imagined him scrutinizing my automobile and could hear him discern, correctly, "Your chariot." He then looked out at our freeways and added, "For use on your highway system."

I next imagined that same ancient soldier, standing in front of Grauman's Chinese Theatre in Hollywood. A red carpet flowed onto the sidewalk, and hundreds of people lined up for the next show. "Ah,

---

Mitch Davis, an independent filmmaker, wrote, directed, and executive-produced The Other Side of Heaven. *He has been an executive at Disney, Touchstone, and Columbia studios. He served as a missionary in Argentina and, more recently, as a bishop. He and his wife, Michelle, are the parents of five children.*

yes," the centurion surmised, "your temple, where your people come to worship and to be instructed."

Sitting there in that traffic jam in Los Angeles, I realized that, in taking the movie theater for a temple, the centurion was much more right than wrong. In our modern culture, the movie house has, in fact, become a rarefied place where god-like heroes are created, then worshiped, and where filmmakers are given enormous power to instruct vast, global audiences.

Suddenly, my reverie was over. As capriciously as he had come, the centurion vanished from my imagination, and I was left to ponder the enormous powers of the movie gods, powers which begin but hardly end inside the theaters. Those who create the movies create our popular culture, and those who create popular culture create the world you and I live in.

That the world will be shaped by powerful men and women in these last days should come as no surprise to those of us who revere the Word of Wisdom, which was given "in consequence of evils and designs which do and will exist in the hearts of conspiring men in the last days" (D&C 89:4). It is my belief this verse of scripture is not merely a warning against those who would harm us physically, but also against those who would destroy us spiritually in order to get gain. The same "conspiring men" who would spike the world's cigarettes with extra nicotine would also spike our entertainment with extra sex and violence. In both cases, the objective is the creation of large numbers of consumers blinded by addiction.

I had an experience with blindness during the making of a recent movie, *The Other Side of Heaven*. The movie tells the story of Elder John H. Groberg's missionary experiences in Tonga in the 1950s. Among the more dramatic scenes is one in which Elder Groberg and his Tongan companion, Feki, are caught in a violent hurricane. Filming that scene was particularly challenging since we had to create the entire hurricane from scratch. We commandeered all of the island's fire trucks and stationed a crew with fire hoses around the edges of the set.

We shipped in rain towers from New Zealand, along with three huge fans powered by car engines.

But my favorite effect came from the large mounds of trash we piled alongside those fans. Whenever I yelled, "Action!" a group of guys I called the debris huckers picked up that trash and threw it into the fans, which, in turn, blew it into our actors' faces. Our actors definitely earned their money that day!

The scene's climax occurs when our actors run through a small village and the winds reach such intensity that two huts are literally blown away. We created that effect by connecting each of the huts to huge spring-loaded cords, which would pull them away on cue. For obvious reasons, we saved that shot until the very end of the day. Once those huts were gone, we would have no set to shoot on anymore. As the sun dipped behind the tropical mountains, the time came for our final shot. With only half an hour of good light left, if we didn't get the scene in one take, we would have to come back the next morning, which would put us behind schedule. Four cameras were positioned to record the stunt from various angles.

First, the rain towers and fire hoses began spewing water over the set, then the fans started blowing hurricane force winds, and the debris huckers starting hurling their trash in the air. Our actors stood bravely in the midst of it all, awaiting their cue from me.

I was about to call "Action!" when I noticed a huge torrent of water cascading perilously close to our actors. I followed its source to find one of our special effects technicians up in a scaffold tower, holding a fire hose under one arm. But rather than paying attention to where that hose was pointed, he was holding his personal camcorder to his eye, intent on recording this moment for all posterity.

I asked my assistant director to call him on the radio. No luck. The noise from the fans and rain towers was too loud for him to hear his radio. He tried the radio again, shouting this time. Still no use.

Frustrated, I waved my arms to get this fellow's attention when, suddenly, out of the corner of my eye, I saw our actors starting to run toward me enthusiastically. They charged heroically through the wind and mud as the debris huckers blew trash in their faces. Then I watched in horror as the first hut was blown away, followed by the second. The actors ran up to me, panting but proud of their performance.

"Well," they asked, "how'd it look?"

I turned to our director of photography, who could only shrug haplessly. None of the cameras had been rolling! Furious, I ordered our assistant director to find out who had set off this horrible chain reaction, then retreated to my corner to pout.

A few moments later, the assistant director, a New Zealander, ventured over to me. "I don't know how to tell you this," he said, "but it was you, mate." Evidently, when I waved my arms to get the attention of the guy with the fire hose, the actors thought I was cueing them. The special effects crew saw the actors running and pulled the trigger to blow the huts away.

Our crew had to spend that night rebuilding the set. We all had to return the next day to get the shot that almost was. And it was all my fault. Or was it?

Was it not really the fault of the cad with the camcorder whose misdirected fire hose started the house of cards falling? Or was it not the fault of the actors, who didn't wait for their proper cue?

On reflection I have decided it was none of our faults. The fault, I have decided, was with the hurricane. It was all the debris in the air, which made it impossible for our actors to see clearly and make correct decisions. It was the fault of the debris huckers, enthusiastically filling the air with their trash.

Isn't this exactly what the "conspiring men" do in these last days? They make it hard for you and me—and our children—to see clearly to make correct decisions. They create a hurricane of popular culture whose sole purpose is convincing us we need the things they have for sale. They create psychological, if not physical, addictions in as many consumers as possible.

Let's go back to the idea of spiked movies and spiked cigarettes. From a purely financial point of view, spiking movies with sex and violence is actually more justifiable than spiking cigarettes with nicotine.

It costs only a penny or two to make the average cigarette. It costs tens of millions of dollars to make the average movie.

Let me repeat that last statement for emphasis: *It costs tens of millions of dollars to create the average movie*. As a result, the gatekeepers to cinematic power are, ultimately, always the same people. They are the moneychangers who will do whatever it takes to turn a profit, even if it means selling their audiences' souls by turning theaters into temples of doom.

But it is all too easy for those of us who have never been in their shoes to judge these moneychangers too harshly.

Following my studies at USC, I worked as a junior executive at a major Hollywood studio. One day one of the division presidents grabbed me in the hall and told me he urgently needed me to read a screenplay an agent had just slipped him. He had received the script on a "sneak peek," "first-look" basis and had only three hours to make a preemptive offer.

I dutifully locked myself in my office and dived into the script. As promised, the executive was at my door exactly two hours later for a full report. I began to summarize the script for him, to describe characters and plot points and motivations. After a few moments, the executive stopped me mid sentence. "Enough of that," he snapped. "Let's get to the bottom line. I don't care what this movie is about. I just want to know one thing: Would you spend fifty million dollars to make it tomorrow?"

At that moment, I felt simultaneous sympathy and contempt for this poor, high-level executive. Contempt for the obvious reason: He didn't care one bit what this movie was about! Sympathy for a less obvious reason: I saw the fear lurking behind his eyes, along with the loaded question, should he spend fifty million dollars to make this movie tomorrow?

Suddenly, I realized what this man's life was like, all day, every day. The sum total of his existence was contained in that fearsome conundrum: to spend or not to spend tens of millions of dollars creating seven reels of celluloid, which may or may not have any magic in them. He knew better than I that once the money is all spent, once the cast and crew have gone their ways, all you have to show for a fifty million dollar movie can be carried around inside two small metal containers.

I heard on the news the other day that the Empire State Building was recently sold for fifty-seven million dollars. I ask you to honestly answer this question: Faced with the choice, which would you purchase with your fifty million dollars? Two cans of film, or one of the world's truly great and spacious buildings?

But perhaps I've posed a trick question because this decision is not about the building, but the people for whom it was built. It is the souls of the children of men that are bought and sold in the marketplace of popular culture, and we have been told by one who knows that "the worth of souls is great" (D&C 18:10). How great?

As far as the world's movie producers are concerned, the worth of a soul is seven or eight bucks, even less during matinees. At the end of the day, what they care about most is getting that soul into one of their seats. In order to make that happen, many producers do what many of us would do: They hedge their bets by pandering to humanity's lowest common denominators in hopes that something, anything about their movie will appeal to as many people as possible.

This unfortunate tendency has been fortified by the disintegration of the Iron and Bamboo Curtains. Suddenly, Hollywood is not merely creating popular culture for North America, but for almost the entire planet. Producers now seek to load their movies with even lower common denominators that cross all cultures, regardless of subtitles. In a self-reinforcing, vicious cycle, movies dumb themselves down to lower and lower levels, leading their global audience carefully down to hell.

For years I assumed that prophetic warnings against unworthy movies were merely designed to protect us from polluting our own hearts and minds. I have since realized that our responsibility goes far beyond those narrow confines, particularly in the United States, which, in fact, has become a sort of test market for the much larger global audience. Movies that are embraced by only a few million people in U.S. theaters are routinely delivered to hundreds of millions, even billions of people worldwide in subsequent years. The U.S. box office has become a sort of voting booth where relatively few audience members in a relatively small place vote in or out the cultural icons that will subsequently be exported to all the world.

Never mind that you and your husband only went to see that movie because "there was nothing else to see." Never mind that you covered your children's eyes during all the bad parts. All that Hollywood knows is that *American Pie* played really well in Provo. And if it played well in Provo, well, then, there aren't many places on earth it won't play well. Hollywood executives therefore decide they should make more movies just like it.

For a more extreme example, consider *Hannibal*, a movie about a Chianti-sipping, gentleman cannibal. The world watched that movie become a whopping success in the United States and mistakenly assumed *Hannibal* must therefore be a good movie. The world swallowed *Hannibal* whole, and pundits from every nation, kindred, tongue, and people pontificated on all that was artful about the cannibal's complex character.

As discouragingly negative as these trends may seem, my message to you today is actually one of hope and encouragement. You see, you and I face an historic opportunity: Rather than choosing to live in a lowest common denominator world, to raise our children in a culture inexorably circling the drain, we can choose to change that world.

That choice may seem overwhelming, but the truth is, we don't really have a choice. The scriptures make clear that we have been created "to act, not to be acted upon" (see 2 Nephi 2:14). Prophets, ancient and modern, have decreed that good will ultimately triumph over evil. The morning will break! The shadows will flee![1] But this will not happen until we more effectively follow the Savior's command to lift our light high, that it might give light to all within the house (Matthew 5:15).

The prophet Isaiah foresaw the day when we will, in fact, succeed in replacing popular culture with a millennial culture. In that day, "They shall not hurt nor destroy in all my holy mountain: for *the earth shall be full of the knowledge of the Lord, as the waters cover the sea*" (Isaiah 11:9; emphasis added).

The Prophet Joseph Smith declared, "The truth of God will go forth boldly, nobly, and independent, till it has *penetrated every continent, visited every clime, swept every country, and sounded in every ear.*"[2]

President Spencer W. Kimball prophesied that "our moving picture specialists, with the inspiration of heaven, should tomorrow be able to produce a masterpiece which would . . . run for months *in every movie center, cover every part of the globe.*"[3]

Do you see how President Kimball's prophecy helps fulfill the others? Can you envision the day when hundreds of millions, even billions of people, will be brought light through the same pervasive delivery systems that now routinely deliver darkness?

Either we envision that day, or we envision our inevitable doom.

No longer can we sit in the safety of the sidelines and hurl epithets at a popular culture we have failed to replace or change. No longer can we decry all the world has to offer without stepping onto the stage and providing a viable alternative. "As well might man stretch forth his puny arm to stop the Missouri River in its decreed course" (D&C 121:33) as might we expect to supplant popular culture with the mere absence of culture.

Who can deny that today, as anciently, there is "a famine in the land, not a famine of bread, nor a thirst for water, but of hearing the words of the Lord"? (Amos 8:11). Who can walk through one of our modern multiplexes and not mourn for the muddled masses, wandering "to and fro," seeking and not finding? (Amos 8:12). Who can deny that, in our day, on our watch, "the fair virgins and young men faint for thirst"? (Amos 8:13). Who can deny our imperative duty to speak to those young men and women "after the manner of their language, that they might come to understanding"? (D&C 1:24).

In his time, the Savior found himself in a predicament much like ours, as he also encountered moneychangers in the temple, perverting the hearts and minds of the people. His course of action is both instructive and inspirational: "And Jesus went up to Jerusalem, and found in the temple those that sold oxen and sheep and doves, and the changers of money sitting: and when he had made a scourge of small cords, he drove them all out of the temple . . . and poured out the changers' money, and overthrew the tables" (John 2:13–15). "And he taught, saying unto them, Is it not written, My house shall be called of all nations the house of prayer? but ye have made it a den of thieves" (Mark 11:17). "And the blind and the lame came to him in the temple; and he healed them" (Matthew 21:14).

I think it is significant that he who was without sin fiercely defended the sanctity of the temple in his time. It is poignant that the creator of heaven and earth sat down and, with his own hands, created "a scourge of small cords" with which to drive out the trespassers. And it is exemplary that the first thing he did upon reclaiming the temple was turn it into a place of healing and instruction.

May we also make the urgent effort necessary to take back the secular temples of our time. May we "boldly, nobly, and independent[ly]" do our part to fill the earth with the knowledge of the Lord, "as the waters cover the sea." May we pay the necessary price to take our place on the world stage, from which vantage we may speak to all of God's children, "after the manner of their language."

Notes

1. See Parley P. Pratt, "The Morning Breaks," *Hymns of the Church of Jesus Christ of Latter-day Saints* (Salt Lake City: The Church of Jesus Christ of Latter-day Saints, 1985), no. 1.
2. Joseph Smith, in *Church History and Modern Revelation*, by Joseph Fielding Smith, 4 vols. (Salt Lake City: The Church of Jesus Christ of Latter-day Saints, 1946–49), 4:98; emphasis added.
3. Spencer W. Kimball, "Education for Eternity," *Speeches of the Year, 1967–68* (Provo: Brigham Young University Press, 1968), 12–19; excerpted in "The Gospel Vision of the Arts," *Ensign*, July 1977, 2; emphasis added.

Politics and the Atonement

Thomas B. Griffith

The year is 1830. The Prophet Joseph Smith has just published the Book of Mormon and organized the restored Church of Jesus Christ. He is engaged in an intensive study of the Bible, part of his ongoing effort to organize the fledgling Church according to the model the Lord is revealing to him. While studying, pondering, and praying over the book of Genesis, Joseph learns from the Lord the remarkable story of a prophet who is mentioned only briefly there. The prophet was Enoch, and his story was to become a model for the infant Church. "And the Lord called his people Zion, because they were of one heart and one mind, and dwelt in righteousness; and there was no poor among them. And Enoch continued his preaching in righteousness unto the people of God. And it came to pass in his days, that he built a city that was called the City of Holiness, even Zion" (Moses 7:18–19). As far as we know, what Enoch and his people achieved has never been duplicated.

Enoch and his people fired the heart, mind, and soul of the early Church. What was it about the people of Enoch that allowed them to model perfectly what it means to prepare to meet the Lord? The key, I believe, is in verse 18: "They were of *one* heart and *one* mind, and dwelt in righteousness; and there was no poor among them" (emphasis added). The people of Enoch achieved at-one-ment with God, with themselves, with their families, and with their community. They set the mark for true spirituality.

Spirituality begins when we allow Christ's atoning sacrifice and his

---

Thomas B. Griffith is assistant to the president and general counsel at Brigham Young University, having served previously as Senate legal counsel of the United States. A stake president, he and his wife, Susan Griffith, are the parents of six children.

awe-inspiring grace to heal the wounds that sin has inflicted upon our broken hearts, thereby uniting us with God. But from Enoch and his people, we learn that the highest form of spirituality is radiating the effects of the Atonement beyond ourselves and our families to unite our communities. The work of community building is, I believe, the crowning spiritual work to which we are called. All other work is preparatory.

Now, here is the thought I offer: Building a community that extends beyond your family or congregation involves politics. Properly understood, the highest role of a politician is to build communities. A key contribution that emerges from the world's experience with democratic governance is the understanding that successful political communities must be built on the rule of law.

The rule of law is the idea, of staggering importance in the progress of humankind, that a political community should not be organized according to the principle that *might makes right*. Rather, a community and its laws should reflect the reality that each person is a child of God and, by virtue of that fact alone, is entitled to be treated with dignity, respect, and fairness. The most famous expression of this radical idea came from the pen of Thomas Jefferson: "We hold these truths to be self-evident, that all men are created equal, that they are endowed by their Creator with certain unalienable rights, that among these are Life, Liberty, and the Pursuit of Happiness—that to secure these Rights, Governments are instituted among Men, deriving their just powers from the consent of the governed."[1]

Jefferson was correct to ground the rule of law in the fact that a creator has endowed each human with rights. But Christians understand more. We know that every human being has dignity, not only because we have been created by God, but because we have also been redeemed by God. The Lord Jesus Christ suffered, bled, and died for each member of the human family so that all who accept his act of gracious love would have access to the power of his redemption.

As Latter-day Saints, we, of all people, should value the worth of souls because we have revelations that teach us the depth of the Lord's love for each member of the human family (D&C 19:16–19). If our Savior has been willing to endure such incomprehensible suffering for our fellowmen, how can we do anything but exert all our efforts to serve them, too?

The great C. S. Lewis, with uncommon understanding, wrote: "It is a serious thing to live in a society of possible gods and goddesses, to remember that the dullest and most uninteresting person you can talk to may one day be a creature which, if you saw it now, you would be strongly tempted to worship. . . . It is in the light of these overwhelming possibilities, it is with the awe and circumspection proper to them, that we should conduct all our dealings with one another, all friendships, all loves, all play, all politics. There are no ordinary people. You have never talked to a mere mortal. . . . Next to the Blessed Sacrament itself, your neighbour is the holiest object presented to your senses."[2]

Community building, the proper aim of politics, assumes its proper importance when we approach an understanding of what the Savior has done for each human being. That is the calling of politicians: to build communities that lead us in the direction of a Zion society, a place where the power of the Atonement unites us.

I realize that the picture of politics I have just painted is, shall we say, idealized. I am well aware that most politicians are hardly the primary emissaries of the Atonement. But, many Latter-day Saints make two equal and opposite mistakes about politics. First, those involved are all heroic role models. This is a mistake common among the young who are looking for icons to emulate. The danger here is obvious. When the young discover that political leaders are, and always have been, fallible humans, they become disillusioned. No one can measure up to the idealized histories we mistakenly use to fan the flames of patriotic fervor. Naivete is not a virtue. We should abandon it. Remember, our Lord taught us to be as "wise as serpents" (Matthew 10:16; D&C 111:11).

The second mistake is more common to the experienced: cynicism. It finds its expression in the persistently low view most people have of politicians, as shown in such jokes as "How can you tell when a politician is lying? When he moves his lips." The danger of this cynical view is disengagement.

When I was Senate legal counsel, I was frequently asked what I thought about the character of the senators. I responded that the one hundred members of the United States Senate are different from any one hundred people taken randomly from the pages of the phone book in only one regard: each is extremely ambitious. Some are gentlemen; some are knaves. Some are brilliant; others less so. Some are earnest; others are not. Some are devout; others profligate.

Why should the rather unremarkable realization that politicians are fallible and act mainly in their own self-interest be allowed to justify a lack of engagement in politics? That they act this way is an assumption the Framers took to be the starting point of wisdom in governance. If I am correct that the highest purpose of politics—community building—is an extension of the work of atonement, how can we possibly justify not participating in this work because the people involved are imperfect? If dealing with messy humanity exempted us from the work of the Atonement, then preaching the gospel, redeeming the dead, and perfecting the Saints would be more like the activities of an elite social club instead of the work of universal salvation.

Interestingly, at the very core of the Atonement is the suffering Redeemer surrounded by fallible mortals acting in their own self-interest. On the eve of Christ's suffering and after having spent three years in training with the Savior, the Twelve argued over who was the greatest (Luke 22:24–27); one of them betrayed Christ for money (Luke 22:3–6); the chief apostle and soon-to-be presiding authority in the Church denied that he knew Christ when it was too dangerous to acknowledge him, and, to add insult to injury, swore in doing so (Mark 14:66–72). If the Savior shrank not from carrying out the work of atonement in the midst of fallible humans motivated by greed and selfishness, how can we excuse our involvement in politics simply because—surprise, surprise—politicians, like all other human beings, have not yet attained perfection? Like the work of salvation, politics, too, is messy.

Yet, we should not be naive. The work of politics is fraught with spiritual dangers. Robert Bolt's play *A Man for All Seasons*, based on the last years of the life of St. Thomas More, the patron saint of politicians, illustrates those dangers. The lord chancellor of England (akin to today's prime minister), More was also the most widely respected person in England because of his piety and erudition. He was a leader of the New Thinking that was the hallmark of the Renaissance. More was a devoted family man actively involved in the education of his sons and, most remarkable for his time, his daughters. A passionate, devout Roman Catholic, More saw much in the church that needed reform, yet he was committed to the church that he believed was founded by the Lord.

More found himself caught between his allegiance to the crown and the church when King Henry VIII declared himself head of the church in England and renounced the authority of the pope. To secure his position, Henry required each of his subjects to swear an oath of allegiance recognizing him as supreme head of the church in England. More refused, resigned his office, and was eventually imprisoned for his recalcitrance. The climactic scene of Bolt's play is his trial. The charge is treason; the penalty is death. Thomas Cromwell, his political enemy and prosecutor, knows that More has done nothing worthy of the charge of treason, not having voiced his reasons for refusing to swear to the oath. Under the law, his silence should protect him. Cromwell's ruse is to find a witness who will perjure himself and accuse More of speaking out against the king. He finds Richard Rich, an aspiring young man who earlier in the play had visited the More household, hoping to win an appointment to government office. More, however, saw in Rich the weakness of character that would make him ill-suited to hold a position of power where he would be the target of bribes.

The stage is now set for the climax. More, the accused, beaten down from months of imprisonment in the Tower of London, sits alone, dressed in a simple monk-like tattered gown. Rich, decked out in the finery of a dandy, is called as the witness. He takes an oath to tell the truth and then perjures himself by falsely testifying that More made treasonous statements to him. Cromwell excuses Rich from the stand. As Rich steps down, More, knowing that this testimony will lead to his death, says:

"**MORE:** I have one question to ask the witness. (Rich stops) That's a chain of office you are wearing. (Reluctantly Rich faces him) May I see it? (Norfolk [the judge] motions him to approach. More examines the medallion) The red dragon. (To Cromwell) What's this?

"**CROMWELL:** Sir Richard is appointed Attorney-General for Wales.

"**MORE:** (Looking into Rich's face with pain and amusement) For Wales? Why, Richard, it profits a man nothing to give his soul for the whole world . . . but for Wales!"[3]

Now, my ancestors are from Wales, but I get the point. What is it that we are willing to gain in this world at the price of losing our souls? If our participation in politics is, in the words of Doctrine and Covenants 121:37, for "our pride, our vain ambition, or to exercise control or dominion or compulsion upon the souls of the children of men, in any degree of unrighteousness," we will lose our souls.

Remember the words of the Savior to his disciples after they had seen a rich young man turn down a call to join them because he was unwilling to sell his many possessions, give the proceeds to the poor, and follow Jesus and the disciples. "I tell you the truth," Jesus said. "It is hard for a rich man to enter the kingdom of heaven. Again, I tell you, it is easier for a camel to pass through the eye of a needle than for a rich man to enter the Kingdom of God" (NIV Matthew 19:23–24).

C. S. Lewis notes that the riches referred to by the Lord here cover more than riches in the ordinary sense. They "really cover . . . riches in every sense—good fortune, health, popularity, and all the things one wants to have."[4] If Lewis is right (and C. S. Lewis is almost always right when it comes to matters of discipleship), each of us stands in peril when we are motivated by anything other than a profound sense of gratitude to the Savior for his atoning sacrifice. President Spencer W. Kimball had strong words for us on this point. If we are motivated by "riches," he said, we are latter-day "idolaters."[5] Few human activities are more susceptible to this form of idolatry than politics.

In his mercy, where the Lord gives such an ominous warning, he also provides a sure means of escape, although it is rarely an easy way out. Let's return to the book of Moses. If the people of Enoch are to be our role models for how we should work to carry out the effects of the Atonement in society, Moses 7:18 describes what we should be doing. Four characteristics of their Zion society are noted. They were of "one heart" and "one mind." Those qualities underscore that Zion building is at-one-ment at work, but I am not exactly certain what these traits, susceptible to many interpretations, mean. So, too, with the third trait: They "dwelt in righteousness." The fourth trait, however, is clear: "There was no poor among them." One of the most consistent themes in the revelations given to the Prophet Joseph is the message that we are, in the words of Doctrine and Covenants 38:35, to "look to the poor and the needy, and administer to their relief that they shall not suffer." We extend the effects of the Atonement to its farthest reaches by creating a society that has as its goal helping those who have been left behind.

Let me clarify that I find nothing wrong, and indeed see much good, in the creation of wealth. The issue is the purpose for which the wealth is sought and the ends to which wealth is put.

Remember the counsel of Jacob, the brother of Nephi: "Think of your brethren like unto yourselves, and be familiar with all and free with your substance, that they may be rich like unto you. But before ye seek for riches, seek ye for the kingdom of God. And after ye have obtained a hope in Christ ye shall obtain riches, if ye seek them" (Jacob 2:17–19). That is a great promise: The material wealth we spend so much of our lives pursuing will be ours. But, as you might have guessed, there is a catch, revealed in a close examination of what Jacob said. The promise is only to those who seek riches "for the intent to do good." But what does that mean? Doesn't the phrase "do[ing] good" allow considerable room to maneuver? Jacob closed that loophole in the very next phrase. By "do[ing] good" with riches, the Lord means "to clothe the naked, and to feed the hungry, and to liberate the captive, and administer relief to the sick and the afflicted" (v. 19).

Are those our goals as a people? Are those our goals in pursuing our vocation? They must be. Our participation in society, something we are called to do by our understanding of the Savior's love for all humankind, must have as its primary purpose this definition of doing good.

Let me conclude with the words that first inspired me to get involved in public life. They come from my boyhood hero, Robert F. Kennedy, and, although they remind me of how far short of the mark I have fallen, I hope they remain a lodestar. "There is discrimination in New York, apartheid in South Africa, and serfdom in the mountains of Peru. People starve in the streets of India; intellectuals go to jail in Russia; thousands are slaughtered in Indonesia; wealth is lavished on armaments everywhere. These are differing evils, but they are the common works of man. They reflect the imperfection of human justice, the inadequacy of human compassion, the defectiveness of our sensibility towards the sufferings of our fellows; they mark the limit of our ability to use knowledge for the well-being of others. And, therefore, they call upon common qualities of conscience and indignation, a shared determination to wipe away the unnecessary sufferings of our fellow human beings at home and around the world."[6]

"[Let no one be discouraged by] the belief there is nothing one man or one woman can do against the enormous array of the world's ills—against misery and ignorance, injustice and violence. . . . Few will have the greatness to bend history itself; but each of us can work to change a small portion of events, and in the total of all those acts will be written the history of this generation. It is from numberless diverse acts of courage and belief that human history is shaped. Each time a man stands up for an ideal, or acts to improve the lot of others, or strikes out against injustice, he sends a tiny ripple of hope, and crossing each other from a million different centers of energy and daring, those ripples build a current which can sweep down the mightiest walls of oppression and resistance."[7]

We must get involved in our society to help those who have been left out or behind. We have a robust debate about the best way to do that. And, as a political conservative, I am certain that I would strongly disagree with my boyhood hero's views about how to get there. But I believe that the goal must be the same.

Notes

1. Declaration of Independence, paragraph 2.
2. C. S. Lewis, *The Weight of Glory and Other Addresses*, rev. ed. (New York: Macmillan, Collier Books, 1980), 18–19.
3. Robert Bolt, *A Man for All Seasons* (New York: Random House, 1960), 5.
4. C. S. Lewis, *God in the Dock: Essays on Theology and Ethics*, ed. Walter Hooper (Grand Rapids, Mich.: Eerdmans, 1970), 51–52.
5. Spencer W. Kimball, "The False Gods We Worship," *Ensign*, June 1976, 4–5.
6. William J. Vanden Heuvel, "Day of Affirmation Address," 6 June 1966, University of Capetown, in *On His Own: Robert F. Kennedy, 1964–1968* (Garden City, N.Y.: Doubleday, 1970), 156.
7. Arthur M. Schlesinger, Jr., *Robert Kennedy and His Times* (Boston: Houghton Mifflin, 1978), 745–46.

Patience—in the Process of Time

Coleen K. Menlove

When I shared with my husband that I had been asked to speak on patience, his spontaneous reply was, "Oh, the Lord really knows you and what you need." That was a humbling but accurate statement. My first impression was that if the Lord had instructed the BYU Women's Conference committee to help me focus on understanding and developing patience, it must be important and I had better be about it. It has become a research project for me. The Lord has gently guided me with daily opportunities to learn more about my attitudes and my habits related to patience and impatience. My family has been assisting me, or better said, checking up on me. A public declaration of your desire to work on a virtue can come back to haunt you. Let me share with you three things that I have learned as I have focused on patience, and perhaps this can be the take-home message. First, patience is part of Heavenly Father's plan; second, we can learn to be more patient; and third, we can start right now to become patient.

Patience Is Part of Heavenly Father's Plan

We might assume we know what patience is, and we could even hastily assume we are patient. Let's look more closely and see if there is need to improve. The dictionary defines *patience* as the bearing of pain

---

Coleen K. Menlove was sustained as general president of the Primary in October 1999. She previously served on the Young Women General Board and as a member of several Church writing committees. She and her husband, Dean W. Menlove, are the parents of seven children and the grandparents of eight.

or sorrow calmly or without complaint; not being hasty or impetuous; being steadfast despite opposition, difficulty, or adversity.

Children say that patience is waiting, waiting nicely, waiting nicely for a long time. At our house, we have a saying about patience that has been passed down from generations before. It is, "Every dog has his day, and you're still a pup." Elder Neal A. Maxwell has said that patience is "accepting a divine rhythm to life"—allowing Heavenly Father's plan to unfold. "Patience is . . . being willing . . . to submit . . . to what the scriptures call the 'process of time.'"[1]

However you describe patience, it is important in the scriptures, as the word *patient* or *patience* appears more than eighty times. Patience is a virtue attributed to God the Father and Jesus Christ. In Mosiah we are asked if we have "come to a knowledge of the goodness of God, and his matchless power, and his wisdom, and his patience, and his long-suffering towards the children of men" (Mosiah 4:6).

The apostle Paul said, "Let us run with patience the race that is set before us, looking unto Jesus the author and finisher of our faith" (Hebrews 12:1–2). As in all things, we look to Jesus Christ and his life for understanding and for an example of how to run the race with patience. As we take the yoke of Christ upon us, we learn of him and how to be like him (Matthew 11:29). Elder Maxwell reassures us that "even though our experiences are micro compared to [the Savior's,] the process is the same."[2] The Prophet Joseph Smith learned that patience has a refining role in preparing us for "a more exceeding and eternal weight of glory" (D&C 63:66). After Joseph Smith's experience in the Sacred Grove, he was required to wait. He waited patiently for more than three years before the angel Moroni appeared to him. And then more waiting and more patience were required in order to learn necessary lessons.

Knowledge of the eternal plan of happiness gives us hope and reassurance for today and for eternity. Elder Maxwell teaches that patience is being willing "to watch the unfolding [process] of God with a sense of wonder and awe—rather than pacing up and down within the cell of our circumstance."[3] We have been given the amazing gift of the Holy

Ghost to teach, guide, calm, and comfort us. As we seek, listen, and respond to the Spirit, it will testify to the truth of the plan of happiness. Feelings of panic can be replaced with peace and joy because we know our potential for eternal life with Heavenly Father and his Son Jesus Christ. This knowledge makes enduring to the end—and all through the middle—a much more meaningful and enjoyable experience.

We need to trust that the Lord will fulfill his promises in his own due time. "When we are . . . impatient, we are suggesting that we know what is best" and that all should march to our timetable and not rely upon Heavenly Father and his divine plan.[4] In the stage production *Savior of the World,* Zacharias and Elisabeth proclaim, "[I will] give God forever to make me what I am—give my plans, and give my dreams, [and] give up all my fretful schemes."[5]

Elder Jeffrey R. Holland helps us understand the significance of submitting our will to the Father's. He described the appearance of the Savior to those on this continent: "In an initial and profound moment of spellbinding wonder, when surely [Christ had] the attention of every man, woman, and child, . . . his submission to his Father is the first and most important thing he wishes us to know about himself.

"Frankly, I am a bit haunted by the thought that this is the first and most important thing he may want to know about *us* when we meet him one day in similar fashion. Did *we* obey, even if it was painful? Did *we* submit, even if the cup was bitter indeed? Did we yield to a vision higher and holier than our own . . . ?"[6] As we follow the example of the Savior, we will learn to submit our will to the Father's will and do his will in his way.

You know, it's not fashionable in today's world to submit to anyone or anything. Submission will appear to many as wimpish and feeble. A popular fast-food chain motto promotes, "Have it your way." Our way may not be consistent with the Lord's way. It takes conviction to submit patiently. It takes trust that the Lord knows best the purpose of our life. Oh, there will be many who will say, "You can't do it," or "Give it up," or "It's too hard," and even "It isn't worth it." But our best guidance doesn't come from the voices of the world. It comes from the sweet Spirit of the Holy Ghost confirming the purpose of our patience.

We must take care, though, that our abilities do not interfere with our humility and our desire to submit to the Lord. A mission president told me about a missionary who came to his mission. A well-accomplished young man, he was physically attractive, an athlete, and an excellent scholar. He was determined to be the best missionary ever, according to his definition of "best missionary." When things didn't go well, his solution was to put in more time, to work harder. In the past, it had seemed that his abilities and natural talents had been sufficient for success. But missionary work had a lesson for this elder to learn. He began to understand what it means to patiently submit to the will of the Lord.

We Can Learn to Be More Patient

The second part of the take-home message is that we can learn to be more patient. A few years ago, I opened a fortune cookie and found this message inside: "What you are doing now is insufficient for the future." It is not good enough to claim that patience is not in our genes, or that we are a type A personality and we can't help our nature. Let's look at what is needed to develop the godly virtue of patience. But I want to warn you that the more I have tried to develop greater patience, the more aware I am of how impatient I am and how patient others are.

Here are two suggestions to consider: first, we need to adjust our expectations to our knowledge of Heavenly Father's plan; and second, we need to learn to wait upon the Lord.

Adjust your expectations to your knowledge of Heavenly Father's plan. There seems to be an unending supply of challenges for all of us. There are so many opportunities for us to learn the kind of patience that requires us to "be still and know that [he is] God" (D&C 101:16). Even patience with a deadline will give opportunities to learn. I spent considerable time studying and pondering what would be important to say today. I patiently waited for what a friend calls "the talk angels" to deliver the pages, at least hint at the words, and finally just to give comfort. And I was really calm until this deadline came uncomfortably close. The Lord has so much to teach me about patience with a deadline. It is humbling to realize that the best thoughts for this talk may come to me as I'm driving home today.

We often expect instantaneous solutions. We want immediate rescue, which is the very thing that will remove our opportunities to develop that which we have been sent to become—like the Savior.

Elder Richard G. Scott reminds us: "You are here on earth for a divine purpose. It is not to be endlessly entertained or to be constantly in full pursuit of pleasure. You are here to be tried, to prove yourself so that you can receive the additional blessings God has for you. The tempering effect of patience is required. Some blessings will be delivered here in this life; others will come beyond the veil. The Lord is intent on your personal growth and development. . . . If you question everything you are asked to do, or dig in your heels at every unpleasant challenge, you make it harder for the Lord to bless you."[7]

God's commitment to agency requires commitment to patience. As God has patience with us, we need patience with ourselves and with others. We can't override the agency of others and take from them that which God has given. Angela, a fifth-grade student, learned about the agency of others when she took the counsel of her mother and she fasted and prayed that another fifth-grade girl would stop being mean to her. But the next day at school did not go as Angela had planned. The girl she had prayed for was instrumental in framing Angela as the culprit who vandalized the girl's restroom. Angela was stunned when the principal called her into his office and accused her of the crime. When she arrived home, she was very upset. She had fasted and prayed. She had used all her faith that Heavenly Father would make this girl be nice. Mother's response was, "Angela, we can't pray away another person's agency, no matter how much faith we have. When we pray for our enemies, it changes how we feel about them and brings us peace. *We* change for the better, and sometimes our goodness helps our enemies to change. Sadly, some never change. But we should never let our enemies choose how we will act."[8] We, too, can learn patience with others as we honor their use of agency.

Wait upon the Lord and allow for the process of time. But "patience is not indifference. Actually, [it's] caring very much, but being willing, nevertheless, to submit both to the Lord and to what the scriptures call the 'process of time.'"[9] "While the scriptural phrase 'in process of time' means 'eventually,' it also denotes an entire spiritual process: 'The Lord showed unto Enoch all the inhabitants of the earth; and he beheld, and lo, Zion, in process of time, was taken up into heaven (Moses 7:21).'

"By itself, . . . the passage of time does not bring an automatic advance . . . we often need the 'process of time' in order to come to our spiritual senses. . . . Many spiritual outcomes require saving truths to be mixed with time."[10]

As we have said, Joseph Smith learned to wait upon the Lord. He waited for the plates, he waited in prison—he waited for the Lord's purposes. And what did he do while he was waiting upon the Lord? He prayed, he sang, he wrote, he obeyed, and the Lord was with him. Waiting time can be productive time. It is a time to pray, to fast, study the scriptures, renew covenants, obey, ponder, and learn from others.

During my years as a young mother of seven children, I was a Relief Society visiting teacher to an older sister who was suffering with a terminal illness. She sat in her chair most of the day with a table piled high with medications by her side. She had been very generous with her means and her home. She had children and grandchildren living with her, and she often tended one or two of her grandchildren while their parents worked. But her response to this pain was, "I love being alive, and I love being with these children." They called her "Grandmother Dear." She was an inspiration to me as I was struggling in good health to meet the needs of my young children. I have since adopted the title of Grandmother Dear—to remind me of this dear sister's good works even while she was patiently suffering.

Another lesson in patience came from a neighborhood child, Rebecca. Rebecca is now eight years old, but when she was a toddler she occasionally wandered into my yard and became a regular visitor by the time she was three. One fall I invested money and time in purchasing and planting numerous flower bulbs. The next spring I woke up early each morning and walked around the yard to inventory and enjoy the progress of the daffodils, the tulips, and the hyacinths.

And then the morning came when the flowers were in full, glorious bloom, and I felt I had truly achieved the status of a master gardener. But that afternoon as I turned into my driveway, there was not a blossom to be seen. When my car reached the end of the driveway, I saw where my flowers had gone. My Alberta spruce was covered with an extensive floral arrangement. The name *Rebecca* came to my mind. This was a serious test for me. I had to decide whom I loved most, the neighbor's child or my precious flowers that I had so lovingly planted and whose beauty I had so hopefully imagined during those long, cold winter months.

The decision was made—I could love both. I knew from that moment that I could continue my love for flowers and also develop a loving relationship with Rebecca. In fact, the flowers would be the way to develop that relationship. We obviously had something in common—we both loved flowers! The only difference was that I liked flowers in the ground connected to their bulbs, and she liked them without stems stuck on a tree! I might be able to share my love of flowers with her, and I knew she had much to teach me—starting with patience and mercy. Magic began to happen between us. That same spring Rebecca helped me take the marigolds out of the pony packs so I could plant them in the ground. And the following spring, when Rebecca was five, she helped me clear the ground and prepare it for planting. The next year she helped me very carefully plant the flowers. She stayed and worked until bedtime while my own children were off with their friends. Even I was ready to quit long before Rebecca lost interest. Again, Rebecca taught me patience.

Rebecca has often left things on my doorstep. One afternoon, as I rushed home with much on my mind, I was surprised by more Rebecca magic on my porch. This time it was a picture Rebecca had made of flowers and a rainbow. On the back of the picture, she had written the words "I love you" and "I love being me." Thank you, Rebecca. You have taught me much about patience. And we, like Rebecca, can love being who we are as we feel the joy of learning lessons we have been sent here to learn.

I realize that this experience is not as challenging as many of the events some of you have faced. But I have shared it because it may be a "while we are at it" moment—one of the seemingly insignificant opportunities that go unnoticed and underestimated and even undervalued for development of patience.

We Can Start Right Now to Become Patient

The third part of the take-home message is that we can start right now to become patient. It's not enough to know what patience is and how to be more patient; we need to become more patient, to become Christlike. What is it that challenges your patience? Is it loneliness due to the death of a loved one? Is it physical or spiritual pain? Or is it as simple as the monotony of daily problems such as the lack of sleep because of an infant's crying or a youth out late at night? Is it a child with a disability who requires more focused attention, or perhaps a son of missionary age who is not ready to go on a mission? Does the neighbor's dog bark night and day? Has your long-range planning experienced a shortfall? Do you have parents who are aging and need your patient assistance?

We can learn to find purpose and joy in whatever season of life or circumstances we find ourselves. Elder Scott tells us that "after their noble husbands were called home, Sister Camilla Kimball, Amelia McConkie, and Helen Richards learned to paint. They not only left legacies of art, but they never saw a sunset, a face, or a tree the same again."[11] We, too, can develop talents that sharpen our capacity to reason, to act, and to find purpose in life. They give a renewal, a spark of enthusiasm, and a zest for life. Make a list of things you can do to bring happiness to yourself and to others while you are waiting upon the Lord's own due time. Experiences such as writing a thank-you note, adding an extra few minutes of ponder time to scripture study, and maybe just smiling more will be part of your process of time.

The Lord has said, "Be patient in afflictions, for thou shalt have many; but endure them, for, lo, I am with thee, even unto the end of thy days" (D&C 24:8). "As you are patient, you will come to understand what the statement 'I am with [you]' means. God's love brings peace and joy."[12]

Yesterday has passed, and tomorrow is not yet here, but today is our day to live. Harold B. Lee counseled, "Don't try to live too many days ahead. Seek for strength to attend to the problems of today. . . .

"Do all that you can do and leave the rest to God, the Father of us all. [It's] not enough to say I will do my best, but rather, I will do everything which is [in] my power; I will do all that is necessary."[13]

Elder Maxwell's talk on patience that I referred to earlier was given a few years before he was diagnosed with leukemia and spent forty-six days and nights in the hospital enduring debilitating chemotherapy. He found comfort in a scripture that he'd often quoted to others who were suffering: "I know that [God] loveth his children; nevertheless, I do not know the meaning of all things" (1 Nephi 11:17).[14]

What do we do when things are not as we wish? We seek strength from the Spirit to keep trying. "Sometimes that which we are doing is correct enough but simply needs to be persisted in—patiently—not for [just] a minute or a moment but sometimes for years."[15] When we go to bed at night, we can say prayers of thanks as we think about the opportunities we have been given to practice patience, and we can smile at our step-by-step growth to "run with patience the race that is set before us." Success will come by daily hanging onto the desire to look "unto Jesus the author and finisher of our faith" (Hebrews 12:1–2).

The take-home message for this time together is this: Patience is part of Heavenly Father's plan, we can learn to be more patient, and we can start right now to become patient. We have received a mighty promise in the Book of Mormon: "Because of your diligence and your faith and your patience . . . ye shall pluck the fruit . . . which is most precious, which is sweet above all that is sweet . . . ye shall reap the rewards of your faith, and your diligence, and patience" (Alma 32:42–43).

We are on a journey to exaltation. Earthly experiences have a purpose and will bring opportunities to fulfill our divine potential. "God's court is filled with those who have patiently overcome—whose company we do not yet deserve."[16] The godly virtue of patience will bring the power to overcome challenges, the assurance of the Savior's love as we seek his help, and genuine joy in his eternal plan. I testify that Heavenly Father will always be there to guide, to lift, and to love us.

Notes

1. Neal A. Maxwell, "Patience," *Ensign*, October 1980, 28.
2. Neal A. Maxwell, "'Endure It Well,'" *Ensign*, May 1990, 33.
3. Maxwell, "Patience," 28–29.
4. Maxwell, "Patience," 28.
5. "I'll Give God Forever," *Savior of the World*, musical drama, The Church of Jesus Christ of Latter-day Saints.
6. Jeffrey R. Holland, "The Will of the Father in All Things," *Brigham Young University 1989–99 Devotional and Fireside Speeches* (Provo: Brigham Young University Press, 1999), 76–77; see also Jeffrey R. Holland and Patricia T. Holland, *On Earth As It Is in Heaven* (Salt Lake City: Deseret Book, 1989), 126; emphasis added.
7. Richard G. Scott, "Finding Joy in Life," *Ensign*, May 1996, 24.
8. Lisa H. Fernelius, "Fiction: Prayers and Faith," *Friend*, November 1999, 44; emphasis in original.
9. Maxwell, "Patience," 28.
10. Maxwell, "'Endure It Well,'" 34.
11. Scott, "Finding Joy," 24.
12. Scott, "Finding Joy," 24.
13. Harold B. Lee, Conference Report, October 1970, 117–18; or "Time to Prepare to Meet God," *Improvement Era*, December 1970, 28–30; see also *Harold B. Lee*, [vol. 3] in *Teachings of Presidents of the Church* series (Salt Lake City: The Church of Jesus Christ of Latter-day Saints, 2000), 8.
14. Bruce C. Hafen, *A Disciple's Life: The Biography of Neal A. Maxwell* (Salt Lake City: Deseret Book, 2002), 11–12.
15. Maxwell, "Patience," 28.
16. Maxwell, "Patience," 29.

DIVINE TIMING

Elaine S. Marshall

I have a timing dysfunction. I've come to believe that timing is a talent or gift probably distributed at some meeting I missed. The problem is best expressed in my inability to get on or off an escalator. It doesn't seem natural to me that stairs should move. When I was young, it didn't matter. The only escalator in my universe was at Grayson's Department store on Washington Boulevard. But now they are everywhere—at airports, in hotels, in subway stations. I can't tell when to get on and when to get off. I stand and wait, and rock back and forth, and hesitate. Everyone in my family has tried to help. My son Chad once rocked with me, saying gently, "Mom, you can do this." My husband says with poorly veiled impatience, "Just close your eyes and step on!"

Unfortunately, my anxiety has been confirmed by other events on the conveyor belts of my life. Those moving steps of life seem to come too early or too late, and I often trip getting on or off. I sometimes mistake divine timing as either heavenly interference in my personal plan or endless waiting on the Lord for something I think I deserve now. Earlier this year, Elder Dallin H. Oaks reminded me that "we cannot have true faith in the Lord without also having complete trust in the Lord's will and the Lord's timing."[1]

As members of the Church, we know the commandments. We are goal oriented, and we believe in "working out our salvation." "We live

---

Elaine S. Marshall is professor and dean of the College of Nursing at Brigham Young University. She served a mission in Colombia and has served on a general Church writing committee. Her book, Children's Stress and Coping: A Family Perspective, *won the New Professional's Book Award from the National Council on Family Relations. Married to Dr. John Marshall, she is the mother of four children.*

in a world of quick fixes and instant gratification."[2] We're drawn to day planners and palm computers. We sometimes think we know and may even deserve specific blessings at scheduled times, that our lives should unfold in a self-prescribed order. When we quarrel with the Lord's timing, it's usually because we think events occur too early or too late. Elder Neal A. Maxwell warned, "When we are unduly impatient with an omniscient God's timing, we really are suggesting that we know what is best . . .—we who wear wristwatches seek to counsel Him who oversees cosmic clocks and calendars."[3] When we are impatient, "we are suggesting that we like our timetable better than God's."[4]

Contrary to logic, life doesn't progress in strict chronological order. Or, to put it another way, life is not one-dimensional like a string with knots tied at assigned distances. Most of the profound lessons in life are not self-scheduled because life is multidimensional, dynamic, and eternal. It includes our life before; the past, present, and future of this mortal life; and our life hereafter; all with overlapping and interacting events, people, and reminders of the divine.

No specific time clock governs life's most precious moments, nor are they remembered or cherished in chronological order. Our past life and its key events flow in our memory unarranged and timeless: the birth of a child, a first day of school, a kiss from Grandmother. We don't care in what order they happened. In our hearts and memories, timing and sequence do not matter. As we reflect on our lives in a larger perspective, time is neither linear nor measured. I need only try to interpret Isaiah or the Revelation of John the Beloved to know that my measures of time are irrelevant to eternity.

As we learn lessons of waiting, patience, hope, and faith, we begin to gain an eternal perspective. Without that perspective, our plans are small and uninspiring, or, as one author put it, we are "measuring out of life in tepid teacups."[5] When we have an eternal perspective, we recognize the divine rhythm in our own personal lives. When the Lord extends blessings in his own due time, he is not withholding his favor in punitive judgment. By requiring us to wait and submit, God may be allowing us to mature spiritually. Just as grain seed requires time to germinate and ripen, we require time to mature. We "know not" the Lord's time (Mark 13:33). The scriptures say, "All is as one day with God, and time [is] only . . . measured unto men" (Alma 40:8). "For a thousand years . . . are but as yesterday when it is past, and as a watch in the night" (Psalm 90:4; see also 2 Peter 3:8).

Gaining an eternal perspective, however, is rarely easy. Trials or losses often come as sudden, crashing, wrenching, untimely, and unfair surprises. They blindside us. They challenge all our notions of heaven, our hopes, and even faith. Fourteen years ago, I lost my eight-year-old son, Todd, in such a jolting ambush. That shock still stings. For years, as I set one less plate at the counter, washed and folded one less stack of play clothes, passed birthdays with no cake or candles, and hung the Christmas stocking that remained empty in the morning, time did not matter. For a time, even eternity did not matter because I only knew that he was gone from me here and now. I didn't know where he was. I had lost that personal knowledge.

But after a wait of almost exactly seven years, a sweet miracle occurred. My mother's passing, though sudden and sad, was also gentle, tender, and attended by angels. She was able to share a courageous farewell with each family member and leave us peacefully on Thanksgiving night. My father and sisters and brother and I had surrounded her with love around the clock for the preceding four days. Like young children, we fluttered around her bed. We sang hymns and brought roses. We assisted as midwives to her dying, watching the intense powers of nature as body and spirit struggled to separate. During this transition, it was a profound spiritual experience to care for her, to wash her face and brush her hair, to talk to her, and to pray over her. I felt like she was, as the poet described, a "deep weathered basket" in which I longed to linger.[6] Every hushed and reverent moment was a gift. Never was there so much love and peace, or so little concern for time in our family.

Throughout that sweet passing, I thought often of the contrast between her departure and the departure of my Todd. I learned about "the Lord's own due time" (1 Nephi 10:3). I learned that God had actually waited with me in my years of grief. I don't know why that lesson came after so long. But understanding the Lord's timing is not so important to me now because I also learned that the greatest gift of the Savior and his atonement is that he lives, and we live in eternity. In our mortal time, sorrows and losses will come, life won't happen as we hope or plan. We will suffer, sin, and regret and need to try again, and we will wait, but his gift is always there for us. He watches over the timing and events of our lives. He knows of our waiting and its purposes. We are as impulsive children who must learn delayed gratification and the fruits of waiting in order to gain spiritual maturity. Isaiah offers these beautiful promises: "But they that wait upon the Lord shall renew their strength; they shall mount up with wings as eagles; they shall run, and not be weary; and they shall walk, and not faint" (Isaiah 40:31). "Blessed are all they that wait for him" (Isaiah 30:18).

Notes

1. Dallin H. Oaks, "Timing," Brigham Young University Devotional Address, 29 January 2002, Provo, Utah.
2. BYU Women's Conference (program brochure), May 2002, Provo, Utah, Brigham Young University.
3. Neal A. Maxwell, "Hope through the Atonement of Jesus Christ," *Ensign*, November, 1998, 63.
4. Neal A. Maxwell, "'Endure It Well,'" *Ensign*, May 1990, 34.
5. "Must There Always Be a Red Brick England?" *Time Magazine*, 26 March 1965, 60.
6. Jane Relaford Brown, "Finding Her Here," n.d.; available online at www.geocities.com/bkw22.geo/finding.html (retrieved 11 April 2002).

"With Healing in His Wings"

Stephen E. Robinson

I'd like to share with you my testimony of the healing power of the Son of God. In Malachi 4:2 we read: "But unto you that fear my name shall the Sun of righteousness arise with healing in his wings." It has been my privilege all of my life to teach about the Savior and about his atonement. I've been fortunate in helping my wife; my children; as a bishop, my ward members; as a teacher and a counselor, my students and others. I have been able to help them through spiritual distress, through depression, and through pain.

Five years ago, I found out how those things felt—not by walking someone else through them, but by experiencing them myself. I found out what it was like to lie on the bottom looking up and to pray to the Lord for deliverance only to feel the floor give way and to fall into a hell deeper and more awful than the one from which I had prayed to be delivered. I know what it is like to be defeated by the task of calling the bishop on the telephone, or to be unable to make it from the hallway back into my bedroom or out into the living room, and to pray to God for help and be told, "Not yet."

Malachi's promise is true, and I testify of the healing power of Jesus Christ. But this promise is about the messianic Christ, about the Second Coming when the Son of Righteousness will arise with healing in his wings. It is at the Resurrection that every tear will be dried and that every wrong will be righted. In this world, we will suffer

---

Stephen E. Robinson received his doctorate in biblical studies from Duke University. A professor of ancient scripture at Brigham Young University, he has written several books, including Believing Christ *and* Are Mormons Christians? *He has served as a bishop and Gospel Doctrine teacher. He and his wife, Janet Bowen Robinson, are the parents of six children and the grandparents of six.*

tribulation. There is no guarantee of protection against the sufferings of mortality while we are here in this time of trial, for this life *is* trial. That is its purpose. We are here to experience the opposition and the pain and to know good from evil. The Lord will keep every promise. He will right every wrong. He will dry every tear. But he will do it on his schedule, not on ours.

Furthermore, we need to distinguish between suffering that is caused by sin (by our own agency) and suffering caused by mortality (by the Fall), which is the common lot of us all. The former suffering, which comes through the unwise use of our agency, through bad choices, through sin, can be eased almost immediately and removed fairly quickly through the atonement of Christ, by faith, repentance, and baptism. Then we receive the gift of the Holy Ghost. However, suffering that is the common lot of mortality often cannot be eased now. Sickness, infirmity, pain, death—these are common trials of mortality, which will be removed only at his coming, when the Son of Righteousness comes with healing in his wings for every problem, for every ill.

Let me give just one example of the importance of knowing the difference between the suffering caused by our own sins and the suffering caused by mortality. Our emotions are the common ground of both our spirits and our bodies. We lose track of that. We get used to thinking of our emotions as the place where the Spirit talks to us, and when we feel emotions we identify them with the Spirit. But we forget, sometimes, that our body can also cause emotional states. Every woman—and even married men—knows how emotions can be subject to biology. Grief, despair, guilt, and depression can be caused spiritually by sin. But grief, despair, guilt, and depression can also be caused physically by hormones and by body chemistry. If our depression is caused by sin, no amount of counseling or medication will make it go away. We must repent. But if our depression is caused by our chemistry and by our hormones, no amount of prayer or fasting or faith or scripture study will make it go away.[1] We must seek professional help. I have learned this myself. When we are wrong, we must repent; when we are ill, we must seek the help that the Lord has made available for us in these latter days in counseling and in medication.

Under these conditions, the broken heart is little different from the broken leg. Just as we cannot fast and pray and study a broken leg into wellness, neither can we fast or pray or study a broken heart into wellness if its cause is chemical and part of our mortality. In this case, depression is not the result of failing the test. Understanding this concept is crucial. Depression—body-caused depression, not spirit-caused depression—is not the result of having failed spiritual tests. It *is* the test. And to have faith under those circumstances while we are being tried with body-caused depression is to have faith that God is there when I can't hear him, and that he still loves me though I cannot feel him, and that for whatever purpose, he is saying, "Not yet." The time *will* come when he will reach me with healing in his wings.

In my own case, I cheated a bit. When I fell into clinical depression, I was able to step outside of myself intellectually, look at myself, and say, "Wow! How about that! Your body can make you feel guilty! And your body can you make you feel responsible for everything in the universe!" There is some comfort in understanding that. It doesn't make the pain go away, and it doesn't even really lessen it, but to know that this is chemistry and not rejection by God makes the pain much easier to bear. It may be the challenge of our time to learn the difference between spirit-caused depression and body-caused depression and to apply the remedy appropriate to each at the proper time. I say again, if your depression, if your guilt, if your despair is caused by sin, repent. If it is caused by chemistry, seek help, as I did. And now five years later, I am somewhat better and can bear testimony that the arms of the Lord can reach us no matter how far we fall.

There is one other restriction that applies to the promise found in Malachi: If God has placed limitations upon us, we must accept them in humility and obedience. So many of us don't want to do this. Are you reading this article hoping to learn how to overcome every obstacle and solve every problem because you cannot *bear* having a limitation? If so, repent and accept with humility and obedience those limits the

Lord has placed upon you. It is a false teaching of our age that we can personally overcome anything. It's just not true. No matter how much we pray, no matter how much faith we have, God will not make us eighteen again.

King Benjamin said to his people: "And see that all these things are done in wisdom and order; for it is not requisite that a man [or a woman] should run faster than he [or she] has strength" (Mosiah 4:27). To the Prophet Joseph Smith, the Lord commanded: "Do not run faster or labor more than you have strength and means provided" (D&C 10:4). This commandment followed Joseph's loss of 116 pages of the Book of Mormon translation. Do you think he wanted to make up for lost time? Do you think he wanted to repent and double his speed to make up for his mistakes? Of course. But the Lord said as he gave him back the plates, "Don't give in to the temptation to run faster than you have strength and means provided." We can't keep this commandment not to exceed our limits unless we recognize, realistically, our limits. This is the law of stewardship. To be righteous stewards, we must understand what our resources are and make sensible decisions about how we are going to use those resources. It is not a righteous or a wise steward who expends all the resources at the outset and then turns to the Master and says, "Now, it's your turn." We must be wise stewards.

You can do anything God wants you to do, but you can't do anything you want to do. You can't even do anything *you wish* God wanted you to do. The apostle Paul learned this lesson. Paul was a giant among men, not in stature but in intellect. He was as bright and as dynamic as anyone in the early church. Yet, having received gifts and revelations and all the wonderful blessings that he had access to as an apostle, he admits: "And lest I should be exalted above measure through the abundance of the revelations, there was given to me a thorn in the flesh, [God laid upon him some limitation], the messenger of Satan to buffet me, lest I should be exalted above measure [lest I think too much of myself, be too proud of myself, be too happy with my accomplishments]. For this thing I besought the Lord thrice [three times] that it might depart from me. And he said unto me, My grace is sufficient for thee:

for my strength is made perfect in weakness" (2 Corinthians 12:7–9). In essence, the Lord said to Paul, "No, Paul, you need this weakness to remind you *every day* that you rely on me." Sometimes our weaknesses are given to us for that purpose, to remind us that we rely upon the Lord and to *train* us to rely upon the Lord, instead of behaving as if the gospel were a Celestial Eagle Scout program where we are to earn merit badges and check off items on the list until finally *we* have perfected ourselves. Through our weaknesses, we learn that our victory comes through Christ, that we must rely upon him and be content to trust him to make our weaknesses strong instead of demanding in our pride that he grant us immediate victory over all our limitations and difficulties.

In the Book of Mormon, the Lord tells us: "I give unto men [and women] weakness that they may be humble; and my grace is sufficient for all men [and women] that humble themselves before me" (Ether 12:27). Notice that the focus is on our learning humility and not on the *overcoming* of weakness and the achievement of more spiritual merit badges. Learn who you rely on ultimately to enter the kingdom. Learn whose task salvation is ultimately and why the word *long-suffering* is given us in the gospel as a virtue. That's a horrible word. We are to cultivate the virtue of long-suffering. In other words, some of our limitations, some of our pains, some of our weaknesses will not be quickly removed from us. If we are given weaknesses and pains for our own sakes, then our lot is to accept them in humility and obedience. God gives us weaknesses to teach us to rely on his atonement—his grace—for that perfection that we seek.

Why is humility so important? Some of us don't want to be saved. We want to save ourselves. We want to be coached and trained and prepared and taught and instructed about how to save ourselves. If you think of the Fall as falling down a fifty-foot well and breaking both legs, there are two approaches to what salvation is. For some people, salvation is to notice that someone is at the bottom of a fifty-foot well with broken legs and to write a handbook and drop it down to them: "Here are the instructions about how you climb out of wells with broken legs. Good luck!" We laugh, but we believe it. When we find that we are in a fallen state, that we are less than celestial in our performance, we start looking for the handbook. "Okay, now, where are the rules? What do I do next?" We start wanting to check things off on that gospel of lists, an attitude which, according to Elder Bruce R. McConkie, is one of the seven deadly heresies of the modern church.[2] The other approach is that when you fall down a well and break your legs, someone climbs down, puts his arms around you, and carries you out. You are saved not under your power but under his. That is the superior understanding of the nature and purpose of the gospel of Jesus Christ. We will overcome all things through Christ but in his way and in his time.

Furthermore, we overcome by faith in Christ. In Doctrine and Covenants 76:53, we learn about those who inherit the celestial kingdom: "These are they who overcome by faith," not by performance. They have turned to Christ and have faith in him. That relationship of faith gives them victory. His victory is shared with them. They do not personally overcome every obstacle in this life and thus merit the celestial kingdom. Rather, as we are told in verse 69, "These are they who are just men [and women] *made* perfect through Jesus Christ" (D&C 76:69; emphasis added).

Moroni's final plea in the Book of Mormon is: "Yea, come unto Christ, and be perfected in him" (Moroni 10:32). Notice he does not say "perfect yourself in him." The verb form is passive; perfecting is something that he does to you when you come to him. If you can understand the distinction between these two tasks, there is nothing more important I can teach you. One task is horizontal and one is vertical. Our task is to come to Christ; that's the horizontal task. Come to Christ, make a relationship with him. Then his task is to make you celestial, to take you to the kingdom and enthrone you there. For that vertical task, we all—even the best among us—rely on his merit, mercy, and grace. Too many of us are straining at our boot straps, trying with our willpower to perfect ourselves and make ourselves celestial. That is not our task. Our job is to come to him, to give him everything. "It's not much, but it's all I've got. . . . I'm not much, but I'm yours. . . . I might be a mess, but I'm your mess." Once we've done our part, we can trust him to do all that he can do, which is to set us on a throne in his Father's kingdom. We have to trust him to do the vertical part—to perfect us, to make us worthy, to make us celestial.

Every once in a while, some of my colleagues, recognizing that I'm the spiritual pygmy on the faculty, will point out a few of my flaws and say to me, "Robinson, you're such a rough old guy. How do you expect to be exalted in the kingdom of God?" To which I respond, "Not my problem." My problem is to come to Christ, to be sealed to him, and then wherever he goes, I go. I don't know how he is going to do it, but I'm sure I'm going to be happy and my wife is going to be surprised.

Of course, once we are his, to try to serve him better becomes our desire. To strive to be better partners in the covenant relationship is right and proper, as long as we understand that we are not perfecting ourselves thereby. What we are doing is coming closer to him and sealing ourselves more perfectly to him. We are trusting him, then, to do what remains undone, to overcome all our enemies, and to take us to the celestial kingdom. How in the world, or out of it, is he ever going to make us—you and me, wretched us—celestial beings? Not our problem. Our problem is to come to him, in faith, in repentance, and to offer him all that we have in return for all that he has, that greatest bargain in all eternity.

Finally, I think that we must remember that all suffering is redemptive. In fact, I believe there are occasions when we unknowingly suffer to ease the burden for others. And if we knew of it, we would not have it stop, because we would choose to suffer for their sakes. I believe that such suffering is part of our being saviors on Mount Zion (see Obadiah 1:21; D&C 103:9). We just don't remember that we volunteered to do that.

As we go through this life, we must not expect that the gospel gives us a guarantee against suffering, against the common lot of what this life is—mortal probation, trial, experiencing opposition. We must not expect that everything is going to be done, that all problems are going to be solved, that all obstacles are going to be overcome. We just commit ourselves to do what we can do. We make ourselves his and then trust the outcome to him. We know that through the Atonement our suffering for our own sins and choices can be remediated, either immediately or ultimately at the resurrection when all enemies are overcome, when the Son of Righteousness will arise with healing in his wings and *every* tear will be dried and *every* problem will be solved.

In 1 Corinthians, Paul closes his letter with an Aramaic phrase, *maran-atha*, which means, "May our Lord come." Apparently it was a frequent prayer of the early Church. *Maran-atha*, may our Lord come. I'd like to share a poem with you entitled "Maran-atha," which looks forward to that glorious second coming, to the drying of every tear and the righting of every wrong. (Let me point out also that *Shiloh* is a term in the Hebrew Old Testament for the glorious Messiah at his coming, meaning "He whose right it is.")

The path for some is never lighted
Their love poured out all unrequited
And wrongs they suffer never righted,
—'til Shiloh comes.

Some promises remain unspoken
To faithful hearts that lie all broken
Instead of coins, they get a token,
—'til Shiloh comes.

Some old wounds are never healed
While answers sought but not revealed
Leave God's purposes concealed,
—'til Shiloh comes.

And some noble souls seem quite forsaken,
Their dreams and hopes like plunder taken,
Their looted hearts left empty, aching,
—'til Shiloh comes.

From such pains, Oh God, keep me secure,
But if not, through hell let me stay sure,
And in the dark, let me endure,
—'til Shiloh comes.[3]

I bear testimony of the healing power of Christ, whether now, in the intermediate future, or at his coming. He will overcome all enemies. He will remove every obstacle. He will dry every tear. He earned the power to do so in his great atonement in Gethsemane. He has the love and the desire to do so for you personally. I bear testimony that his power and his love have reached me. And I pray that we may be faithful and long-suffering . . . 'til Shiloh comes.

Notes

1. I am not saying that we should not also ask for priesthood administrations, nor am I discounting the miracles of healing that sometimes occur.
2. See Bruce R. McConkie, "The Seven Deadly Heresies," in *Devotional Speeches of the Year, 1980* (Provo: Brigham Young University Press, 1981), 74–80.
3. Copyright © 2002 by Stephen E. Robinson.

"I Know My Sheep, and They Are Numbered"

Elaine Walton

I grew up in a strong Latter-day Saint family. As a child, I was a serious-minded achiever. I was a straight-A student and the kind of youth that bishops and Young Women presidents love. I guess in a sense I saw myself as a valiant spirit on the fast track to the celestial kingdom. But divorce derailed my journey, and now, instead of speeding down the success track, I'm painstakingly trying to rebuild my track, one tie, one rail at a time.

As a single parent dealing with the aftermath of divorce, I took comfort that my children were young and innocent. I expected their pure hearts to recognize and cling to goodness. I naively thought that the choice between their father's gay, worldly lifestyle and my gospel-centered lifestyle would be easy. So I was devastated when, one by one, three of my four children turned away from the Church.

Now adults, those children are still as loving as they were as children. They work hard at honoring me, especially on Mother's Day, and letting me know that they care. We enjoy spending time together, teasing each other, and reminiscing. They are responsible, productive people who manifest the basic values of Christian charity and honesty. But three of my four children have made their home in a culture that is foreign to me. Without question we love each other, but sometimes finding common ground is difficult.

Elaine Walton is an associate professor and director of the School of Social Work at Brigham Young University. She and her husband, Wendel Walton, are the parents of a blended family of ten children and the grandparents of eighteen. She serves at the Missionary Training Center in Provo with her husband, where he is a branch president.

I go back and forth in my feelings, between missing them and wanting to be a part of their lives, and being relieved at not having to always be a part of their lives. It's sometimes painful to remember the dreams I used to have for them, for me, for us. But I don't want to torture them or me with my disappointment, so I try to live in the present instead of the past. Even so, I face a perpetual battle between wanting to love my children as they are and wanting desperately for them to change.

In 3 Nephi 18, Jesus is about to leave the Nephites after sharing remarkable experiences with them, experiences so powerful they defy description. He tells them he has to go back to his Father because he has other work to do. Then, almost as a postscript, he gives them one final instruction. Because he knows the sweetness of the moment will not last indefinitely, he warns them about how to treat those of their congregations who fall away—like my children and maybe some of yours. In verse 31 he says, "If he [the wayward soul] repent not he shall not be numbered among my people, that he may not destroy my people, for behold I know my sheep, and they are numbered." Then in verse 32, he adds, "Nevertheless, ye shall not cast him out of your synagogues, or your places of worship, for unto such shall ye continue to minister; for ye know not but what they will return and repent, and come unto me with full purpose of heart, and I shall heal them; and ye shall be the means of bringing salvation unto them."

I am struck with the force with which Jesus instructed the Nephites regarding wayward souls, both in terms of condemning their behavior and in terms of ministering to them. His counsel highlights a contradiction I feel as I interact with wayward souls. Should I be careful not to number them among the Saints for fear they might do damage, as in verse 31? Or should I go out of my way to minister to them, as in verse 32? I struggle with myself in this regard every time I visit my children. Have I polluted myself by spending time in Babylon? Have I given them a false message of tacit approval by sharing parts of their questionable lifestyles? Or have I been ministering to them? What meaning does 3 Nephi have for *me?*

The last time I visited my oldest daughter, I turned down her invitation to go to an amusement park on Sunday. Instead, I attended sacrament meeting in the local chapel. It felt strange to be attending church in my daughter's neighborhood in what should be her ward, participating in an experience now foreign to her. I sat there with her neighbors, realizing that they would see my daughter as foreign and likely feel uncomfortable around her. It probably would not occur to them that she was raised in a Latter-day Saint home, the descendant of Mormon pioneers. As these thoughts raced through my mind, I felt torn. I was sympathetic with their discomfort and probable desire not to include my daughter—verse 31. But there was also a voice inside me crying out to these people to recognize her as a daughter of God and to minister to her—verse 32.

This was a testimony meeting, and as my thoughts took over I could not restrain myself. I walked to the pulpit and spoke to the congregation about my children, their choices, and my hopes for them. As nearly as I can reconstruct it, I concluded with this request: "The next time you are confronted with someone in your neighborhood whose appearance or behavior offends you, remember that person has a mother and it might be me. So let me thank you in advance for not avoiding eye contact, for not judging, and for remembering that this child of mine is also a child of God."

My comments in that testimony meeting synthesized the struggle that I've had for many years, going back and forth between verse 31 and verse 32. That balancing act pretty much sums up my life. When I was younger and idealistic, I used to think that my faith would be sufficient to bring my children back. I could be like Alma, who through his prayers caused an angel to appear to his son, Alma the Younger, and in a miraculous, dramatic way convert him. I thought if I could just exercise *enough* faith, I could call down a miracle from heaven on behalf of my husband and then later my children. But I wasn't successful. My heart was broken because of my children and my husband. And in a very real sense, my life fell apart.

But I learned three lessons from that falling apart. Perhaps the best way to explain these lessons is to use the fourth Article of Faith, which identifies the first principle of the gospel as faith in the Lord Jesus Christ. I discovered that *faith* and *faith in the Lord Jesus Christ* are two different principles. I used to think of faith as the power to accomplish anything: to move mountains, to walk on water, and certainly to bring my children back. But I learned that faith, no matter how powerful, will not take away agency. In contrast, faith in the Lord Jesus Christ allows me to acknowledge his mercy and long-suffering as those gifts relate to me and to my children.

Lesson number one was the realization that I cannot change others, I can only change myself. As I have matured, so have my prayers. I used to try to exercise faith by saying, "Heavenly Father, please help my children to change. Help them to become aware of the harmful effects of alcohol or being sexually active. Help them to recognize the truth of the gospel." Now I'm more likely to exercise faith in the Lord Jesus Christ by saying, "Heavenly Father, I know you love my children. Help me to feel about them the same way that you do. Help me to love them more. Help me to understand your plan for them. And help me to be patient." As Elder Maxwell taught, we should pray not only "thy will be done," but also "thy timing be done."[1]

Lesson number two, for me, was that becoming stripped of pride freed me to make spiritual progress. It was humiliating, when I divorced, to go from being a strong, admired member of the ward to being the ward charity case. I was embarrassed when people found out that my fourteen-year-old daughter had chosen to live with her gay father instead of me. What was I doing wrong? I was a good mother. I was paying tithing, fasting and praying, going to the temple. What else could I do? It was even more embarrassing to admit that my daughter had chosen an alternative lifestyle for herself. Exercising faith, I trusted that my friends and family would support me and not judge me. But later, when exercising faith in the Lord Jesus Christ, my broken heart become a broken heart and a contrite spirit. Not a crushed heart, but a heart broken open to receive help, guidance, wisdom. I was opened to learn and grow and change. Pride was no longer a barrier. During that time when my heart was so tender, I could hardly sit through a sacrament meeting without weeping. I'm sure that people looked at me and felt sorry for me. But those tears were not just tears of grief because of my losses. I was overwhelmed with many feelings, including gratitude, joy, love. The Lord was aware of my plight, and his grace was at work in my heart.

Lesson number three was that Christ will never stop loving his children and neither should I. Exercising faith, I took comfort in reading any scripture that helped me understand that profound love Christ has for all his children. Loving my children will never be inappropriate no matter what they may have done to cut themselves off. But by exercising faith in the Lord Jesus Christ, I focus on additional scriptures that give me hope. One of my favorites is Isaiah 49:15–16: "Can a women forget her sucking child, that she should not have compassion on the son of her womb? yea, they may forget, yet will I not forget thee. Behold, I have graven thee upon the palms of my hands; thy walls are continually before me." While Christ was hanging on the cross, he was engraving the images, the names of my children and me, in the palms of his hands.

Faith is believing that through fasting and prayer all things are possible, even a change of heart in our children so that they will repent and return to Christ. Faith in the Lord Jesus Christ is trusting in the reality and power of Christ's love for all of God's children, regardless of their mistakes, my mistakes, our mistakes, and knowing that the Atonement makes repentance possible. I am so grateful for my testimony of the power of the Atonement. I will never quit hoping that my three children will again embrace the gospel, but I know that my job right now is to love them.

I love to ponder 3 Nephi 18:32: "For unto such shall ye continue to minister; for ye know not but that they will return and repent, and come unto me with full purpose of heart, and I shall heal them; and ye shall be the means of bringing salvation unto them." I particularly appreciate the promise "and I shall heal them." I can imagine Christ healing the damaged skin where my daughter has a tattoo, or repairing the rather large hole in my son's earlobe. I believe in that kind of literal healing. But that healing will be a mere symbol of the real healing, which is spiritual. That's the healing I long for.

I want to conclude with a confession. It is often difficult for me to listen to so-called faith-promoting stories in testimony meeting. Hearing how through fasting, prayer, and faith a surprising conversion occurs, a spouse is healed, or a son or daughter comes back to Church, I could become cynical. What about all the righteous people who end up dying? Faith doesn't always heal. And why does Heavenly Father answer prayers of other parents but not mine? Do I lack sufficient faith? Is my fast not long enough? But instead I have chosen not to be cynical. I rejoice with my brothers and sisters when their prayers are answered. And I accept the fact that faith in the Lord Jesus Christ is much more than being able to pray down a miracle from heaven. In the final analysis, such faith is really faithful-ness. All that really matters is that I remain true to the knowledge and testimony I have, and that I stay open to growing and learning by acknowledging my limitations and by seeking divine guidance.

Along with my decision to avoid cynicism, I have decided not to wallow in guilt and misery. I could torture myself with the "if onlys." You know, if only I had married someone else. If only I had been a stronger influence with my children. If only I had recognized their concerns earlier. But "if only" doesn't make a difference now. And beating myself doesn't accomplish anything. If I truly believe that the gospel of Jesus Christ is the plan of happiness, then it is my responsibility, my duty, to be happy. The best way I can be a missionary to my children is to radiate the joy of the gospel by the way I live each day. I no longer see myself on the fast track to the celestial kingdom. In fact, I've decided that there is no such thing. When I was skimming along the surface of the strait and narrow path as a youth, I had lofty goals and I knew success, but I didn't know Christ until I was confronted with some of the potholes in that road. I am sorry my children left the Church, but I am not sorry for the potholes that brought me to my knees.

I would like to share one final scripture that has come to have great meaning for me: "All things work together for good to them that love God" (Romans 8:28). My heartbreaking losses, instead of undermining my testimony, have deepened it. And I believe that I have become a better disciple. There is no way to get through life unscathed. For each of us, the only track to the celestial kingdom is a humble recognition of our dependence on the atoning sacrifice of our Savior Jesus Christ. We must recognize the love of our Heavenly Father and develop an unwavering commitment to keep all his commandments. I will continue to exercise faith in the Lord Jesus Christ by loving the Lord, by loving my children, and by striving to be an example of the gospel as the true plan of happiness.

Note

1. Neal A. Maxwell, "Hope through the Atonement of Jesus Christ," *Ensign*, November 1998, 63; also "'Endure It Well,'" *Ensign*, May 1990, 34.

His Most Precious and Enduring Creation

Janet S. Scharman

Last year my husband surprised me by announcing that we were going to build a playhouse in our backyard. I had wanted a playhouse since I was a young girl and, as grandchildren began coming, I wanted one even more. I had dared not hope for such a luxury, so as soon as my husband told me of his plans, I knew immediately there was a very real possibility that this would be my Mother's Day, anniversary, birthday, and Christmas present for the rest of my life. I was thrilled anyway.

Watching the development of the playhouse from an empty space on the ground to the finished product was an adventure for the entire family. During some stages of construction, the playhouse was much more attractive to our grandchildren than it was safe. At one point, there were two openings from the second floor to the outside where slides would be attached, two little balconies, and the open stairwell connecting the top and bottom floors—all without railings or protection of any kind.

One day during that period, I was tending two of my grandchildren: McKinnley, who was almost six years old, and his two-and-a-half-year-old sister, Kennedy. We were playing outside in the backyard when I remembered I needed to run into the house for a quick errand. I said to McKinnley, "Your sister is going to want to go up to the playhouse. I need you to watch her." McKinnley is very good with younger

---

Janet S. Scharman has served as the vice-president of student life at Brigham Young University. The Gospel Doctrine teacher in her ward, she chaired the BYU Women's Conference for 2001 and 2002. She and her husband, S. Brent Scharman, have a blended family of one son and nine daughters.

children, and he readily agreed to my request. When I returned, probably only a minute later, McKinnley headed towards me from the direction of the playhouse with no Kennedy. Just then I heard her little voice call to me from the top of one of the small balconies of the playhouse, and there she was, teetering on the edge, waving and blowing kisses. Directly below her was a cement slab, which was soon to become the front porch, and to the side were several large boulders.

I ran as fast as I could to the playhouse, up the stairs, and snatched that little girl into my arms. McKinnley was right behind me. As I sat down with her, breathless on the floor, he gently put his hand on my shoulder and said, "You didn't have to worry, Grandma. Before I left Kennedy up here, I showed her all the holes not to fall through."

I can picture our Father in Heaven, preparing us for our transition to this earth, with all of us promising him that we would look out for our brothers and sisters here. Because of our varying maturity and limited perspectives, he must have known that we wouldn't always get it just right. And yet, he apparently had confidence in us and trusted that we would get his work done.

The Lord has told us, as recorded in the book of Moses, that "this is my work and my glory—to bring to pass the immortality and eternal life of man" (Moses 1:39). His work and his glory is to bring his children back home, and he has enlisted all of us, assigned to family units, to help in that process. There is nothing more important to the Lord than having his children return to his presence. As creator, he could structure our environment and opportunities here any way he chose, and we must assume that his plan was designed to give each of us the greatest opportunity for success, as he views success. As imperfect as most of our families are, families must be where and how we are most likely to have experiences that will prepare us for eternal life. Perhaps this is why Elder Marion G. Romney referred to the family as "[The Lord's] most precious and enduring creation."[1]

The enduring quality of families is something that each of us, as members of the Church, is taught from our earliest years. We learn such songs as "Families Can Be Together Forever,"[2] and we talk about the importance of temple marriage so that our families can be sealed together for time and eternity. For many this is a comforting thought, even during those moments when *precious* may not be the first descriptor which comes to mind during some of our particular family interactions. But for others, neither *enduring* nor *precious* seems to be a word which will ever fit our family circumstances, and we can wonder why the Lord would place us in such difficult situations when others around us seem to have every advantage of life and opportunity for success.

This is a fair question to ask, but one for which I have no answer. What I do know is that there is order and purpose to our experience here, although as we live out the details of our existence the unfolding picture is sometimes difficult and perhaps even impossible to accurately see from our limited vantage point. President Gordon B. Hinckley has admonished us to "never lose sight of the fact that the Lord put you where you are according to His design, which you don't fully understand."[3] He placed us in families so that we might help each other, learn from each other, draw strength from each other in times of need, and grow in our understanding of the gospel—together. His promise to us is clear: "Enter thou into the joy of thy Lord," which is "the rest of the Lord" (Matthew 25:21; Moroni 7:3).

Wouldn't it be nice if we really could comprehend how all of that works? Haven't we all wished from time to time to be able to see the end from the beginning, to understand how all the pieces fit together? Sometimes we don't even have all the pieces, let alone know how they fit together. The Lord's way is not to show us the end but to show us the way. That's important to understand. Just because we can't see it, however, doesn't mean there is not a beautifully designed and intricate masterpiece of which we are a part.

Sister Patricia Holland, comparing our earthly experience to a tapestry, suggests that "our heavenly parents are preparing a lovely tapestry with exquisite colors and patterns and hues. They are doing so lovingly and carefully and masterfully. . . . It is very difficult for us to assess our own contribution accurately . . .

" . . . We are confined to the limited view of the underside of the tapestry where things can seem particularly jumbled and muddled and unclear. If nothing really makes very much sense from that point of view, it is because we are still in process and unfinished. But our heavenly parents have the view from the top, and one day we will know what they know—that every part of the artistic whole is equal in importance and balance and beauty. They know our purpose and potential, and they have given us the perfect chance to make the perfect contribution in this divine design."[4]

Elder Jeffrey Holland makes the same point using a different metaphor. He compares our life experience to that of being in the scene of a play. "We—never seeing the play from the outside, and meeting only the tiny minority of characters who are on stage in the same scenes as we, and largely ignorant of the future and very imperfectly informed about the past—cannot tell at what moment Christ will come and confront us." He continues, "Playing it well, then, is what matters most."[5]

Have you ever seen the Bloch painting of Christ healing the sick at the pool of Bethesda? Up close it may seem dark, uninviting, and without form or design. But as you move back some distance, allowing yourself to gain a grander perspective, a masterpiece unfolds which touches your hearts with a reverence for all it represents. This painting, commissioned by Danish priests in 1883, was created by artist Carl Bloch to celebrate the opening of the Bethesda Indre Mission in Copenhagen. It hung there as a focal point until 29 August 2001, at which time it was transported to the BYU Museum of Art, where it is now displayed in a place of prominence. The scriptural account portrayed here is of Christ healing the sick at the pool of Bethesda (John 5:2–9), and it powerfully portrays a message of love, hope, and physical and spiritual healing. Isn't it interesting that when we are very close to something, even as exquisite as this work of art, its appearance can be very unappealing? Just as moving slightly away from it changed its meaning for us, the dark and dreary corners of our lives, if seen from some distance, can be understood as essential parts of the Lord's masterpiece for us. We need to look for the Savior's hand in our lives.

Just as he is lifting the cover from the crippled man in the painting, he invites us to come to him and be healed from our cares.

It is not an easy task to see our own experiences with the meaning the Lord has for them. Our lives are so busy, and demands on our time are so tremendous. But there is a sure way, as Elder Neal A. Maxwell tells us: "Because looking at life and others through the lens of the gospel provides eternal perspective, if we look long enough, as well as often enough, we can see much more clearly. . . . Such things as a mess of pottage and thirty pieces of silver and moments of sensual pleasure totally disappear from view; so does an improved golf swing or tennis serve when compared with progress towards patience. So does redecorating the front room when placed alongside listening to and teaching one's children."[6]

It is impossible to overstate the value of the gospel in our lives. As we look through its lens, as Elder Maxwell suggests, we are able to catch a glimpse of the magnificence of the Lord's creations. We understand how precious each one of our Heavenly Father's children is to him and that each has a place of importance in his grand design. We feel his love for us and the love he wants us to share with those around us. I am reminded of a mother of a large family who was asked which one of her children was her favorite. Her answer was quick and telling: "The one who is sick, the one with a problem, the one who needs me most today."

Our vision of possibilities and potential is sharpened when we are reminded that with God, nothing is impossible (Luke 1:37). Nor is anything inconsequential. Each of us matters to him: our happiness, our potential, our problems, our progress back home to his presence. Keeping focused on the things of most importance, being able to filter out the detractors of the world, and holding steady the gospel lens to our eye—all facilitate our staying the course as we journey along the sometimes treacherous roads of life.

But remember, this is not a solitary journey. Although we will stand before God as individuals to be judged, we do not progress to that point alone, nor will we live in the eternities alone. Tessa Santiago, in a talk to the BYU community in 1997, recounted the experience of thirteen-year-old Mary Goble Pay, an ancestor of Sister Marjorie Hinckley. Mary and her family were fortunate enough to have an ox-drawn wagon as they began their trek across the plains to the Salt Lake Valley. Ox-drawn wagons could go faster, carry more supplies, and were much easier on the travelers who could sometimes ride than were the handcarts used by so many of the Saints who had much less than Mary's family. Mary later wrote in her journal, "We had orders not to pass the handcart companies. We had to keep close to them to help them if we could." The slower journey and ensuing bitter winter conditions exacted its toll on her family, just as it did on all the others in those companies. Mary's six-week-old baby sister and older brother were both buried along the way. Her forty-three-year-old mother died just before their wagon entered the valley. In spite of the tremendous sacrifices, her family understood their responsibility to their brothers and sisters, and they did not desert them, even though it would have appeared to have been in their own best interests to have done so. As Sister Santiago reflected, "As long as there are others on the trail, or those who *might* travel with us, our stewardship is not over."[7]

I am struck by the importance of working and loving and struggling together as I reflect on another group of people who successfully journeyed to Zion, another Zion—the city of Enoch, the only city in recorded history which has ever been translated. This is indeed an amazing account when we remember that at the time of Enoch's calling from the Lord, a large number of people were wicked and Enoch, righteous and capable as he was, felt somewhat reluctant to accept the daunting assignment of helping them turn their hearts to the Lord. "Why is it that I have found favor?" he asks. "[I] am but a lad, and all the people hate me" (Moses 6:31). Enoch was not being overly modest. In truth, he was inexperienced, and the people really did not want to listen to him. Does this sound at all familiar? The very same avenue Enoch used then is open to each of us today, and it's really quite simple. He trusted that the Lord would help him.

We are given little information about how this transformation from wickedness to righteousness and from reluctance to apparent perfection took place, but one verse gives us some insight into the process which evolved. We learn that the people of Enoch "were of one heart and one mind . . . and there was no poor among them" (Moses 7:18). Being of one heart and one mind suggests an openness, a nonjudgmental and selfless attitude of reaching out and of cooperation. "No poor among them" is not a reference primarily to money. I believe that every member of that extended family shared all they had with each other so that there were no poor emotionally, physically, intellectually, and most important, spiritually. For these people, the success of the entire group must have been highly valued over an extended period of time and that required not only willing givers but willing recipients as well. It was the city of Enoch, not the individual of Enoch, that the Lord chose to bring to him in this special way. If the people of Enoch had gathered at the pool of Bethesda, they would not have been clumped together, each one hoping to be the first into the pool. They would have joined hands, supporting those in need, and dipped down into the water together.

The scriptures are rich with messages which continue with an almost uncanny relevance today, centuries and millennia since they were written. It seems that the perennial nature of family relationships transcends time and place, regardless of the variables. Husbands, wives, parents, siblings, and in-laws apparently all shared many of the same feelings in 600 B.C. in the Middle East as they do in A.D. 2002 in Provo, Utah. It is likely no coincidence, then, that the very first stories in both the Book of Mormon and the Bible are about families. The first words of the Book of Mormon remind us of the significance of families, "I, Nephi, having been born of goodly parents . . ." (1 Nephi 1:1).

As I reflect upon what we know of Adam and Eve, two of the Lord's choicest spirits, and then again on Lehi, a prophet of God, and his devoted wife, Sariah, I am reminded that even these most righteous of parents experienced significant family challenges. Because family is what matters most, because it is the Lord's most precious and enduring creation, it should not be surprising to us that this is precisely where the adversary is waging his fiercest attack. If it were not of such importance, Satan and his comrades would focus their efforts elsewhere. This should not be cause for us to fear, but rather an incentive to hold tightly to what we know to be good and true, to be alert to the cunningness and deceptions of the adversary, to see through the confusion of the messages of the world.

The messages of the world demean the family and give little assistance to the work within the walls of our homes. All this can feel overwhelming and, even though our hearts may be in the right place, it can be difficult to know where to start and how to, as President Hinckley has said, "Carry on."[8]

Ironic as this may sound, we can be strengthened by acknowledging our inadequacies and using that understanding to direct us to the Lord. A few weeks ago, I mentioned in a campus meeting with a group of colleagues that it was very apparent to me why each of them had been appointed to their respective positions of responsibility, but I sometimes wondered and worried about how a regular girl like me had ended up in a place like this. Later, much to my surprise, a friend who was in that meeting said he often feels that same way as well. We probably all have situations when we just do not think we are equal to the task, and, if we believe we have to handle everything on our own, we are probably correct. I believe that even the brightest, most talented, creative, beautiful people in the world have those times when they wish they could do better. Part of the Lord's plan is to provide us with opportunities that will test our limits, cause us to try a little harder, and in the process become acutely aware of our dependence on him as we gain new skills. Nothing can provide us with the continuous and dramatic opportunities for testing and growth as much as our family relationships. Each time we turn to the Lord for strength and refuse to give in to Satan's enticements to be discouraged or to give up, we learn a little more, and we strengthen the very bonds which have eternal implications.

The world would have us believe that if we have problems, particularly when they do not seem to be of our own creation, we abandon the situation and look elsewhere for satisfaction; that if a situation is hard, we walk away. We are tricked into thinking that we are entitled to constant pleasure and that our needs should be met. Clearly, we live in a drive-through society. Of course, that sounds appealing, but in the end it's not how we achieve a sense of personal achievement and satisfaction, and it is not a perspective that allows us to have an impact on those around us. The Lord uses words in the scriptures that remind us to be patient when he says, " . . . that [we] might have joy" (2 Nephi 2:25). Oh, if only we could always remember that it is not the perfect, trouble-free moments of life we should focus on but who is at our side. As Paul said in a letter to the Romans, "If God be for us, who can be against us?" (Romans 8:31).

The real message here is to trust the Lord and to never give up. Again, Paul counseled us to "hold fast that which is good" (1 Thessalonians 5:21). The family, during its phases of near perfection and complete imperfection, is ordained of God and is good.[9] We must remind ourselves that we knew each other before, and we rejoiced at the opportunity to be here together. Sometimes that is very easy to forget.

How can we know what to do next? How can we know when to stop doing something that is not working and to try a new strategy? Alma told his people to "counsel with the Lord in all thy doings, and he will direct thee for good" (Alma 37:37). It's such an obvious answer, but sometimes we think of prayer as a last resort instead of a first resort. "Because our Father loves his children," Elder Eyring has told us, "he will not leave us to guess about what matters most in this life concerning where our attention could bring happiness or our indifference bring sadness." Elder Eyring goes on to say, "We may have to pray with faith to know what we are to do, and . . . we must pray with a determination to obey. But we can know what to do and be sure that the way has been prepared for us by the Lord."[10]

I think our experience on earth is like the playhouse in my backyard. It's not too far from the "big" house, so the parents can keep an eye on their little ones and hear their confident calls "Look at me" as they zip down the slide. Sometimes, the voice is a little more plaintive as a younger one hollers for help—the top of the slide, looking down, is much more daunting than the bottom, looking up. The playhouse is a place where the children can practice independence and have picnic lunches, a place where they can learn to obey the rules. It's a place where they can learn to get along, to share, to get sand out of each other's hair, and let everyone into the club, no matter how old they are. At the end of the day, the kids come back, and we are together—as a family.

Elder Robert D. Hales has emphasized: "We are each an important and integral part of a family and the highest blessings can be received only within an eternal family. When families are functioning as designed by God, the relationships found therein are the most valued of mortality. The plan of the Father is that family love and companionship will continue into the eternities. Being one in a family carries a great responsibility of caring, loving, lifting, and strengthening each member of the family so that all can righteously endure to the end in mortality and dwell together throughout eternity. It is not enough just to save ourselves. It is equally important that parents, brothers, and sisters are saved in our families. If we return home alone to our Father in Heaven, we will be asked, 'Where is the rest of the family?' This is why we teach that families are forever. The eternal nature of an individual becomes the eternal nature of the family."[11]

This can seem like a tall order. President Kimball, sensitive to the feelings of discouragement some of us may have as we try hard and still see loved ones who are not progressing as we would hope, said, "Where there are challenges [with family members], you fail only if you fail to keep trying!"[12] It is my prayer that we will not give up, that we can remember that we are on the Lord's errand as we play our part with his most precious and enduring creation.

Notes

1. Marion G. Romney, "Scriptures As They Relate to Family Stability," *Ensign*, February 1972, 57.

2. Ruth M. Gardner, "Families Can Be Together Forever," *Hymns of The Church of Jesus Christ of Latter-day Saints* (Salt Lake City: The Church of Jesus Christ of Latter-day Saints, 1985), no. 300.
3. Gordon B. Hinckley, *Stand a Little Taller: Counsel and Inspiration for Each Day of the Year* (Salt Lake City: Deseret Book, 2001), 5.
4. Jeffrey R. Holland and Patricia T. Holland, *On Earth As It Is in Heaven* (Salt Lake City: Deseret Book, 1989), 4–5.
5. Holland and Holland, *On Earth As It Is in Heaven*, 137.
6. Neal A. Maxwell, *We Will Prove Them Herewith* (Salt Lake City: Deseret Book, 1982), 76.
7. Tessa Meyer Santiago, "Under Covenant toward the Promised Land: Section 136 as a Latter-day Saint Type," in *Brigham Young University Speeches, 1996–97* (Provo: Brigham Young University Press, 1997), 239–49; emphasis in original.
8. Gordon B. Hinckley, *Teachings of Gordon B. Hinckley* (Salt Lake City: Deseret Book, 1997), 255.
9. See "The Family: A Proclamation to the World," *Ensign*, November 1995, 102.
10. Henry B. Eyring, "The Family," *Ensign*, February 1998, 10.
11. Robert D. Hales, "The Eternal Family," *Ensign*, November 1996, 65.
12. Spencer W. Kimball, "Families Can Be Eternal," *Ensign*, November 1980, 5.

"BE STILL, MY SOUL"

Ebony Keith

My father died when I was a baby, leaving my mother to raise three daughters on her own. After my grandmother's death seven years later, my mother lost hope and turned to drugs to "help her heal." They destroyed her life and nearly destroyed ours. We raised each other as we were sent from house to house, living with friends, relatives, and at times complete strangers to avoid being split up in foster care. We learned early that we had to rely on each other because that's all that we had. We were homeless many times, abused in every way, abandoned, unloved, and unwanted. We were what many would consider a burden, I guess. When my oldest sister turned eighteen, we moved into an apartment together and supported each other through school.

In the midst of all of this moving, I was found by the missionaries, taught, and baptized. I am alone in this journey, the only one in my family to join. It was hard to join alone and it still is, but I came to know Christ in a completely new way, relying on him for everything that I needed. As wonderful as it was, however, that reliance did not dispel the anguish I felt on occasion as I contemplated my life and its adversities. I couldn't help but think, *Why me?* I was so young and so desperately wanted to be loved and protected.

I came to BYU determined to leave my past in the past, and I worked hard to keep my background a secret. In time I decided to serve a mission to share with others the joy that I had found in the gospel. While serving as a missionary, I struggled with nightmares and

---

Ebony Keith graduated from Brigham Young University with a bachelor's degree in psychology. She served in the Michigan Lansing Mission and has served as the literacy teacher and family home evening coordinator in her ward.

flashbacks of a life I had tried to forget. Once again I relived the horror I had experienced for so many years. This severe condition, diagnosed as post-traumatic stress disorder, forced me to come home early from my mission.

I share this experience because I want you to remember that there may be times in all our lives when we will lose hope, or our hope will dwindle. That's okay. Sadness and discouragement are a part of life. The question is, Will we let them stay forever? President Ezra Taft Benson said, "Hope is an anchor to the souls of men. Satan would have us cast away that anchor. In this way he can bring discouragement and surrender."[1]

If we want hope to stabilize us in the storms of mortality, to anchor our souls, we must learn to understand the Atonement and appreciate it personally. Moroni said, "And what is it that we should hope for? Behold I say unto you that ye shall have hope through the atonement of Christ and the power of his resurrection, to be raised unto life eternal" (Moroni 7:41). We must have hope *in* and *through* the Atonement. I still struggle at times to understand the Atonement in regards to human suffering, but the words of Sister Chieko Okazaki have helped: "We know that on some level Jesus experienced the totality of mortal existence in Gethsemane," she wrote. "It's our faith that he experienced everything—absolutely everything. Sometimes we don't think through the implications of that belief. We talk in great generalities about the sins of all humankind, about the suffering of the entire human family. But we don't experience pain in generalities. We experience it individually. That means Jesus knows what it felt like when your mother died of cancer—how it was for your mother, how it still is for you. . . .

"His last recorded words to his disciples were, 'And, lo, I am with you alway, even unto the end of the world.' (Matthew 28:20.) What does that mean? It means he understands your mother-pain when your five-year-old leaves for kindergarten, when a bully picks on your fifth-grader, when your daughter calls to say that the new baby has Down's syndrome. He knows your mother-rage when a trusted babysitter sexually abuses your two-year-old, when someone gives your thirteen-year-old drugs, when someone seduces your seventeen-year-old. He knows the pain you live with when you come home to a quiet apartment where the only children who ever come are visitors, when you hear that your former husband and his new wife were sealed in the temple last week, when your fiftieth wedding anniversary rolls around and your husband has been dead for two years. He knows all that. He's been there. He's been lower than all that."[2] This is what we are to hope for: the calm that comes as we understand that he knows us. As Alma said, the Savior's mission was to suffer so that he would know how to succor his people, how to help us in our time of need (Alma 7:11–13).

Understanding his atonement won't make the pain disappear. I had to learn that the hard way. But knowing that he knows what it's like for me does comfort me when I'm feeling no one else could possibly understand. Surely the creator of all the heavens and the earth who knows the fall of each sparrow knows our pain. Surely there is not a tear that we cry that he does not match with his own.

Last fall I was struggling to understand the Atonement and how it helped human suffering. I couldn't understand why children and women are raped and why parents abuse and abandon their children. How could our Father in Heaven who loves us so very much bear to watch his precious sons and daughters be hurt like this? I longed to understand. As I struggled with these questions, I received a blessing from the Lord through a church leader. In the blessing, he told me that there are times when the Spirit just carries us through our trials, and there are other times that we may feel completely alone when we need the Lord the most. He said, "Ebony, as a child we need to be with him. But as an adult we need to be like him. That doesn't mean that he will leave us comfortless, but instead he will walk beside us guiding our path."

To make hope an anchor to our souls, however, we must realize that we need to restore the hope we had within us as we left our Father's arms before we came to mortality. The restoration of our hope will take hard work, time, and patience, the virtue so many of us lack.

Where do we begin? That's a question I have asked myself many times. And the only answer that I have come up with is *Ask for help.* The Savior taught us to ask and we shall receive, as long as we ask in faith and don't become weary in well doing. "Indeed, as Paul wrote of Abraham, he 'against [all] hope believed in hope' and 'staggered not . . . through unbelief.' He was 'strong in faith' and was 'fully persuaded that, what [God] had promised, he was able . . . to perform' (Romans 4:18)."[3]

In a conference talk, Elder Jeffrey R. Holland perfectly summarized my thoughts on hope: "To any who may be struggling to see that light and find that hope, I say: Hold on. Keep trying. God loves you. Things will improve. Christ comes to you in His 'more excellent ministry' with a future of 'better promises.' He is your 'high priest of good things to come.' . . .

" . . . Cling to your faith. Hold on to your hope. 'Pray always, and be believing.'"[4]

Thanks to the restored gospel, I have not only a testimony of Jesus Christ but also a hope in Christ. I know that my Redeemer lives and that he loves me. I know that Christ from "wood and nails built mansions for us all."[5] I know that hope will not only point us to a better tomorrow but to a brighter and happier today.

Notes

1. *Speaker's Sourcebook for Latter-day Saints* (Salt Lake City: Aspen Books, 1999), 198.
2. Chieko Okazaki, *Lighten Up!* (Salt Lake City: Deseret Book, 1993), 174–75.
3. Jeffrey R. Holland, "'An High Priest of Good things to Come,'" *Ensign*, November 1999, 36.
4. Holland, "An High Priest," 36.
5. John V. Pearson, "Behold the Wounds in Jesus' Hands," music by David Naylor, Jackman Music Corp., 1998.

The Family of Christ

Sandra Rogers

On the subject of families, I recall a tracting experience from my mission. When the father of the house answered our knock, we asked if he would like to know more about having his family together for eternity. The gentleman paused to think, then said, "I can hardly stand them now. Why would I want to be with them for eternity?" In a moment of frustration, guilt, or bitterness, any number of us might also wonder, *Why all this focus on family?*

In reality we belong to several families. First, we are the literal spiritual offspring of God the Father. Second, we are born into the family of our mortal fathers when we receive a physical body. Third, we create our own distinct families when we marry and have children. Fourth, through baptism we belong to the family of the Church. And fifth, through obedience we may belong to the family of Christ.

The family of our mortal father, our own distinct family, and our Church family all consist of weak, imperfect mortals who can easily commit trespasses, offenses, and sins. All these families can be a source of great joy, comfort, and well-being. They can also be a source of sorrow, pain, loneliness, grief, and despair. When things are not going perfectly in our mortal family constellations, I hope we each comprehend that we can seek the peace that comes from belonging to the family of Christ and understanding that we can have him as our Father.

At the end of his magnificent sermon to his people, King Benjamin gave the key that opens the door to this last, most important

---

Sandra Rogers has served as dean of the College of Nursing at Brigham Young University. She served as a Welfare Services missionary in the Philippines and has taught in her ward Relief Society.

family: "And now, because of the covenant which ye have made ye shall be called the children of Christ, his sons, and daughters; for behold, this day he hath spiritually begotten you; for ye say that your hearts are changed through faith on his name; therefore, ye are born of him and have become his sons and his daughters" (Mosiah 5:7).

I find great comfort and power in that scripture. Gospel ordinances, temple covenants, and priesthood authority can seal upon us the blessings of family life in eternity if we are faithful. When things are going well in our mortal families, we should, in full humility, be grateful for the plan of salvation that makes it possible for us to enjoy those relationships in eternity. And when things are not going well, we can, in full humility, be grateful for the plan of salvation that promises that no blessing, no gift from God or Christ will be withheld from us if we are faithful. President Spencer W. Kimball said, "If, in the short term, we are sometimes dealt with insensitively and thoughtlessly by others, by imperfect men and women, it may still cause us pain, but such pain and disappointment are not the whole of life. The ways of the world will not prevail, for the ways of God will triumph."[1]

The Savior offers light to all who are in darkened, less-than-perfect circumstances in their mortal families. For those who are there through no fault of their own, he offers comfort and peace, hope, and charity. And for those who are there because of their own poor choices, he offers forgiveness and redemption. Remember the doctrine taught by King Benjamin: through Christ "ye can be made free" (Mosiah 5:8).

I cannot fully know the breadth nor the depth of the challenges you may be facing within your families. I do not know the worry you carry over your disobedient child's poor decisions, or the conflict you may feel as you wrestle with doubts over what course to pursue. I do not know the depth of your sorrow as you struggle with poor communications, frayed relationships, or infertility. I do not know the extent of the guilt you may feel over whatever problems may exist. Most of all, I do not know the answers to the many questions that fill your hearts as you ponder your families and your hopes and dreams for them. I wish there were a recipe for success—one I could give you telling exactly how many cups of sugar or tablespoons of salt to use in your families. But I cannot; I am not wise enough.

But I do know someone who is—someone who knows you and your circumstances perfectly. In the Garden of Gethsemane, a perfect, sinless, error-free man came to know you and me in a way that makes it possible for him, through the ministrations of the Holy Ghost, to guide, to comfort, and to heal us. I know that.

The family of Christ is the most important family to which we can belong. We are his children through obedience to his gospel. Without this special family relationship, none of our earthly families will continue after mortality. Being part of the family of Christ is the foundation for all other eternal family relationships.

This is a profoundly important truth. On one occasion, Jesus taught, "He that loveth father or mother more than me is not worthy of me: and he that loveth son or daughter more than me is not worthy of me" (Matthew 10:37). Elder Bruce R. McConkie explained, "How severe the tests of life sometimes are! Mortals come here to be tried and tested, . . . [a]nd if such necessitates a choice between father and mother, or son and daughter, and the saving power of the gospel of the Lord Jesus Christ, then so be it. But one thing is needful, and that is, to save our souls. No one is justified in maintaining family peace and unity if by so doing he must forsake the gospel and its saving truths."[2]

Please do not mistake my intent. Our families need our devotion, our love, our attention, and our service—now more than ever. But remembering Jesus' answer when asked to name the greatest commandment will bless us as families. He said, "Thou shalt love the Lord thy God with all thy heart, and with all thy soul, and with all thy mind. This is the first and great commandment. And the second is like unto it, Thou shalt love thy neighbour as thyself" (Matthew 22:37–39). Belonging to the family of Christ requires us to put the first commandment first. President Ezra Taft Benson pointed out, "The world largely ignores the first and great commandment—to love God—but talks a lot about loving their brother. . . . But only those who know and love God can best love and serve his children, for only

God fully understands his children and knows what is best for their welfare. Therefore, one needs to be in tune with God to best help his children. . . . [I]f you desire to help your fellowmen the most, then you must put the first commandment first. When we fail to put the love of God first, we are easily deceived by crafty men who profess a great love of humanity."[3]

We might also easily be deceived by crafty men who profess an interest in what families need. Our great adversary, who knows the importance of the family, will promote confusion and half-truths. Any attitude or doctrine which turns our center from the Lord to our family will ultimately destroy the family.

Let me illustrate with two fathers in the scriptures. When Alma learned that his son, Corianton, misbehaved on his mission to the Zoramites, he had a "teaching moment" with him. He pointed out to Corianton that he had been proud and boastful, and worse, unchaste and unfaithful to his missionary assignment in seeking out the harlot, Isabel. "Thou shouldst have tended to the ministry wherewith thou wast entrusted," Alma firmly reminded him (Alma 39:4). Alma then exhorted Corianton to repent of both his pride and his immorality, finishing with this counsel: "Do not endeavor to excuse yourself in the least point because of your sins, by denying the justice of God; but . . . let the justice of God, and his mercy, and his long-suffering have full sway in your heart; and let it bring you down to the dust in humility" (Alma 42:30). After "reproving . . . with sharpness," Alma then showed "an increase of love" (D&C 121:43) by expressing his confidence that Corianton, being "called of God to preach the word unto this people," could eventually complete an honorable mission and "bring souls to repentance, that the great plan of mercy may have claim upon them" (Alma 42:31).

In contrast, consider the Old Testament story of Eli, a priest who served in the temple and had two sons who "knew not the Lord." They profaned the sacrifices of the temple and also, as did Corianton, committed immoral acts. Eli attempted to call them to repentance, but they continued in their wickedness. The Lord sent "a man of God" to rebuke Eli, saying, "Wherefore [do ye treat with scorn] my sacrifice and my offering . . . and honourest thy sons above me?" (1 Samuel 2:27, 29). Still, Eli did not forcefully discipline his sons, and eventually the Lord said, "In that day I will perform against Eli all things which I have spoken concerning his house. . . . For I have told him that I will judge his house for ever for the iniquity which he knoweth; because his sons made themselves vile, and he restrained them not" (1 Samuel 3:12–13).

Both Eli and Alma loved their sons. Both occupied prominent positions in the Church and were probably well known among the people. Which father was looking to the eternal welfare of his sons rather than to ease his relationship with them in the moment? Which one put love of God first in his life? When it is prom-dress time, or worthiness-for-a-mission time, or worthiness-for-temple-marriage time, I hope we will follow Alma's example and love God first and love our children enough to teach, counsel, and, if need be, reprove them.

If for no other reason, we need to belong to the family of Christ to have his direction and guidance in raising our children. We cannot do it alone and be successful. He knows exactly what it is like to have children who have a hard time listening or hearkening, who hope to be excused from the consequences of their choices. He knows exactly what it is like to have children so full of promise and yet so tempted by the adversary. He knows exactly what it is like to have children who think they know better than he does. He knows exactly how to help because he knows your children—and loves them. They are his brothers and sisters, and he wants them to be part of his family.

In Old Testament times, one of the most dreaded circumstances for both men and women was to be without posterity. Countless tragedies and triumphs surround the awful state of being childless. Having one's name held in remembrance by a posterity was so critical that under the Mosaic law, a man had the obligation to marry his brother's widow in order to raise up a posterity for him so that "his name be not put out of Israel" (Deuteronomy 25:6). Imagine, then, what Isaiah felt when he foretold that Jesus, our precious Savior, would have "no beauty that we should desire him," that he would be "despised and rejected of men; a man of sorrows, and acquainted with grief . . . wounded for our transgressions," and imprisoned, and then punctuated that agonizing description with this forlorn and terrible question: "And who shall declare his generation?" (Isaiah 53:2–3, 5, 8).

Sisters, we and our families are Christ's posterity. We can keep his name in remembrance. We can boldly stand and declare his generation. Let us remember: "Ye are a chosen generation . . . that ye should shew forth the praises of him who hath called you out of darkness into his marvellous light" (1 Peter 2:9).

Notes

1. Spencer W. Kimball, "The Role of Righteous Women," *Ensign*, November 1979, 102.
2. Bruce R. McConkie, *The Mortal Messiah: From Bethlehem to Calvary*, 4 vols. (Salt Lake City: Deseret Book, 1979–81), 2:323–24.
3. Ezra Taft Benson, Conference Report, October 1967, 35.

The Family—How Firm a Foundation

Margaret D. Nadauld

I love the wonderful hymn we often sing: "How firm a foundation, ye Saints of the Lord, / Is laid for your faith in his excellent word!"[1] I wonder if that is the song the pioneer workers sang as they tore up the weakening first foundation they had laid for the Salt Lake Temple. Can you remember reading about when that happened? And they replaced it with firm, solid granite which would be enduring in strength and stand the test of time. With such determination to do it right and dedication to excellence, no wonder this magnificent structure took forty years to build.

You and I are today laying foundations which will outlast anything earthly, for we are building families—families dedicated to the work of God. We are building families which are the foundation of society and the foundation of the Church, families which will be enduring in strength and must withstand the tests of our time.

When considered in those terms, the task seems too monumental, too imposing, too grand for mere mortal women to tackle. But you are just the ones to do it! And I am so grateful for the honor of standing with you in these latter days to put our collective hearts and minds and very lives to the attention of this holy endeavor.

I remember trying to do that with our young family. I got up early

---

Margaret D. Nadauld, author of the book Write Back Soon, *has served as the Young Women General President and as a member of the board of trustees of Brigham Young University. She and her husband, Stephen D. Nadauld, previously a member of the Second Quorum of the Seventy, are the parents of seven children and the grandparents of five.*

in the mornings to begin the awesome task. One day I recorded in my journal about how it went: "Got up early. Made German pancakes and hot oatmeal and juice. Practicing violin with James when a baby threw and shattered a glass. Cleaned it up and disciplined him. Fed the boys. Practiced piano with Lincoln while a little one wet on the kitchen floor and another emptied corn flakes on the bedroom floor. All the while Taylor was running wild throughout the house. Sent to his room. Two phone calls—one to go visiting teaching and the other to borrow the boys' snow clothes. All this before 8 A.M. A typical day's beginning." At the end of the day, I recorded in the journal this question, "Have I loved our children enough today?"

Occasionally, it was like the wild, wild west in those frontier days, those foundation-building days of our family. Life was sometimes hectic as we tried to tame and civilize our little ones. With the perspective of years, it appears that the only thing there was to do was to just keep after it, every day. One day you may wake up, sisters, and see that you have high school graduates, missionaries, temple-married children who pay their tithing and serve others. And you may say, "When did such a thing happen?"

The teaching that mothers do takes great patience. It takes a sense of humor and love. And it takes consistent, never-ending effort to build a foundation that is steady and firm. Every time a child kneels at a mother's knee to pray, the child is taught. When going to church is a pleasant event in the week for the family, a child is taught. When a prayer is said and the mother gently helps the child keep arms folded, a child is taught. When classroom teachings are discussed at home, a child is taught—twice. When home teachers are welcomed with appreciation, a child is taught. When tithing is paid first and regarded as important, a child is taught. When parents love the Lord and find joy in living his teachings, a child is taught. When a parent repents and asks forgiveness of a child, a child is taught—and then forgives and forgets. When a parent honors marital vows with complete fidelity, a child is taught—and feels safe. When scriptures are part of teaching in the home, a child is taught—by the Spirit as well as by the word. When a parent is seen reading for enjoyment and information, a child is taught. When parents read to a child, a child is taught—and feels loved.

Teaching in a family is not just mother to child. There is so much to be learned from each other and extended family. Family time together is worth the sacrifice. I recently read a newspaper article describing a family night in a community in New Jersey. It said that when "this commuter village 20 miles from New York decided [that their] jam-packed schedules left no time for families, the calendars came out. It took seven months of planning, but on Tuesday, the upscale community of stately homes and gilt-lettered shops will take a collective night off."[2]

Other communities are doing the same thing. They are coming to understand what a prophet of God foresaw nearly forty years ago when he called upon members of the Church to hold weekly family home evenings. Children and parents need each other. They need planned teaching moments certainly, and they also need just plain old time—time where you work together, play together, laugh together—your time!

Journalist Dick Feagler suggests that "the trouble with [the quality time] notion is that being a [child] is not a profession. [Children] are not colleagues. . . . They lack the brisk efficiency to schedule quality time seminars with their parents.

"What [children] do is hang out. And while they're hanging out, they want to know a parent is available."[3]

Setting aside a weekly family night is a wonderful beginning. I would say that is a minimal requirement for building a strong family foundation. I don't understand how you can build a firm, strong family foundation on one night a week. For many families, the daily mealtime is a must.

Kitchens are an important place for teaching and adding building blocks to a family foundation. Mothers have no idea of the effect of their daily kitchen consistencies in nurturing their children. What is so nice about mealtime is that food and prayers go together like salt and pepper or bread and butter. Whenever we got to eat breakfast at my grandparents' home, I noticed that Grandma, who reared a large family, set the breakfast table the night before with the chairs turned away from the table. In the morning, before eating, we first knelt at our chairs to offer family prayer. "A generation or two ago," said President Gordon B. Hinckley, "family prayer in the homes of Christian people throughout the world was as much a part of the day's activity as were the meals. As that practice has diminished, our moral decay has ensued. I fear that as the quality of our housing has improved, the spirit of our homes has deteriorated."[4]

Isn't it ironic that in a day when the threats of evil in our society are so rampant we are abandoning the very things that could strengthen and fortify us against evil?

One woman said, "Six o'clock was a special hour in our family. Even though the children were outside playing, or working out with teams, or had jobs, or were in student government, everyone knew that at six o'clock there would be dinner waiting—table set, food ready. Those who were late without excuse got to do all the dishes. Otherwise everyone pitched in and we could slick up the kitchen in short order, and it was almost fun. Of course there were exceptions, but usually we all gathered at supper time to pray, share experiences of the day, tell the latest joke, coordinate schedules, discuss sports and current events, and on Sundays we discussed the message of the lessons and the speakers at church."[5] For many successful families, mealtime is an ideal time to teach and add to the firm foundation of the family.

I would like to say a few words about fathers to this audience of women. The stripling warriors who were so famous for following the faith of their mothers were also blessed by their fathers. Alma also tells of the fathers providing for their children (Alma 56:27). These warriors couldn't have been as successful without the provisions brought by faithful fathers. Sisters, do we show appreciation for all fathers do in foundation building?

Recently, my wonderful father passed away. He was the beloved patriarch of our family and of our stake. He had spent his lifetime in the service of his family and others. And in reflecting on the life and goodness of this noble man, I remembered some of the Christmases we had had as children. As I was growing up, my father worked hard and provided well for our family, and every year Christmas morning was the same for us. We got up early—too early—and awakened our parents. We all joined together in the living room as we opened our gifts with unbridled enthusiasm, throwing the wrappings around, exclaiming with delight our joy in all that we had received and then busily (and I must say in retrospect, selfishly) set about playing with and enjoying the abundance our parents had provided. Daddy slipped quietly out and went to the hatchery to do the work which had to be done. Thousands of eggs in incubators, in process of hatching into thousands of baby chicks, had to be carefully attended to and the parent stock fed and cared for. Daddy's employees had Christmas day off to be with their families, but chickens never have a day off. The work still had to be done, and so our good-hearted father did it. In our youthful lack of understanding and appreciation, we were disappointed to have him leave so soon. Didn't he care about us? Did he love to work more than he loved to be with us?

And then one day I understood, and I felt ashamed. Daddy loved us more than anything, and that's why he worked so hard to provide for us without ever, *ever* one word of complaint. I wonder if he ever felt unappreciated or unloved by his thoughtless daughter. We eventually outgrew and overcame that kind of behavior with the help of our wise mother.

The family proclamation teaches that fathers "are responsible to provide the necessities of life . . . for their families."[6] Wives can show gratitude for all that their husbands do to provide for the family. They can express this gratitude within the hearing of their children. When you go out for a hamburger with the family, do you make a point of saying thank you to your husband for doing dinner and dishes that night as he empties the fast food trays into the trash?

When you kneel in prayer as a couple and as a family, do you thank Heavenly Father for a husband who works hard? By their example, wise women teach their children to be grateful for all their fathers do. The husband loves coming home because there he will find peace, refreshment, relief from the pressures of the world. He will find appreciation at home, and there he will be loved.

You can help enhance the relationship between the children and their father. Daddies are so important to daughters in the establishment of their self-esteem. Find ways to help fathers and children keep a close and happy relationship, sisters.

In a newspaper account of the most outstanding girls basketball player in the state, the young woman told a reporter, "'[My dad's] been my coach my whole life,' she said. 'He trains with me, he runs with me, he shoots with me. He helps me set my goals, and he's just always been there for me. He always wants the best for me.'"[7]

One young man named James wrote, "Growing up, every Saturday morning was the same: my father wouldn't say anything, he would simply tap on our bedroom doors and then go outside, and within ten minutes his groggy sons from teenager to toddler would be at his side in our back yard. If there were, in fact, no pressing chores to be done, we would simply move dirt. It was Saturday morning, and we were working, and that's what mattered to him. Eventually he would stop and wipe his brow, and with a broad smile declare, 'It's a fine day for water skiing.' And after a couple of hours of dragging us around the lake in an old boat we shared with another family, he'd stop in the middle of the water for lunch. And then, as we were all sitting there, his captive audience with a bologna sandwich in one hand and a soda in the other, my father would teach us. He taught us the value of hard work and priorities in the context of a well-balanced life. At the time I didn't know it—I was just enjoying my bologna sandwich—but it was during these moments that I learned many of the values I hold dear today."[8]

Mothers, encourage the involvement of fathers in the lives of your children and in the establishment of firm family foundations.

Wise mothers have some vision of what they want their family to become. Teach your children about your vision for the family. When they were apartment dwellers, a young couple would occasionally take

Sunday drives through lovely neighborhoods with fine, large homes, and the wife remembers thinking, *If we could see the spiritual stature of that home out on the front lawn, would it tower over the house or barely fill one little corner of the lot?* And then the time came when this young couple with five growing children took on the project of building a home of their own. As the work progressed, the home began to look larger than they had imagined and had the potential of seeming too wonderful, and the wife worried about where they were placing their values as more and more resources and more and more time were being consumed by this project. And finally one day, she gathered her growing flock around her and said, "It would be sad if people drove by our house and said, 'Oh, look at that beautiful home.' What I would hope is that people would drive by and say, 'Oh, the nicest family of outstanding children live in that home.' This is the home where I want our children to come for love and security—a house wherein they learn the lessons of life and practice living the gospel." She was describing the blueprint of a house of God as outlined in Doctrine and Covenants 88: "Establish a house, even a house of prayer, a house of fasting, a house of faith, a house of learning, a house of glory, a house of order, a house of God" (v. 119).

A vision of what your family can become and what that will require from you is a *must* in establishing a firm foundation to build upon.

Sometimes the vision has to be altered because part of your dream has been destroyed. Don't let a tragic happening destroy your foundation—it may feel shaky for a while, even a very long while sometimes, but if your faith is built upon the solid ground of gospel teachings, upon the rock of Christ, you can eventually steady this family once again, sisters. Look for ways to shore up the footings of faith—faith in the Lord Jesus Christ. He is the foundation upon which our life must be built. It is he who implemented the Father's plan, and it is this plan you voted for. It is the great plan of happiness, a plan for success in meeting life's trials. Alma teaches this: "And he shall go forth, suffering pains and afflictions and temptations of every kind; and this that the word might be fulfilled which saith he will take upon him the pains and the sicknesses of his people. And he will take upon him death, that he may loose the bands of death which bind his people; and he will take upon him their infirmities, that his bowels may be filled with mercy, according to the flesh, that he may know according to the flesh how to succor his people according to their infirmities" (Alma 7:11–12). Our beloved Savior provides succor for sickness, disappointment, tragedy, adversity. He will carry those burdens for you. Ask for his help. He will help you. It is his work and his glory to bring to pass the immortality and the eternal life of all mankind (Moses 1:39). It is his mission to help you be successful in things of eternal worth. Seek his divine help. Turn to him for rest from carrying your heavy burdens. Let faith in him be the basis for your family foundation.

Always remember that the greatest work you will ever do will be within the walls of your own home, as President Harold B. Lee taught.[9] This means the greatest service you will ever give, the greatest leadership you will ever know, the greatest music you will ever make, the greatest lessons you will ever teach will be those that strengthen the foundation of your home and bring your loved ones closer to the Savior.

Like the temple's firm foundation, once the family foundation is firmed up and the strength of the family is established, it can be there for eternity. It can endure forever. Such is our faith, even when you have a child who does not accept your teachings or your examples. The sweet teaching of the Prophet Joseph Smith—and he never taught a more comforting doctrine—said "the eternal sealing of faithful parents and the divine promises made to them for valiant service in the Cause of Truth would save not only themselves, but likewise their posterity. Though some of the sheep may wander, the eye of the Shepherd is upon them, and sooner or later they will feel the tentacles of Divine Providence reaching out after them and drawing them back to the fold."[10]

This is our hope. This is our promise. It is worth our very best effort. It is worth our constant, enduring effort.

"How firm a foundation, ye Saints of the Lord, / Is laid for your faith in [t]his excellent word!"[11] May this be the song of our hearts as we work with our Father in Heaven to build a firm, faithful foundation for our families. God will guide our hands and our minds as we build and strengthen our home and our family. In this I have complete faith, and I testify of his goodness to his children as the master architect and the rock upon which we must build a firm foundation.

Notes

1. Robert Keen, "How Firm a Foundation," *Hymns of The Church of Jesus Christ of Latter-day Saints* (Salt Lake City: The Church of Jesus Christ of Latter-day Saints, 1985), no. 85.
2. Sheila Hotchkin, "New Jersey City Sets aside a Family Night," *Deseret News*, 25 March 2002.
3. Dick Feagler, "Time Spent with Kids Is Truly Quality Time," *SouthCoast Today*, 3 June 1997.
4. Gordon B. Hinckley, *Teachings of Gordon B. Hinckley* (Salt Lake City: Deseret Book, 1997), 213–14.
5. Correspondence, Young Women historical files, Salt Lake City.
6. "The Family: A Proclamation to the World," *Ensign*, November 1995, 102.
7. Amy Donaldson, "Seljaas Is 2002 Ms. Basketball," *Deseret News*, 12 March 2002.
8. Correspondence in author's possession.
9. Harold B. Lee, Conference Report, April 1973, 130; or *Ensign*, July 1973, 98.
10. Quoted by Orson F. Whitney, Conference Report, April 1929, 110.
11. *Hymns*, no. 85.

INDEX